THE AVENGERS

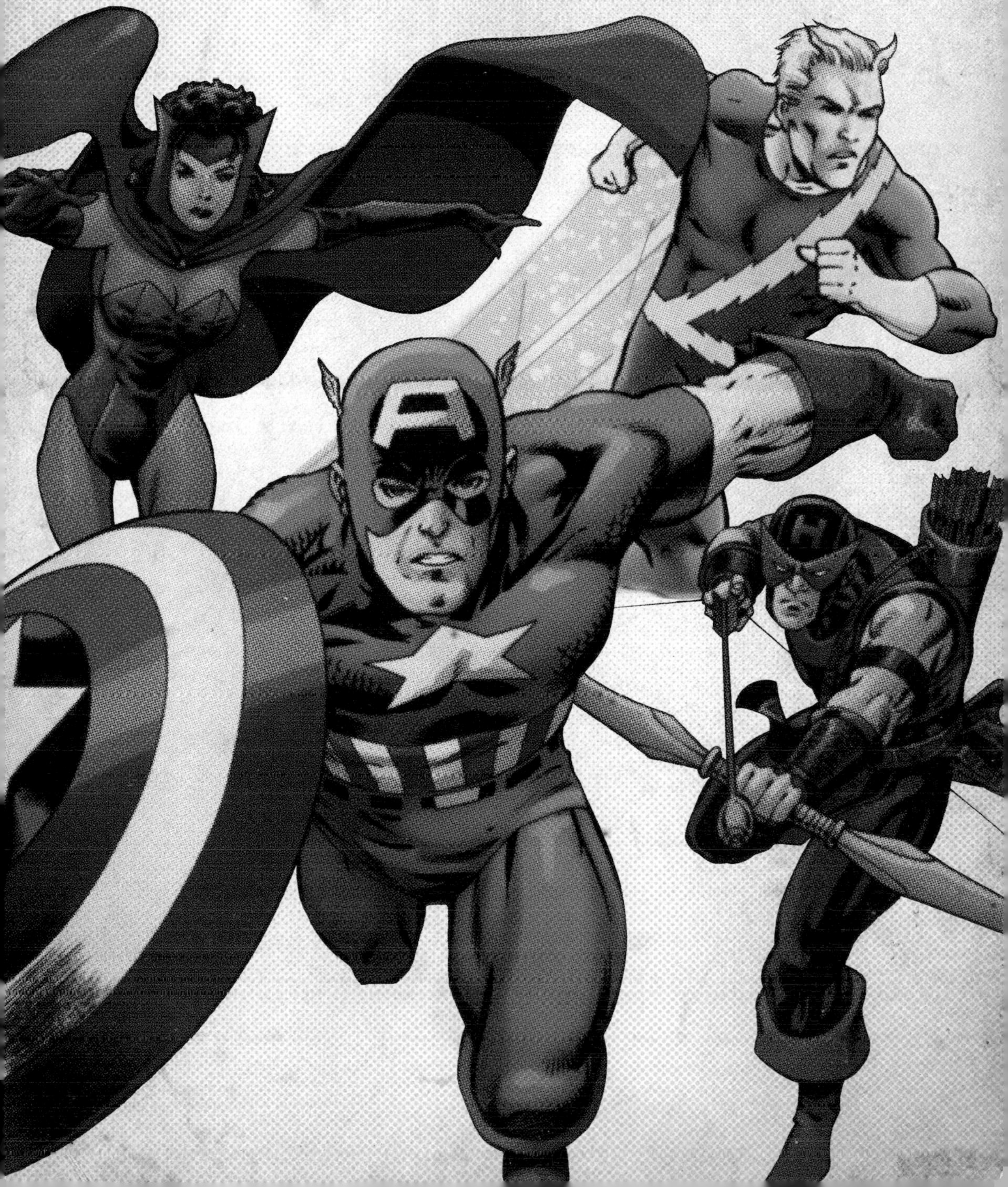

AND THERE CAME A DAY UNLIKE ANY OTHER, WHEN EARTH'S MIGHTIEST HEROES DECIDED TO TAKE SOME TIME OFF AND WERE REPLACED WITH A GROUP OF UNTESTED, UNTRIED NEW RECRUITS: HAWKEYE, A MASTER ARCHER AND REFORMED CRIMINAL, AND TWO OF MAGNETO'S FORMER MINIONS--THE SPEEDSTER QUICKSILVER AND HIS TWIN SISTER, THE MYSTERIOUS SCARLET WITCH.

CAPTAIN AMERICA WAS TASKED WITH TURNING THE MEMBERS OF THIS RAGTAG TEAM INTO AVENGERS, BUT THAT WAS A STORY NEVER REVEALED...UNTIL NOW.

CAPTAIN AMERICA

THE AVENGERS

HAWKEYE

SCARLET WITCH

writer	**MARK WAID**
pencilers	**BARRY KITSON** WITH **MARK BAGLEY** (#5.1), **SEAN IZAAKSE** (#5.1) & **RO STEIN** (#5.1)
inkers	**MARK FARMER** WITH **RAFAEL FONTERIZ** (#3.1-4.1), **BARRY KITSON** (#3.1), **DREW HENNESSY** (#4.1-5.1), **SCOTT HANNA** (#5.1), **MIKE PERKINS** (#5.1), **TED BRANDT** (#5.1) & **SEAN IZAAKSE** (#5.1)
colorists	**JORDAN BOYD** WITH **WIL QUINTANA** (#3.1-5.1) & **MATT YACKEY** (#4.1-5.1)
letterer	**FERRAN DELGADO**
cover art	**BARRY KITSON & JORDAN BOYD**
assistant editor	**ALANNA SMITH**
editor	**TOM BREVOORT**

Avengers created by **STAN LEE & JACK KIRBY**

QUICKSILVER

AVENGERS: FOUR. Contains material originally published in magazine form as AVENGERS #1.1-5.1. First printing 2017. ISBN# 978-1-302-90261-2. Published by MARVEL WORLDWIDE, INC., a subsidiary of MARVEL ENTERTAINMENT, LLC. OFFICE OF PUBLICATION: 135 West 50th Street, New York, NY 10020. Copyright © 2017 MARVEL No similarity between any of the names, characters, persons, and/or institutions in this magazine with those of any living or dead person or institution is intended, and any such similarity which may exist is purely coincidental. **Printed in Canada.** DAN BUCKLEY, President, Marvel Entertainment; JOE QUESADA, Chief Creative Officer; TOM BREVOORT, SVP of Publishing; DAVID BOGART, SVP of Business Affairs & Operations, Publishing & Partnership; C.B. CEBULSKI, VP of Brand Management & Development, Asia; DAVID GABRIEL, SVP of Sales & Marketing, Publishing; JEFF YOUNGQUIST, VP of Production & Special Projects; DAN CARR, Executive Director of Publishing Technology; ALEX MORALES, Director of Publishing Operations; SUSAN CRESPI, Production Manager; STAN LEE, Chairman Emeritus. For information regarding advertising in Marvel Comics or on Marvel.com, please contact Vit QeBellis, Integrated Sales Manager, at vdebellis@marvel.com. For Marvel subscription inquiries, please call 888-511-5480. Manufactured between 4/7/2017 and 5/9/2017 by SOLISCO PRINTERS, SCOTT, QC, CANADA.

10 9 8 7 6 5 4 3 2 1

collection editor	Jennifer Grünwald	vp production & special projects	Jeff Youngquist	editor in chief	Axel Alonso		
assistant editor	Caitlin O'Connell	svp print, sales & marketing	David Gabriel	chief creative officer	Joe Quesada		
associate managing editor	Kateri Woody	book designer	Adam Del Re	president	Dan Buckley		
editor, special projects	Mark D. Beazley			executive producer	Alan Fine		

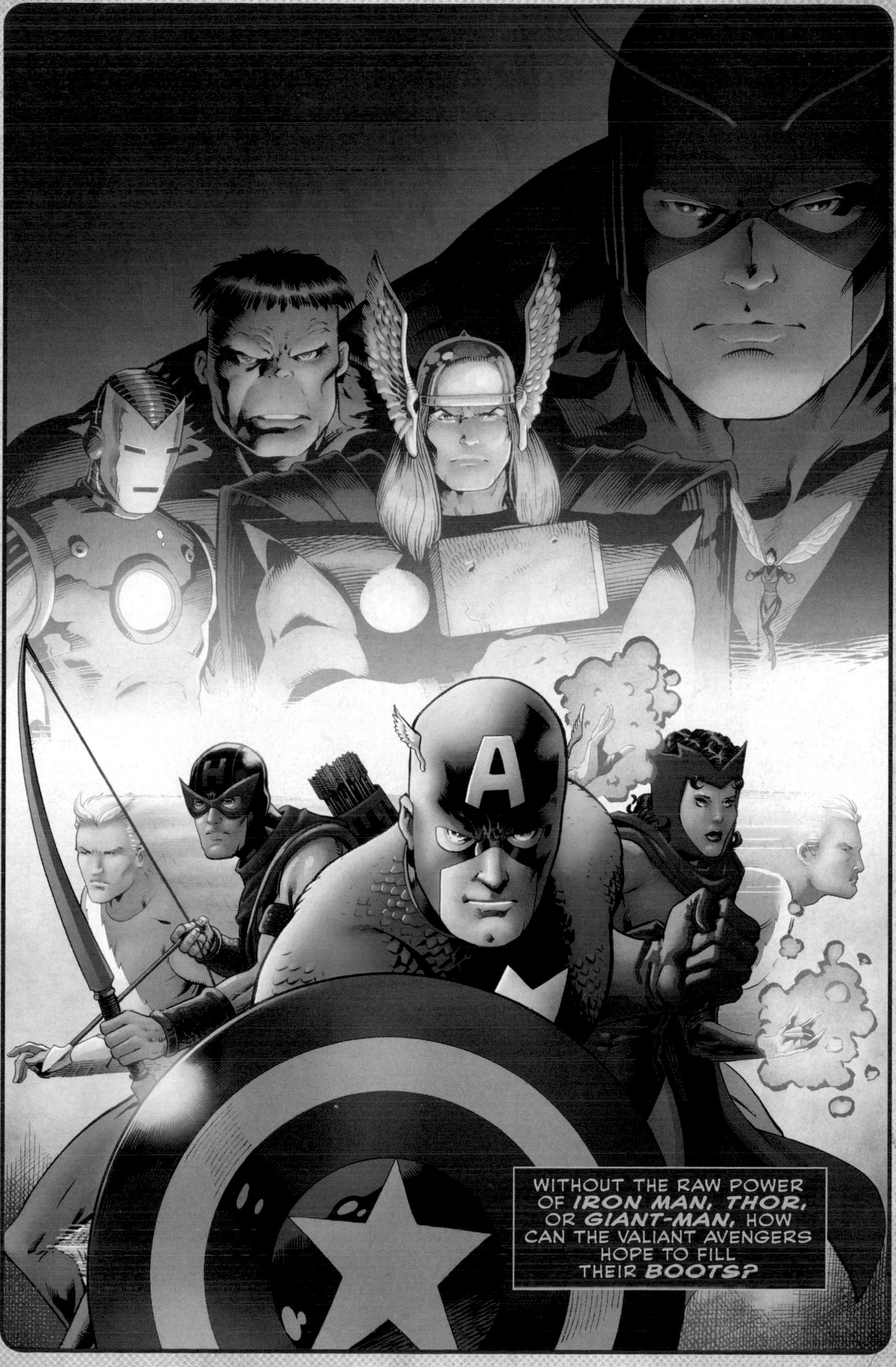
WITHOUT THE RAW POWER OF IRON MAN, THOR, OR GIANT-MAN, HOW CAN THE VALIANT AVENGERS HOPE TO FILL THEIR BOOTS?

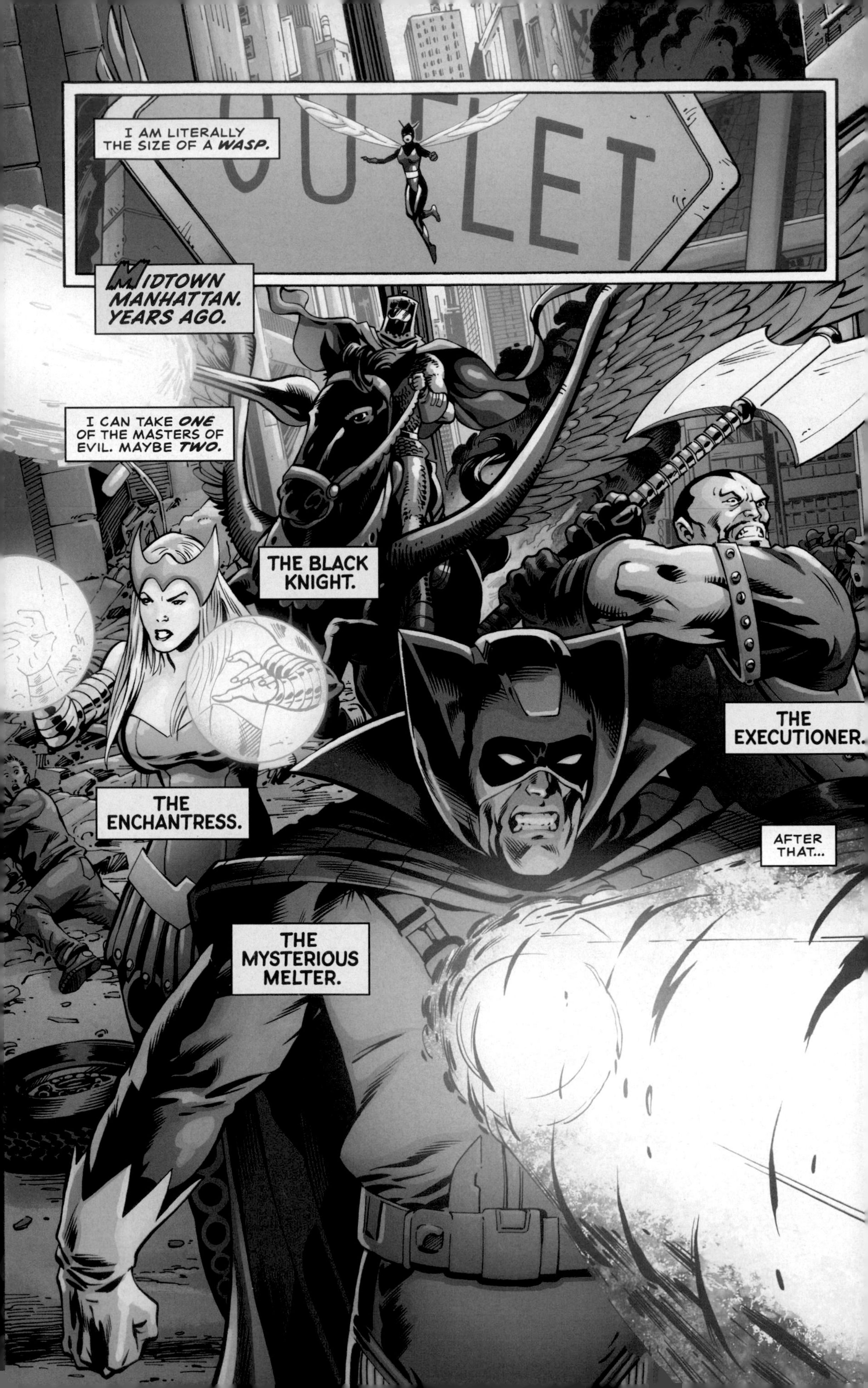

I AM LITERALLY THE SIZE OF A WASP.
OUTLET
MIDTOWN MANHATTAN. YEARS AGO.
I CAN TAKE ONE OF THE MASTERS OF EVIL. MAYBE TWO.
THE BLACK KNIGHT.
THE EXECUTIONER.
THE ENCHANTRESS.
AFTER THAT...
THE MYSTERIOUS MELTER.

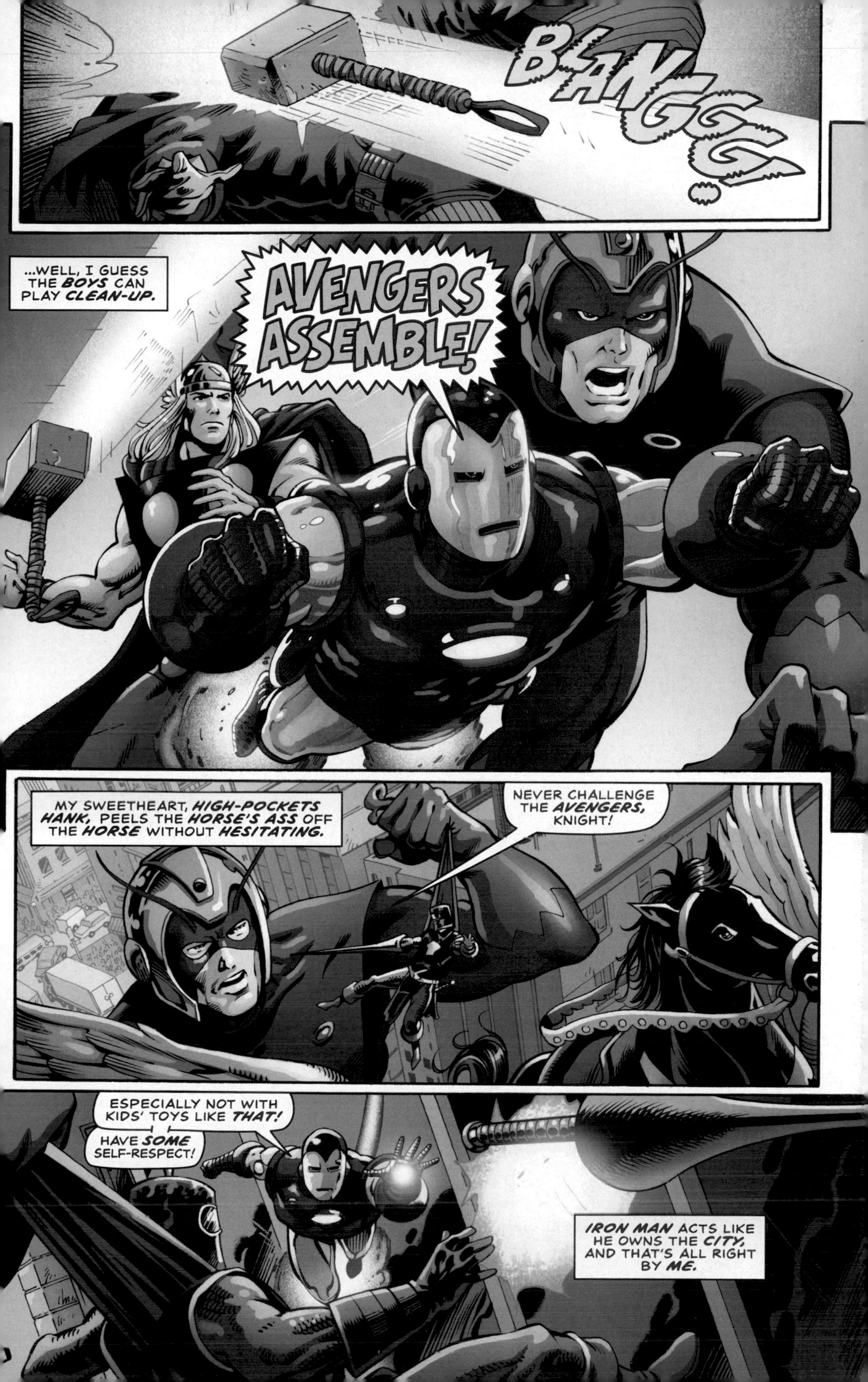
BLANGGG!
...WELL, I GUESS THE BOYS CAN PLAY CLEAN-UP.
AVENGERS ASSEMBLE!
MY SWEETHEART, HIGH-POCKETS HANK, PEELS THE HORSE'S ASS OFF THE HORSE WITHOUT HESITATING.
NEVER CHALLENGE THE AVENGERS, KNIGHT!
ESPECIALLY NOT WITH KIDS' TOYS LIKE THAT!
HAVE SOME SELF-RESPECT!
IRON MAN ACTS LIKE HE OWNS THE CITY, AND THAT'S ALL RIGHT BY ME.

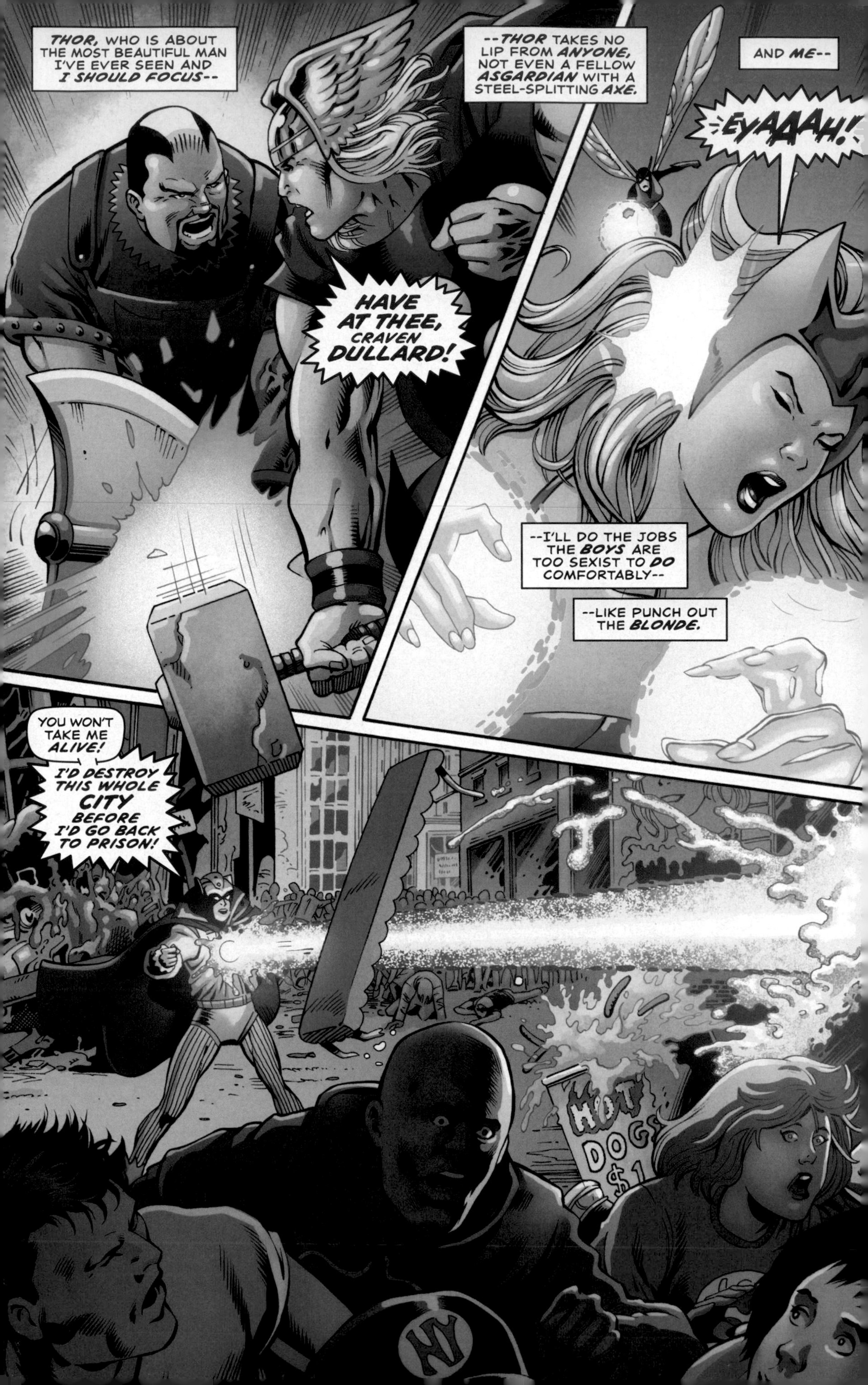
THOR, WHO IS ABOUT THE MOST BEAUTIFUL MAN I'VE EVER SEEN AND I SHOULD FOCUS--
--THOR TAKES NO LIP FROM ANYONE, NOT EVEN A FELLOW ASGARDIAN WITH A STEEL-SPLITTING AXE.
HAVE AT THEE, CRAVEN DULLARD!
AND ME--
EYAAAH!
--I'LL DO THE JOBS THE BOYS ARE TOO SEXIST TO DO COMFORTABLY--
--LIKE PUNCH OUT THE BLONDE.
YOU WON'T TAKE ME ALIVE!
I'D DESTROY THIS WHOLE CITY BEFORE I'D GO BACK TO PRISON!
HOT DOGS $1

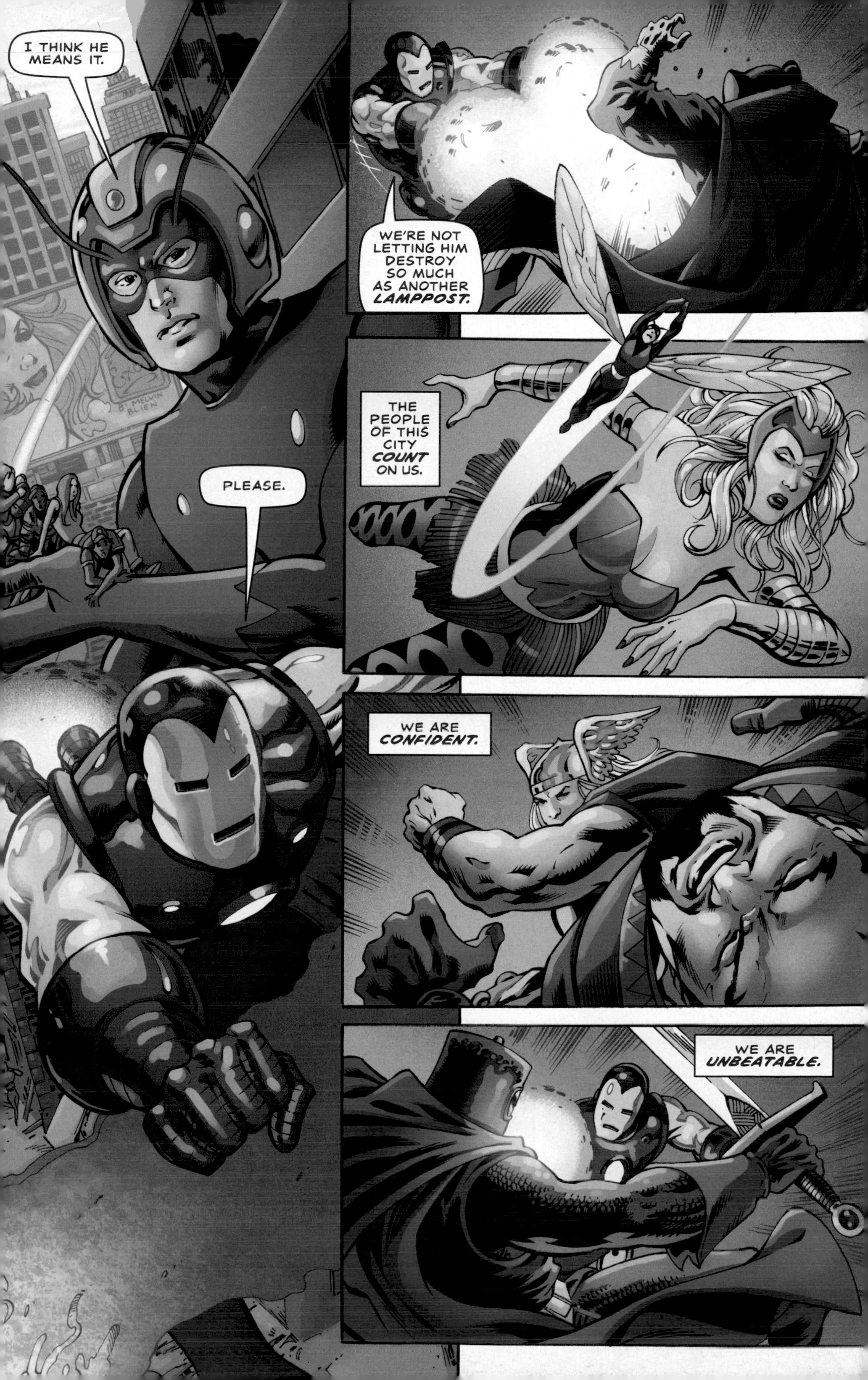

I THINK HE MEANS IT.
WE'RE NOT LETTING HIM DESTROY SO MUCH AS ANOTHER *LAMPPOST.*
PLEASE.
THE PEOPLE OF THIS CITY *COUNT* ON US.
WE ARE *CONFIDENT.*
WE ARE *UNBEATABLE.*

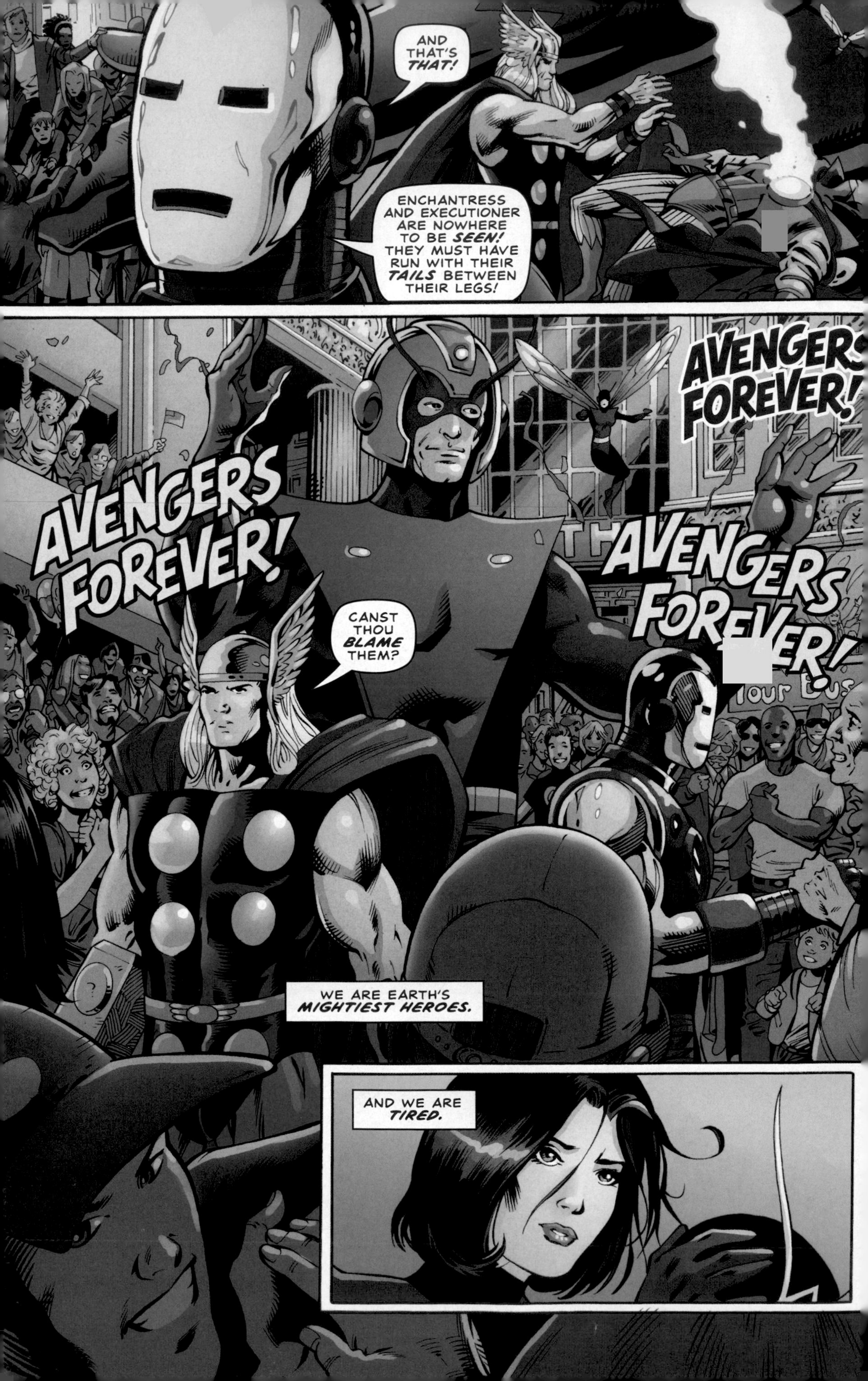
AND THAT'S *THAT!*
ENCHANTRESS AND EXECUTIONER ARE NOWHERE TO BE *SEEN!* THEY MUST HAVE RUN WITH THEIR *TAILS* BETWEEN THEIR LEGS!
AVENGERS FOREVER!
AVENGERS FOREVER!
CANST THOU *BLAME* THEM?
AVENGERS FOREVER!
WE ARE EARTH'S *MIGHTIEST HEROES.*
AND WE ARE *TIRED.*

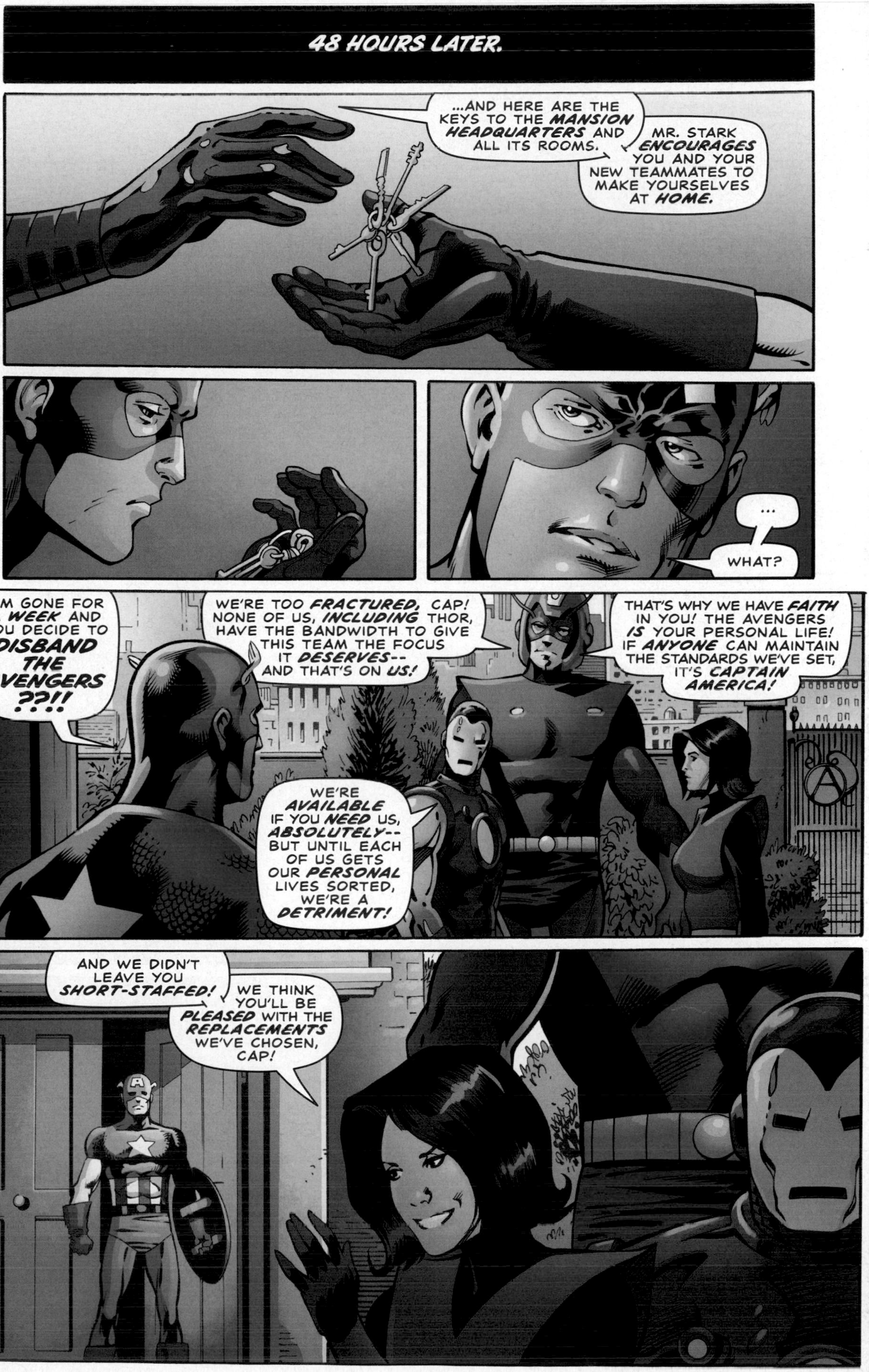
48 HOURS LATER.
...AND HERE ARE THE KEYS TO THE MANSION HEADQUARTERS AND ALL ITS ROOMS.
MR. STARK ENCOURAGES YOU AND YOUR NEW TEAMMATES TO MAKE YOURSELVES AT HOME.
...
WHAT?
I'M GONE FOR A WEEK AND YOU DECIDE TO DISBAND THE AVENGERS ??!! ....
WE'RE TOO FRACTURED, CAP! NONE OF US, INCLUDING THOR, HAVE THE BANDWIDTH TO GIVE THIS TEAM THE FOCUS IT DESERVES-- AND THAT'S ON US!
THAT'S WHY WE HAVE FAITH IN YOU! THE AVENGERS IS YOUR PERSONAL LIFE! IF ANYONE CAN MAINTAIN THE STANDARDS WE'VE SET, IT'S CAPTAIN AMERICA!
WE'RE AVAILABLE IF YOU NEED US, ABSOLUTELY-- BUT UNTIL EACH OF US GETS OUR PERSONAL LIVES SORTED, WE'RE A DETRIMENT!
AND WE DIDN'T LEAVE YOU SHORT-STAFFED!
WE THINK YOU'LL BE PLEASED WITH THE REPLACEMENTS WE'VE CHOSEN, CAP!

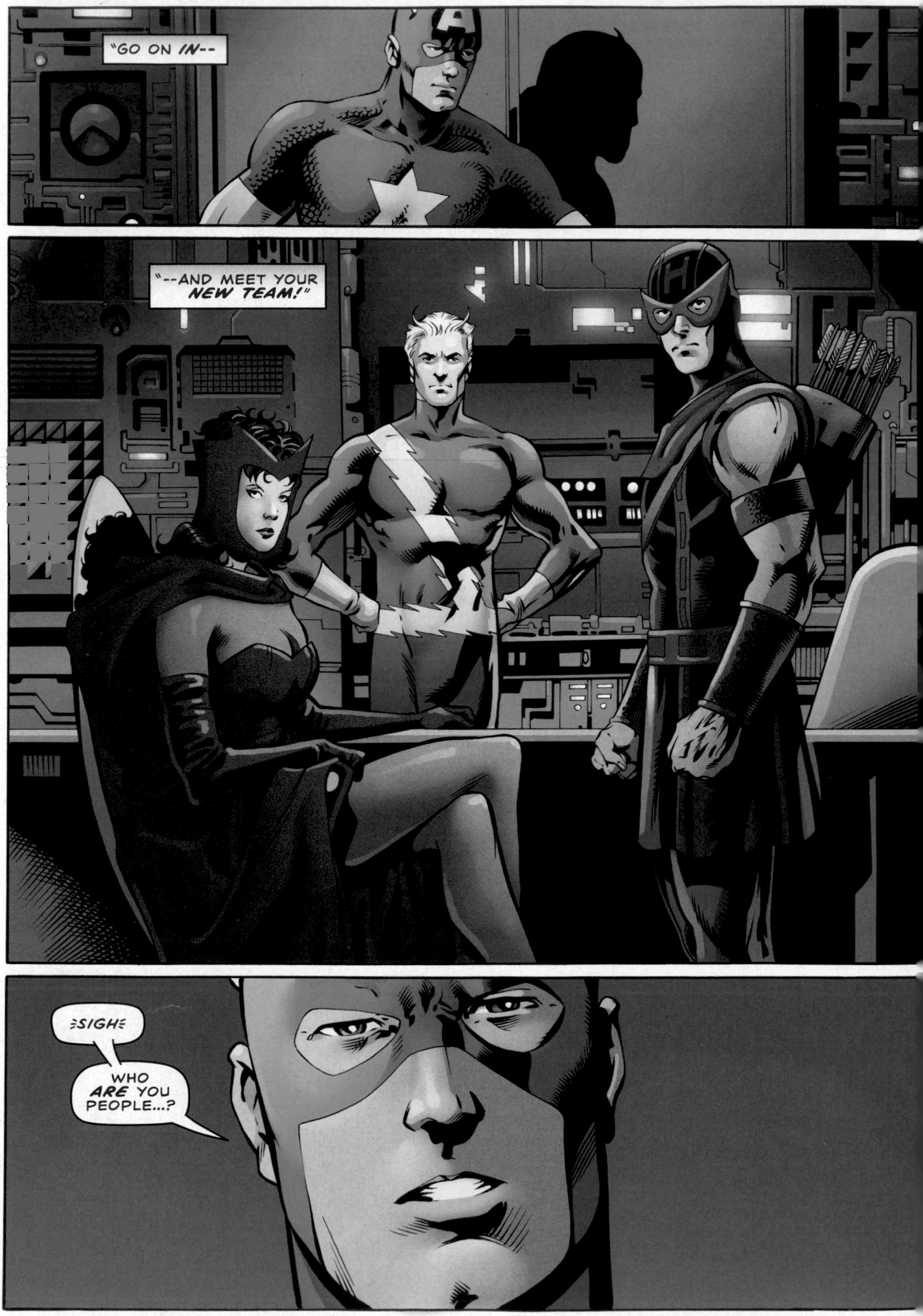
"GO ON IN--
"--AND MEET YOUR NEW TEAM!"
≠SIGH≠
WHO ARE YOU PEOPLE...?

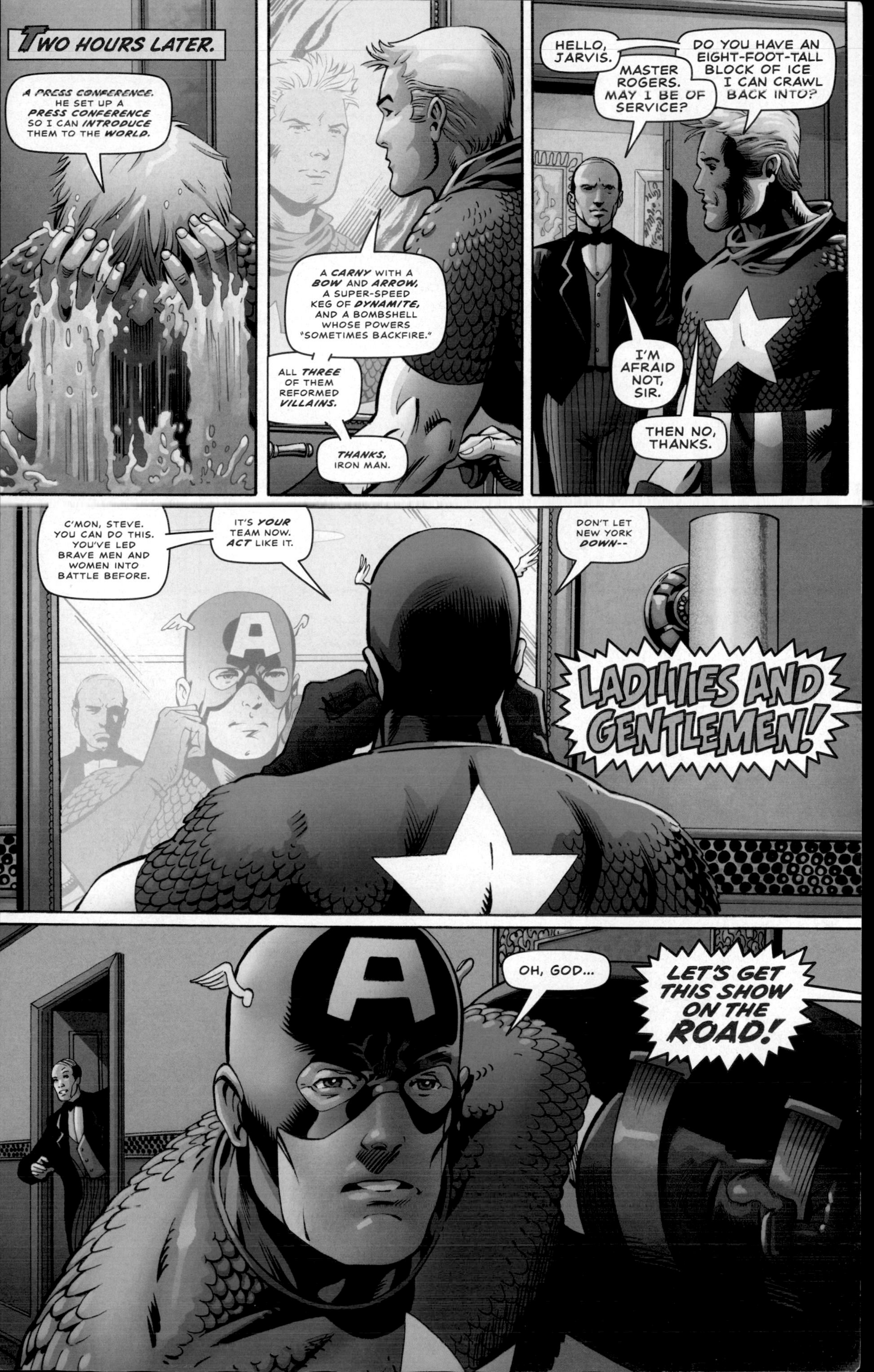
TWO HOURS LATER.
A PRESS CONFERENCE. HE SET UP A PRESS CONFERENCE SO I CAN INTRODUCE THEM TO THE WORLD.
A CARNY WITH A BOW AND ARROW, A SUPER-SPEED KEG OF DYNAMITE, AND A BOMBSHELL WHOSE POWERS "SOMETIMES BACKFIRE."
ALL THREE OF THEM REFORMED VILLAINS.
THANKS, IRON MAN.
HELLO, JARVIS.
MASTER ROGERS. MAY I BE OF SERVICE?
DO YOU HAVE AN EIGHT-FOOT-TALL BLOCK OF ICE I CAN CRAWL BACK INTO?
I'M AFRAID NOT, SIR.
THEN NO, THANKS.
C'MON, STEVE. YOU CAN DO THIS. YOU'VE LED BRAVE MEN AND WOMEN INTO BATTLE BEFORE.
IT'S YOUR TEAM NOW. ACT LIKE IT.
DON'T LET NEW YORK DOWN--
LADIIIIES AND GENTLEMEN!
OH, GOD...
LET'S GET THIS SHOW ON THE ROAD!

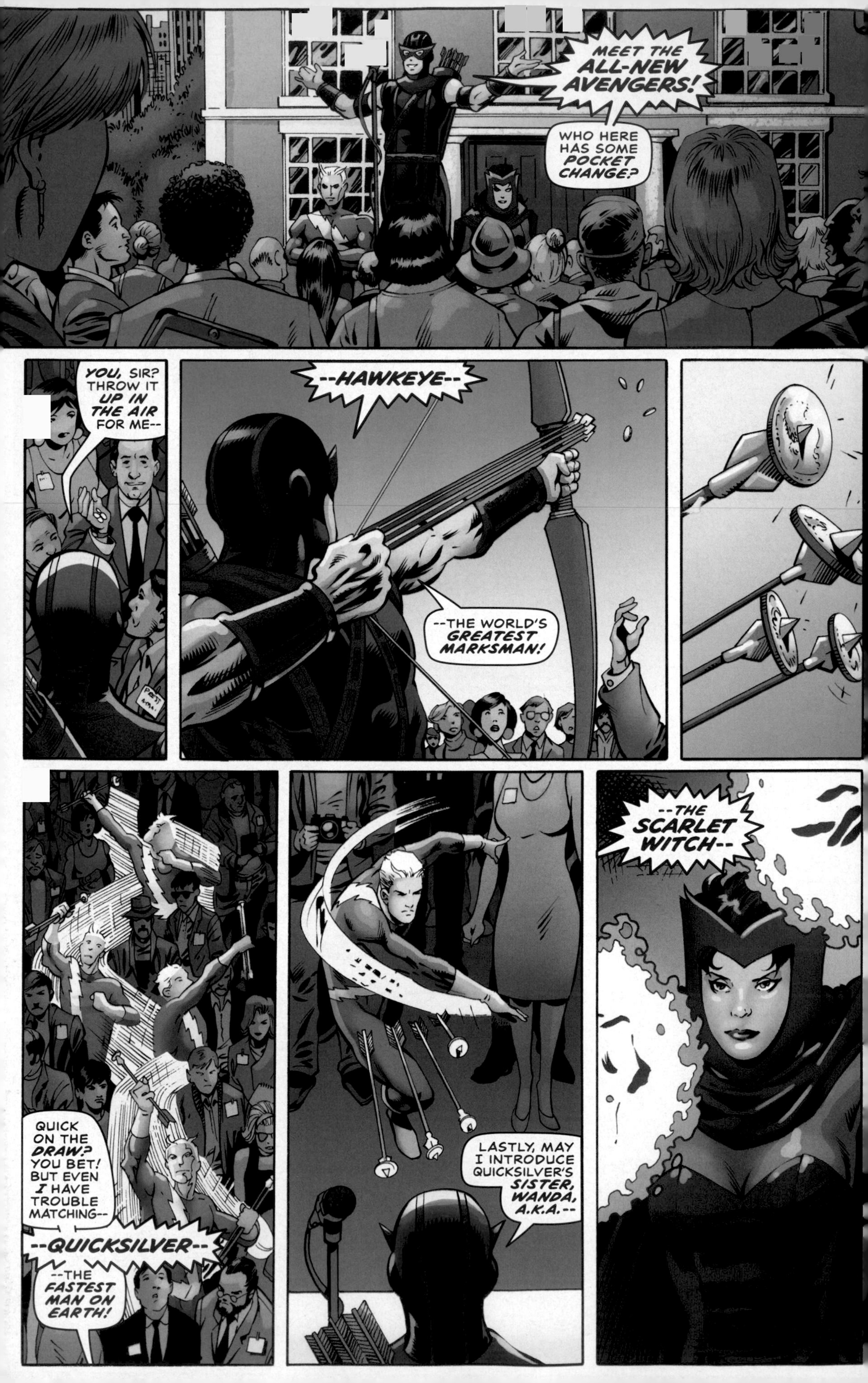
MEET THE ALL-NEW AVENGERS!
WHO HERE HAS SOME POCKET CHANGE?
YOU, SIR? THROW IT UP IN THE AIR FOR ME--
--HAWKEYE--
--THE WORLD'S GREATEST MARKSMAN!
QUICK ON THE DRAW? YOU BET! BUT EVEN I HAVE TROUBLE MATCHING--
--QUICKSILVER--
--THE FASTEST MAN ON EARTH!
LASTLY, MAY I INTRODUCE QUICKSILVER'S SISTER, WANDA, A.K.A.--
--THE SCARLET WITCH--

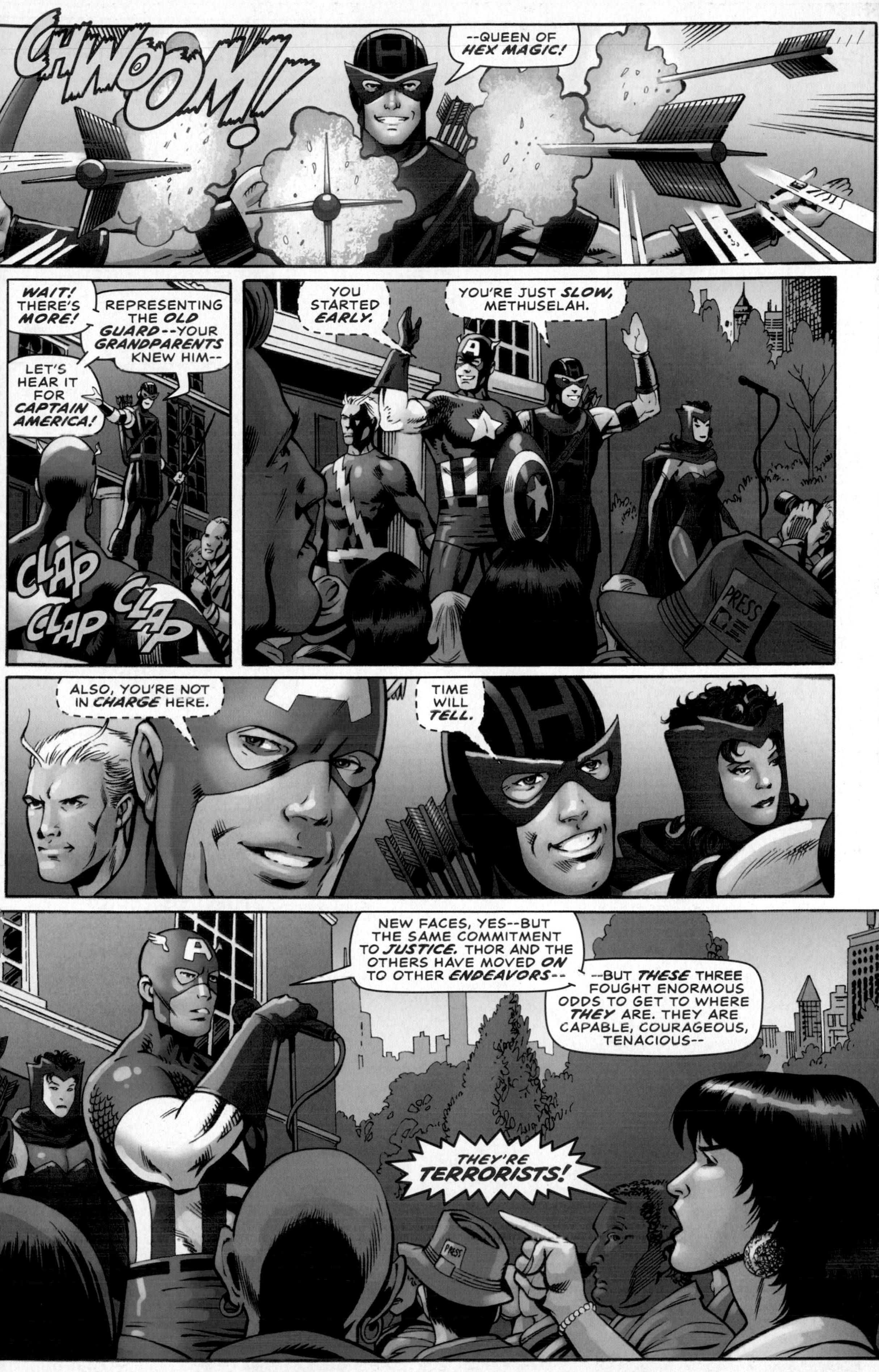
CHWOOM!
--QUEEN OF HEX MAGIC!
WAIT! THERE'S MORE!
REPRESENTING THE OLD GUARD--YOUR GRANDPARENTS KNEW HIM--
LET'S HEAR IT FOR CAPTAIN AMERICA!
CLAP
CLAP
CLAP
YOU STARTED EARLY.
YOU'RE JUST SLOW, METHUSELAH.
PRESS
ALSO, YOU'RE NOT IN CHARGE HERE.
TIME WILL TELL.
NEW FACES, YES--BUT THE SAME COMMITMENT TO JUSTICE. THOR AND THE OTHERS HAVE MOVED ON TO OTHER ENDEAVORS--
--BUT THESE THREE FOUGHT ENORMOUS ODDS TO GET TO WHERE THEY ARE. THEY ARE CAPABLE, COURAGEOUS, TENACIOUS--
THEY'RE TERRORISTS!
PRESS

WHO SAID *THAT?*

IT'S ALL RIGHT, PIETRO. SHE'S FREE TO SPEAK HER MIND.

GO AHEAD, MA'AM.

LAURA MARSHALL, CABLE-1. JUST LAST *MONTH,* THE WITCH AND QUICKSILVER WERE MEMBERS OF MAGNETO'S *MUTANT EXTREMIST CELL!*

THEY WERE *PAWNS,* I ASSURE YOU. I--

HOW *CAN* YOU? WHAT *IS* THE AVENGERS' PROCESS FOR VETTING NEW MEMBERS? WHY ARE *THESE* TWO SUDDENLY ACCEPTABLE?

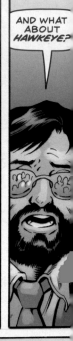

AND WHAT ABOUT *HAWKEYE?*

WHAT *ABOUT* HAWKEYE...?

YOU ONCE ATTACKED *STARK INDUSTRIES,* OUR BIGGEST *DEFENSE* CONTRACTOR.

WHO WERE *YOU* WORKING FOR?

THAT THING WITH ME AND STARK, THAT'S *CLASSIFIED.* AND THE FACT THAT YOU *KNOW* ABOUT IT MEANS THAT I MADE SOME ROOKIE MISTAKES.

BUT ONCE A HERO STARTS TO MATURE, HE LEARNS TO RELY ON *SUPPORT* AND *ASSISTANCE.*

WITH THIS TEAM BACKING ME UP, I LIKE MY CHANCES.

AND THAT'S HOW YOU PLAY TO AN *AUDIENCE,* KIDS. SMILE PRETTY.

HAWKEYE'S MAKING HIMSELF SOUND LIKE THE *TEAM LEADER,* CAP.

IS HE BUCKING FOR *YOUR* JOB?

EVERY ONE OF US UNDERSTANDS THE IMPORTANCE OF COHESION AND DISCIPLINE. NEXT QUESTION.

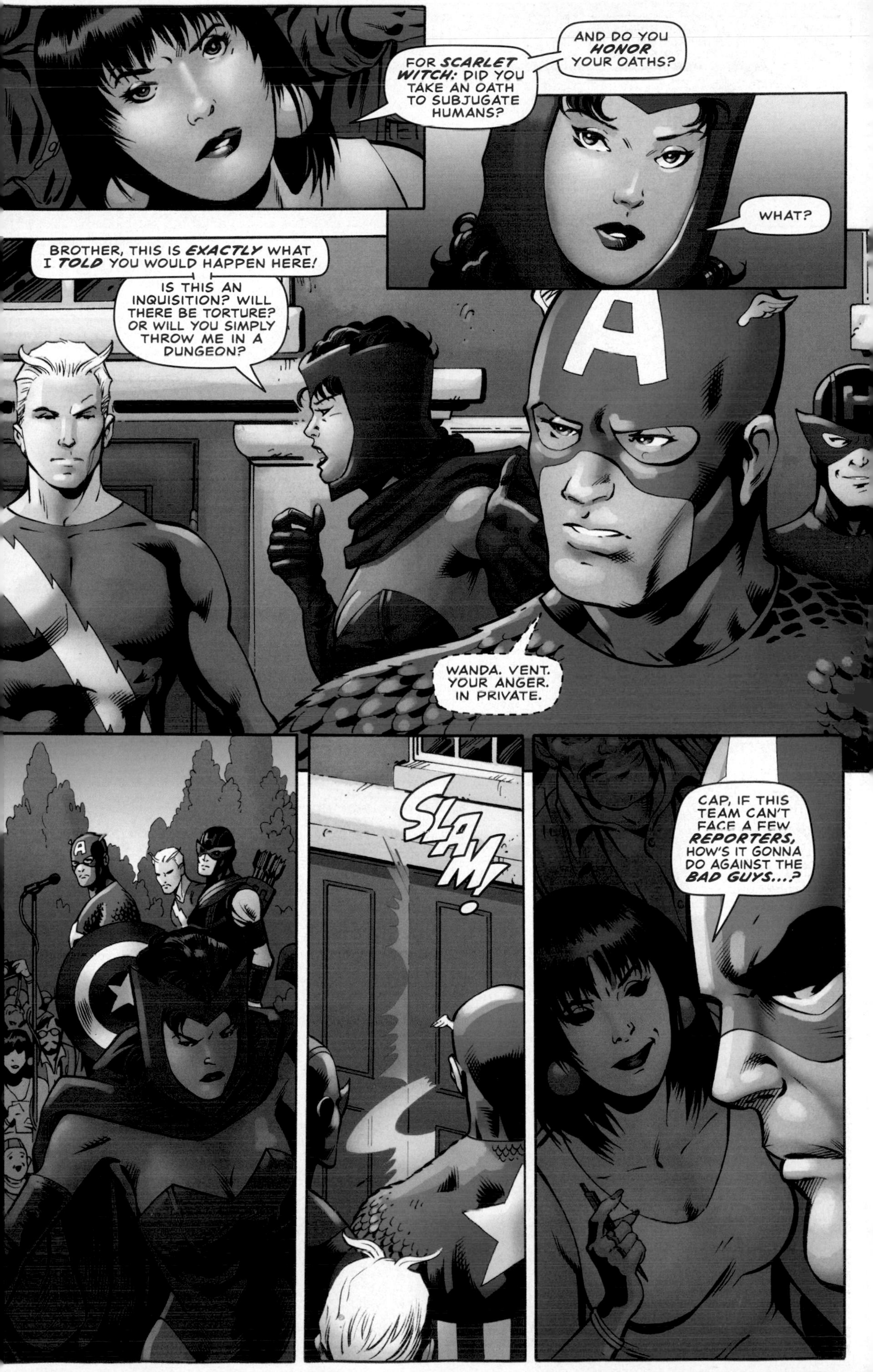

FOR SCARLET WITCH: DID YOU TAKE AN OATH TO SUBJUGATE HUMANS?
AND DO YOU HONOR YOUR OATHS?
WHAT?
BROTHER, THIS IS EXACTLY WHAT I TOLD YOU WOULD HAPPEN HERE!
IS THIS AN INQUISITION? WILL THERE BE TORTURE? OR WILL YOU SIMPLY THROW ME IN A DUNGEON?
WANDA. VENT. YOUR ANGER. IN PRIVATE.
SLAM!
CAP, IF THIS TEAM CAN'T FACE A FEW REPORTERS, HOW'S IT GONNA DO AGAINST THE BAD GUYS...?

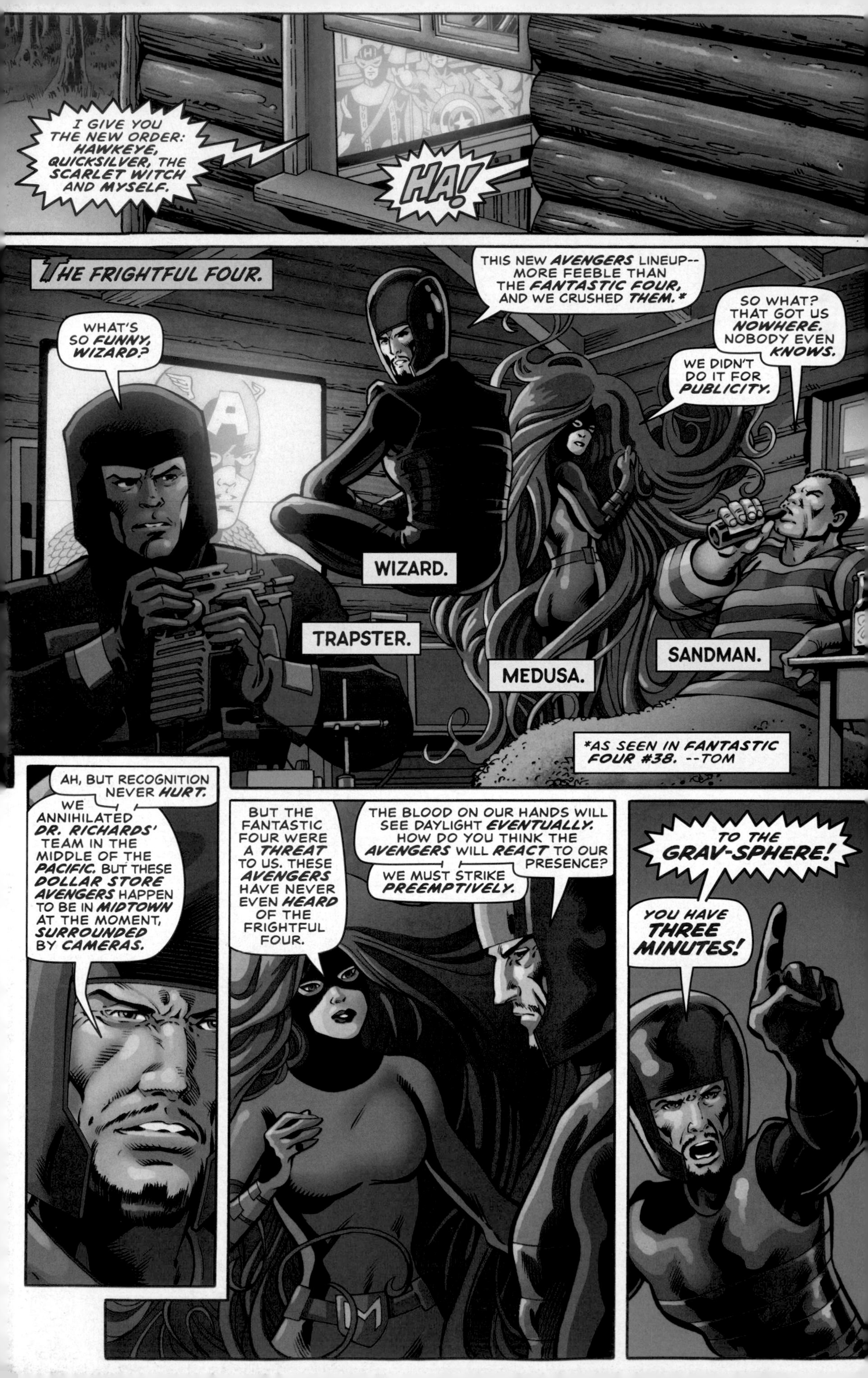

I GIVE YOU THE NEW ORDER: HAWKEYE, QUICKSILVER, THE SCARLET WITCH AND MYSELF.
HA!
THE FRIGHTFUL FOUR.
WHAT'S SO FUNNY, WIZARD?
THIS NEW AVENGERS LINEUP-- MORE FEEBLE THAN THE FANTASTIC FOUR, AND WE CRUSHED THEM.*
SO WHAT? THAT GOT US NOWHERE. NOBODY EVEN KNOWS.
WE DIDN'T DO IT FOR PUBLICITY.
WIZARD.
TRAPSTER.
MEDUSA.
SANDMAN.
*AS SEEN IN FANTASTIC FOUR #38. --TOM
AH, BUT RECOGNITION NEVER HURT.
WE ANNIHILATED DR. RICHARDS' TEAM IN THE MIDDLE OF THE PACIFIC. BUT THESE DOLLAR STORE AVENGERS HAPPEN TO BE IN MIDTOWN AT THE MOMENT, SURROUNDED BY CAMERAS.
BUT THE FANTASTIC FOUR WERE A THREAT TO US. THESE AVENGERS HAVE NEVER EVEN HEARD OF THE FRIGHTFUL FOUR.
THE BLOOD ON OUR HANDS WILL SEE DAYLIGHT EVENTUALLY. HOW DO YOU THINK THE AVENGERS WILL REACT TO OUR PRESENCE?
WE MUST STRIKE PREEMPTIVELY.
TO THE GRAV-SPHERE!
YOU HAVE THREE MINUTES!

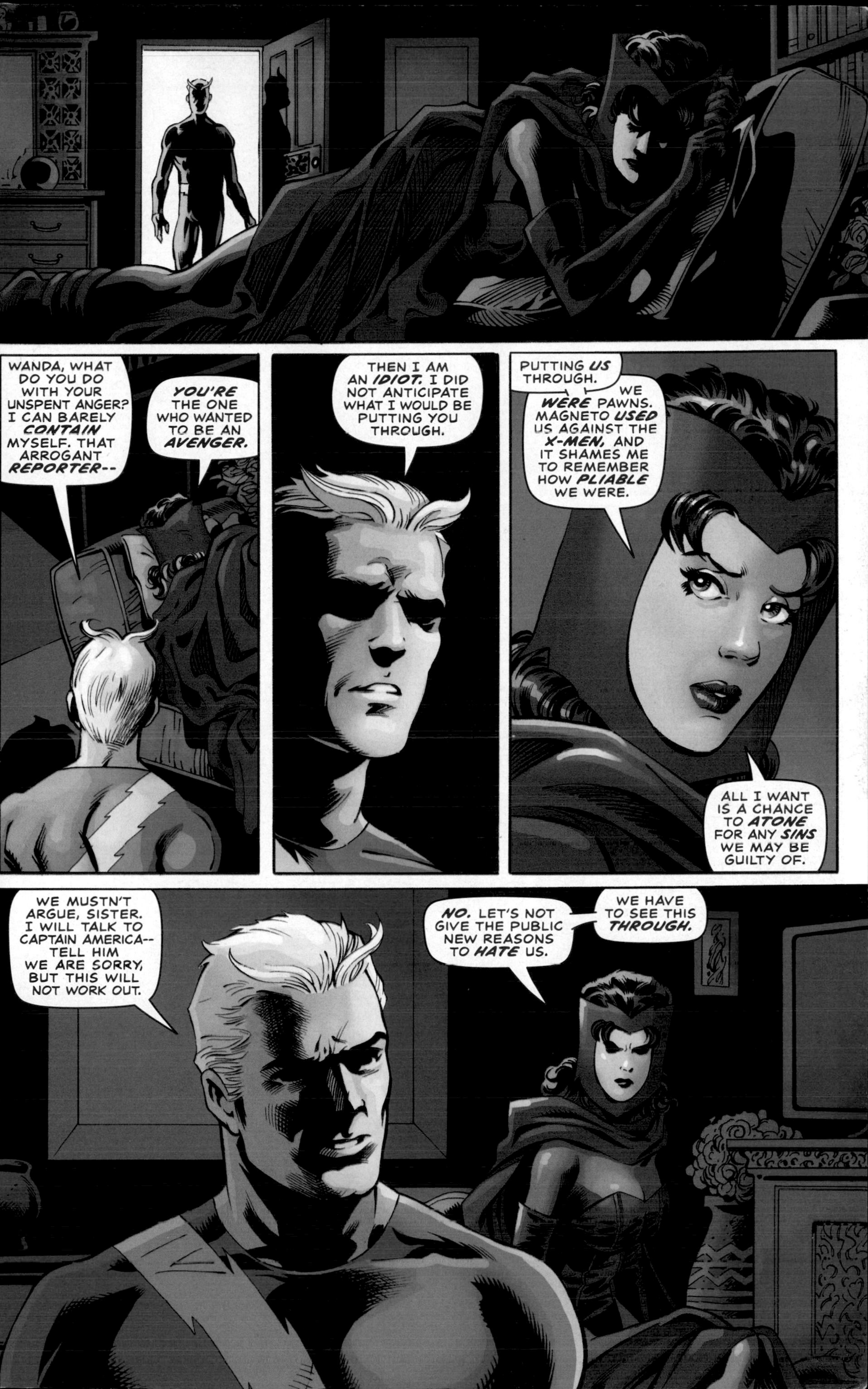
WANDA, WHAT DO YOU DO WITH YOUR UNSPENT ANGER? I CAN BARELY CONTAIN MYSELF. THAT ARROGANT REPORTER--
YOU'RE THE ONE WHO WANTED TO BE AN AVENGER.
THEN I AM AN IDIOT. I DID NOT ANTICIPATE WHAT I WOULD BE PUTTING YOU THROUGH.
PUTTING US THROUGH.
WE WERE PAWNS. MAGNETO USED US AGAINST THE X-MEN, AND IT SHAMES ME TO REMEMBER HOW PLIABLE WE WERE.
ALL I WANT IS A CHANCE TO ATONE FOR ANY SINS WE MAY BE GUILTY OF.
WE MUSTN'T ARGUE, SISTER. I WILL TALK TO CAPTAIN AMERICA-- TELL HIM WE ARE SORRY, BUT THIS WILL NOT WORK OUT.
NO. LET'S NOT GIVE THE PUBLIC NEW REASONS TO HATE US.
WE HAVE TO SEE THIS THROUGH.

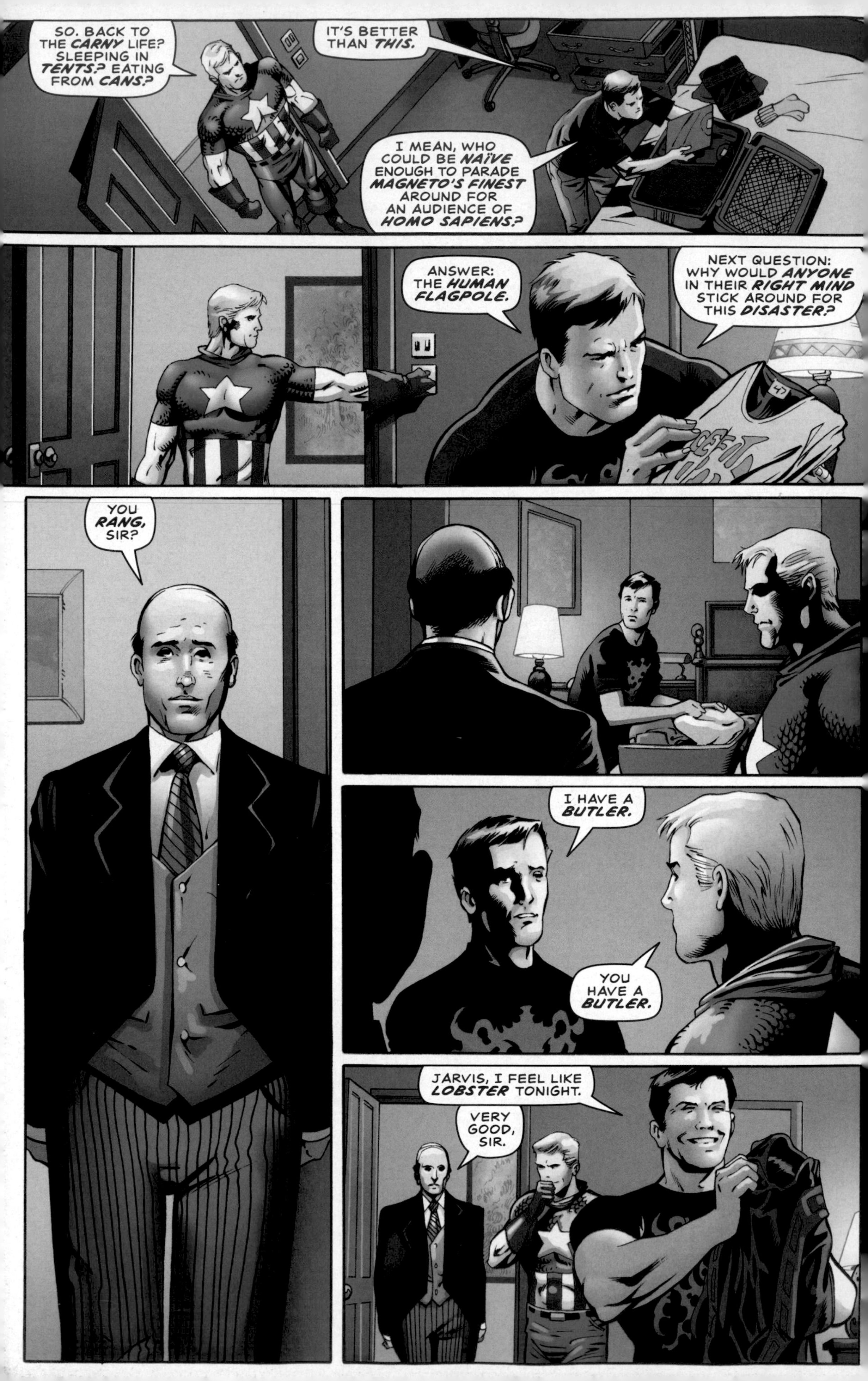
SO. BACK TO THE CARNY LIFE? SLEEPING IN TENTS? EATING FROM CANS?
IT'S BETTER THAN THIS.
I MEAN, WHO COULD BE NAÏVE ENOUGH TO PARADE MAGNETO'S FINEST AROUND FOR AN AUDIENCE OF HOMO SAPIENS?
ANSWER: THE HUMAN FLAGPOLE.
NEXT QUESTION: WHY WOULD ANYONE IN THEIR RIGHT MIND STICK AROUND FOR THIS DISASTER?
YOU RANG, SIR?
I HAVE A BUTLER.
YOU HAVE A BUTLER.
JARVIS, I FEEL LIKE LOBSTER TONIGHT.
VERY GOOD, SIR.

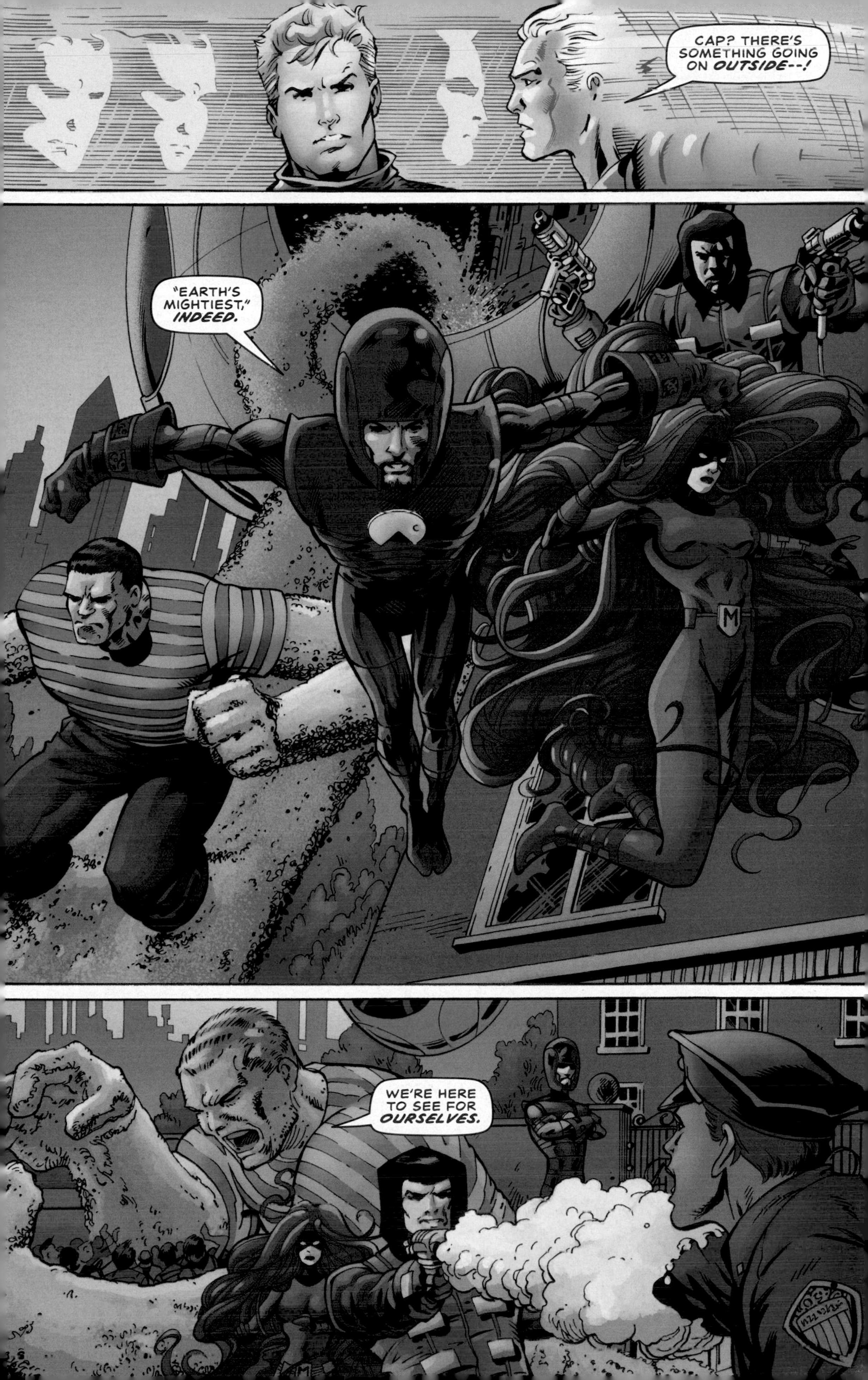
CAP? THERE'S SOMETHING GOING ON OUTSIDE--!
"EARTH'S MIGHTIEST," INDEED.
WE'RE HERE TO SEE FOR OURSELVES.

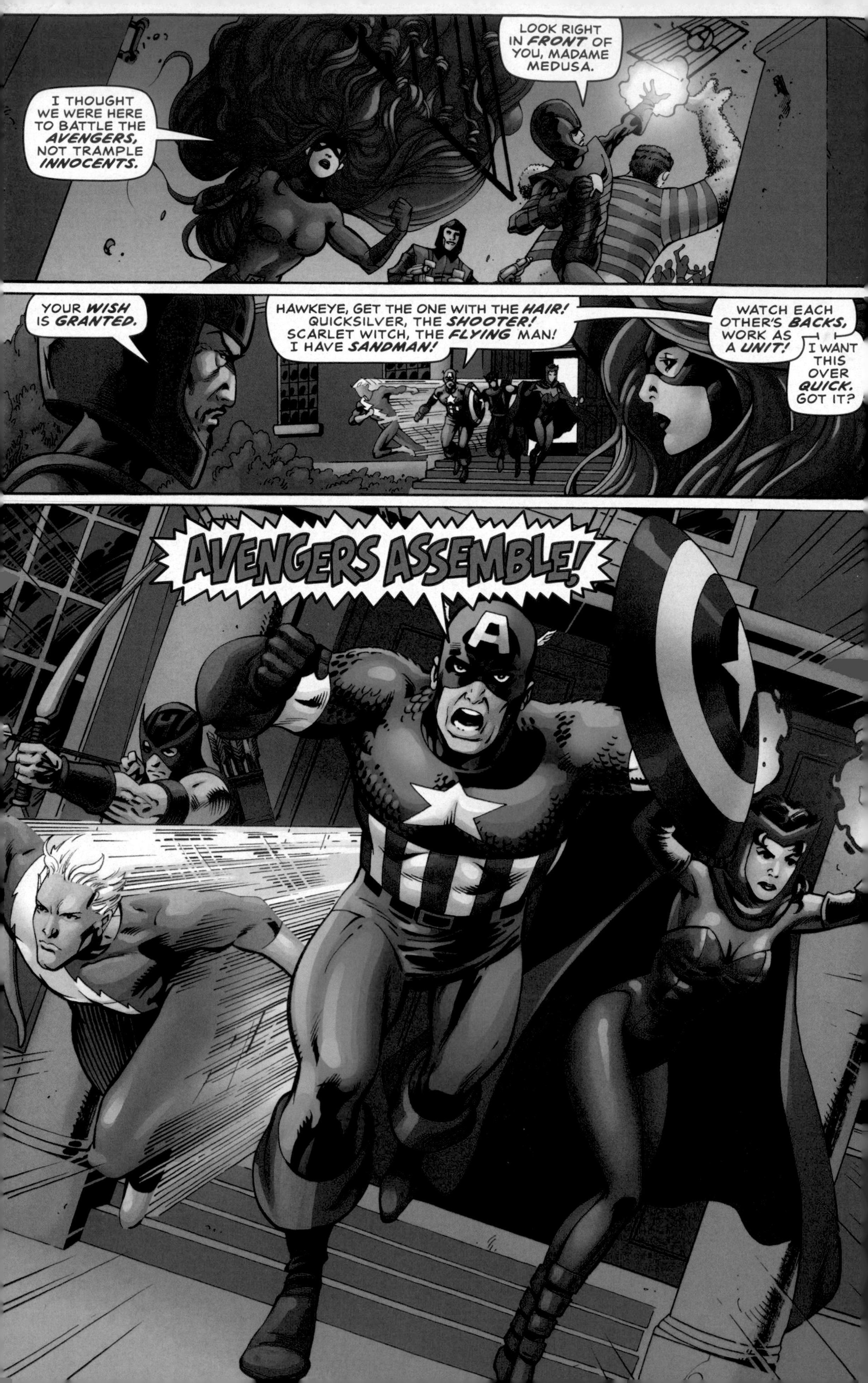
I THOUGHT WE WERE HERE TO BATTLE THE AVENGERS, NOT TRAMPLE INNOCENTS.
LOOK RIGHT IN FRONT OF YOU, MADAME MEDUSA.
YOUR WISH IS GRANTED.
HAWKEYE, GET THE ONE WITH THE HAIR! QUICKSILVER, THE SHOOTER! SCARLET WITCH, THE FLYING MAN! I HAVE SANDMAN!
WATCH EACH OTHER'S BACKS, WORK AS A UNIT!
I WANT THIS OVER QUICK. GOT IT?
AVENGERS ASSEMBLE!

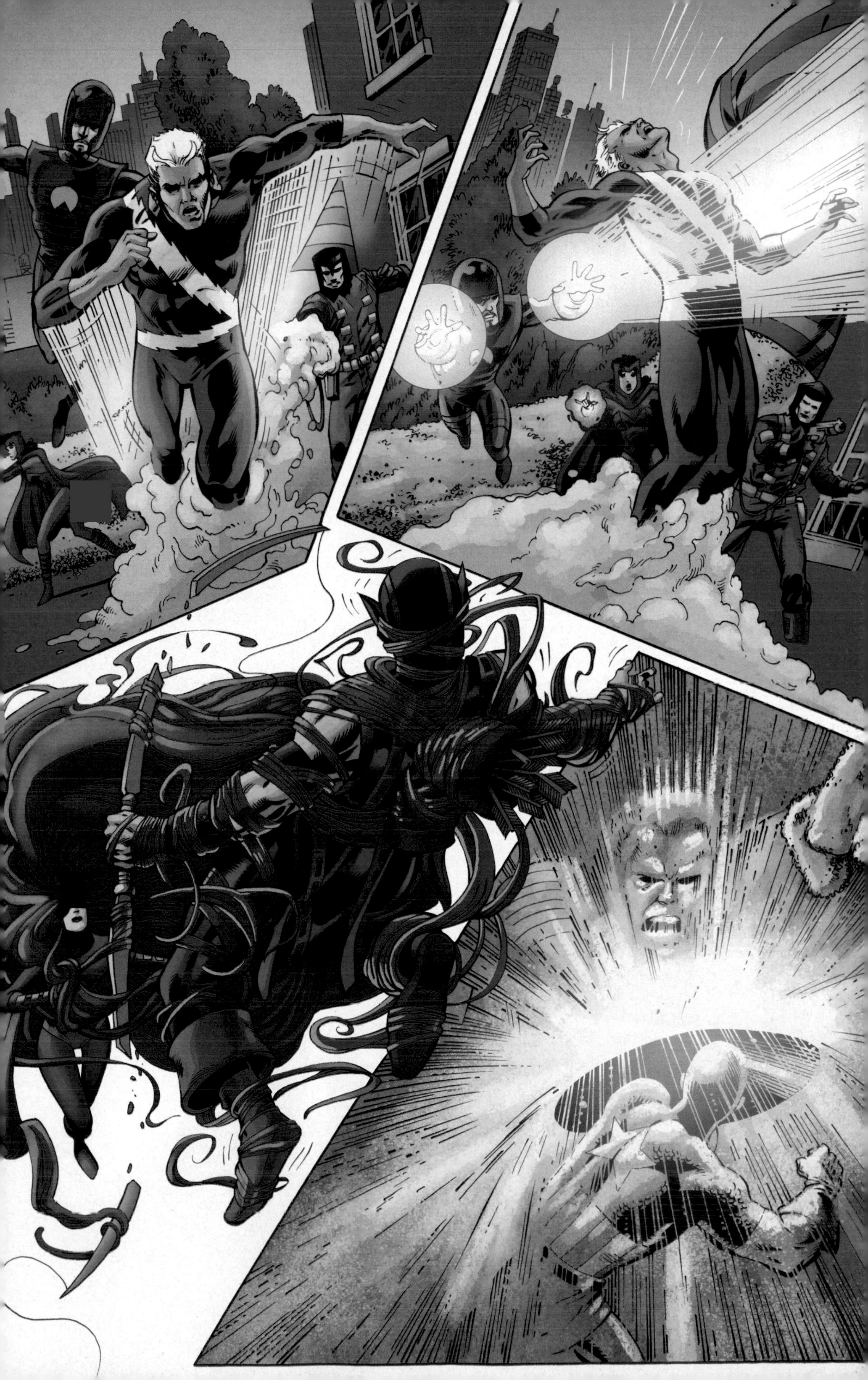

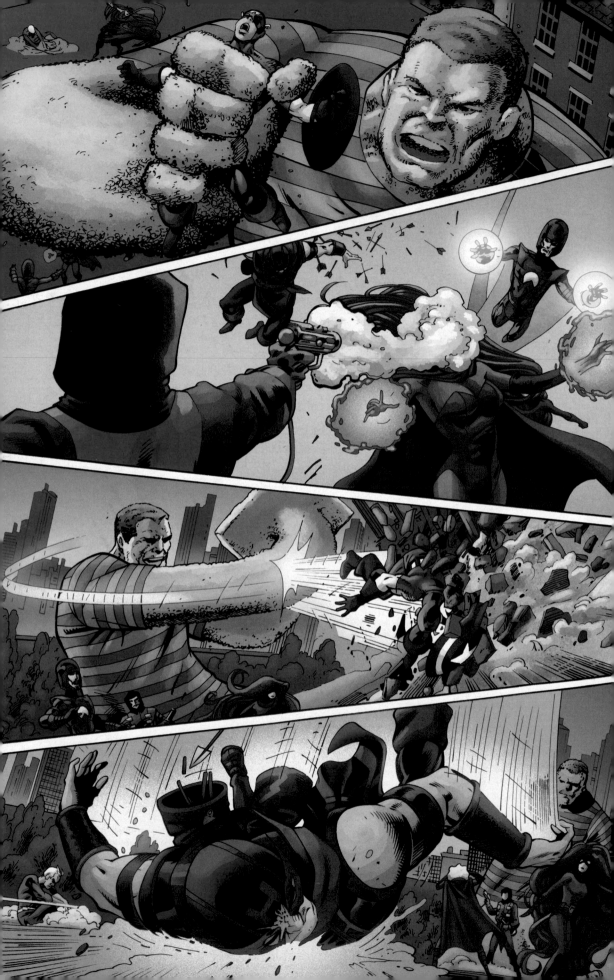

WE'RE FINISHED HERE.

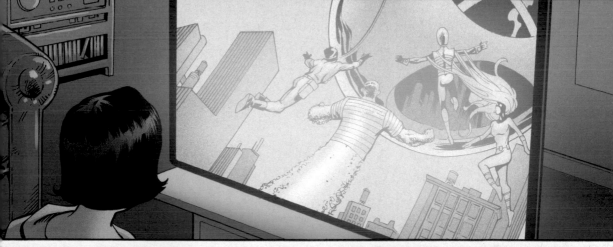

OH, DEAR GOD.

WHAT HAVE WE *DONE...?*

NEXT:
AVENGERS
FIVE

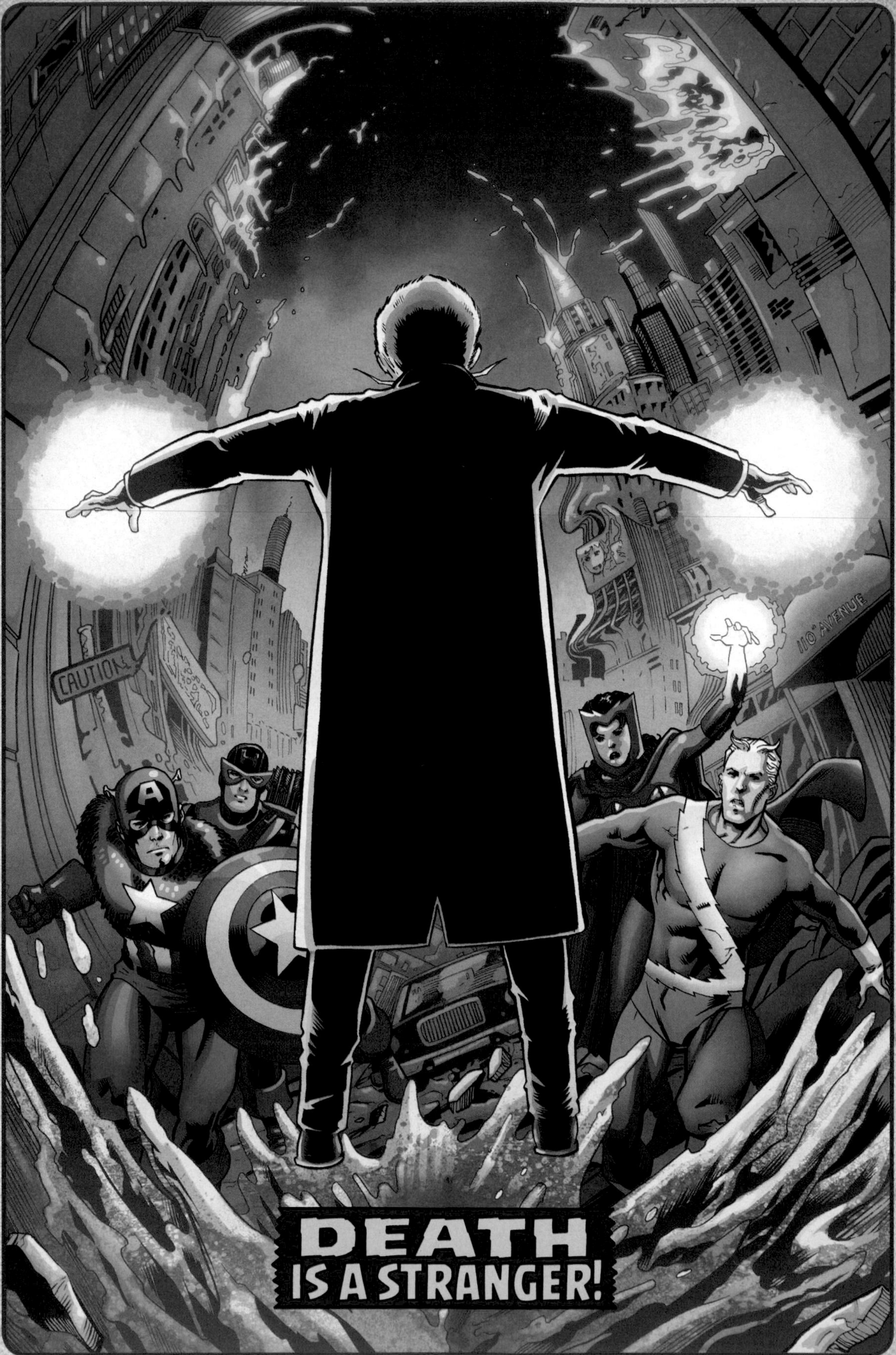
CAUTION
110th AVENUE
DEATH
IS A STRANGER!

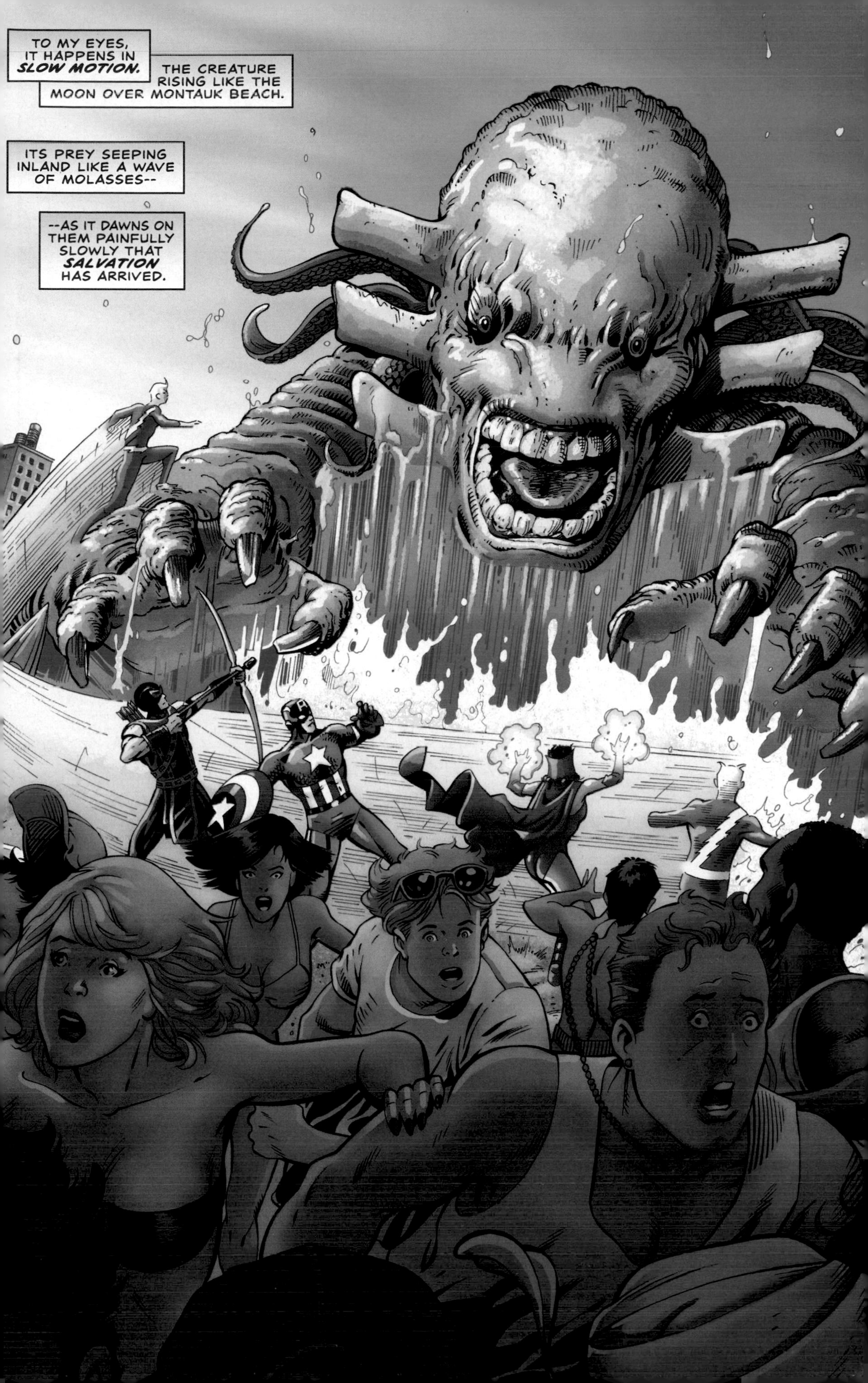
TO MY EYES, IT HAPPENS IN SLOW MOTION.
THE CREATURE RISING LIKE THE MOON OVER MONTAUK BEACH.
ITS PREY SEEPING INLAND LIKE A WAVE OF MOLASSES--
--AS IT DAWNS ON THEM PAINFULLY SLOWLY THAT SALVATION HAS ARRIVED.

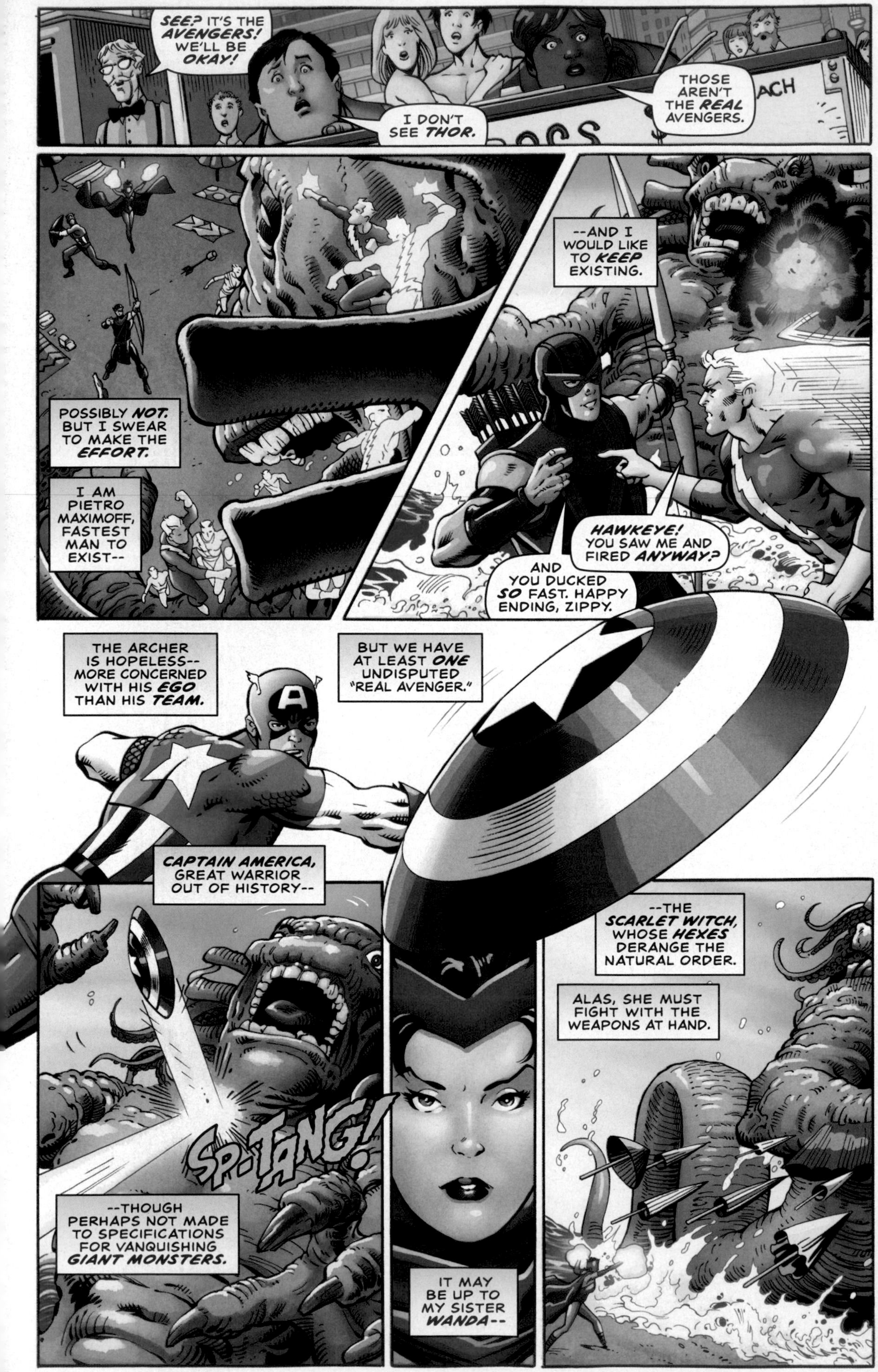
SEE? IT'S THE AVENGERS! WE'LL BE OKAY!
I DON'T SEE THOR.
THOSE AREN'T THE REAL AVENGERS.
POSSIBLY NOT. BUT I SWEAR TO MAKE THE EFFORT.
I AM PIETRO MAXIMOFF, FASTEST MAN TO EXIST--
--AND I WOULD LIKE TO KEEP EXISTING.
HAWKEYE! YOU SAW ME AND FIRED ANYWAY?
AND YOU DUCKED SO FAST. HAPPY ENDING, ZIPPY.
THE ARCHER IS HOPELESS-- MORE CONCERNED WITH HIS EGO THAN HIS TEAM.
BUT WE HAVE AT LEAST ONE UNDISPUTED "REAL AVENGER."
CAPTAIN AMERICA, GREAT WARRIOR OUT OF HISTORY--
SP-TANG!
--THOUGH PERHAPS NOT MADE TO SPECIFICATIONS FOR VANQUISHING GIANT MONSTERS.
IT MAY BE UP TO MY SISTER WANDA--
--THE SCARLET WITCH, WHOSE HEXES DERANGE THE NATURAL ORDER.
ALAS, SHE MUST FIGHT WITH THE WEAPONS AT HAND.

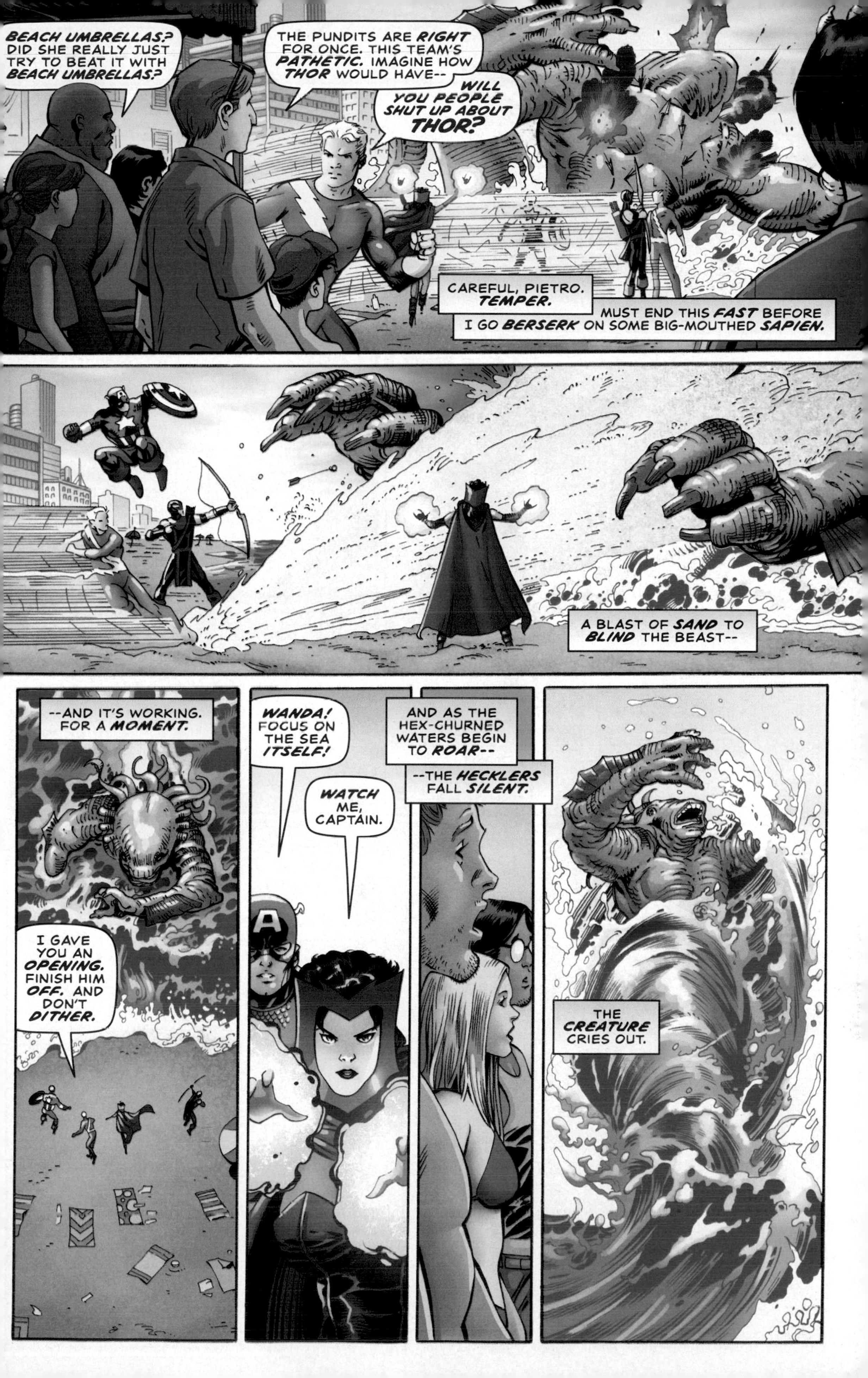
BEACH UMBRELLAS? DID SHE REALLY JUST TRY TO BEAT IT WITH BEACH UMBRELLAS?
THE PUNDITS ARE RIGHT FOR ONCE. THIS TEAM'S PATHETIC. IMAGINE HOW THOR WOULD HAVE--
WILL YOU PEOPLE SHUT UP ABOUT THOR?
CAREFUL, PIETRO. TEMPER.
MUST END THIS FAST BEFORE I GO BERSERK ON SOME BIG-MOUTHED SAPIEN.
A BLAST OF SAND TO BLIND THE BEAST--
--AND IT'S WORKING. FOR A MOMENT.
I GAVE YOU AN OPENING. FINISH HIM OFF. AND DON'T DITHER.
WANDA! FOCUS ON THE SEA ITSELF!
WATCH ME, CAPTAIN.
AND AS THE HEX-CHURNED WATERS BEGIN TO ROAR--
--THE HECKLERS FALL SILENT.
THE CREATURE CRIES OUT.

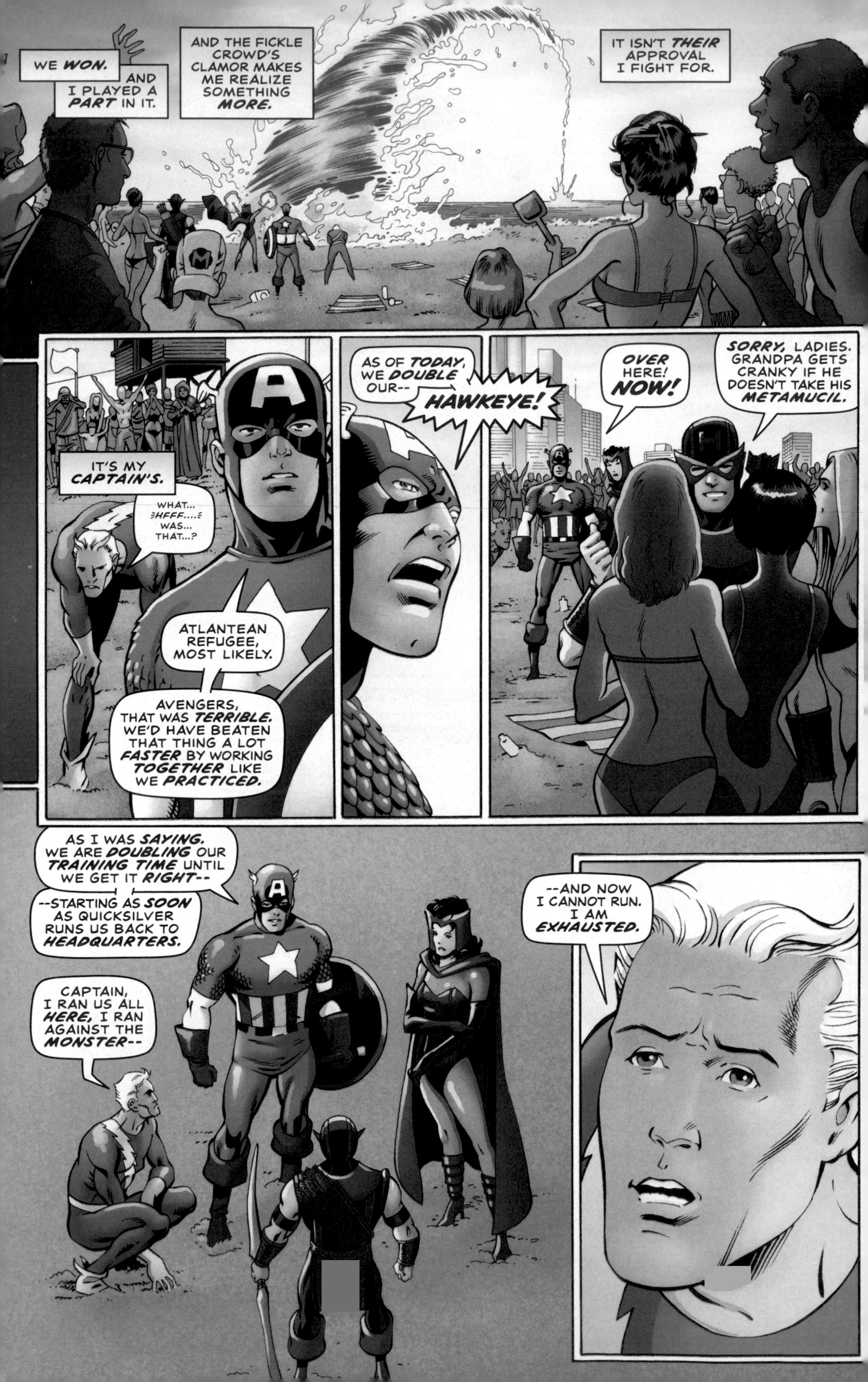
WE WON.
AND I PLAYED A PART IN IT.
AND THE FICKLE CROWD'S CLAMOR MAKES ME REALIZE SOMETHING MORE.
IT ISN'T THEIR APPROVAL I FIGHT FOR.
IT'S MY CAPTAIN'S.
WHAT... HFFF.... WAS... THAT...?
ATLANTEAN REFUGEE, MOST LIKELY.
AVENGERS, THAT WAS TERRIBLE. WE'D HAVE BEATEN THAT THING A LOT FASTER BY WORKING TOGETHER LIKE WE PRACTICED.
AS OF TODAY, WE DOUBLE OUR--
HAWKEYE!
OVER HERE! NOW!
SORRY, LADIES. GRANDPA GETS CRANKY IF HE DOESN'T TAKE HIS METAMUCIL.
AS I WAS SAYING. WE ARE DOUBLING OUR TRAINING TIME UNTIL WE GET IT RIGHT--
--STARTING AS SOON AS QUICKSILVER RUNS US BACK TO HEADQUARTERS.
CAPTAIN, I RAN US ALL HERE, I RAN AGAINST THE MONSTER--
--AND NOW I CANNOT RUN. I AM EXHAUSTED.

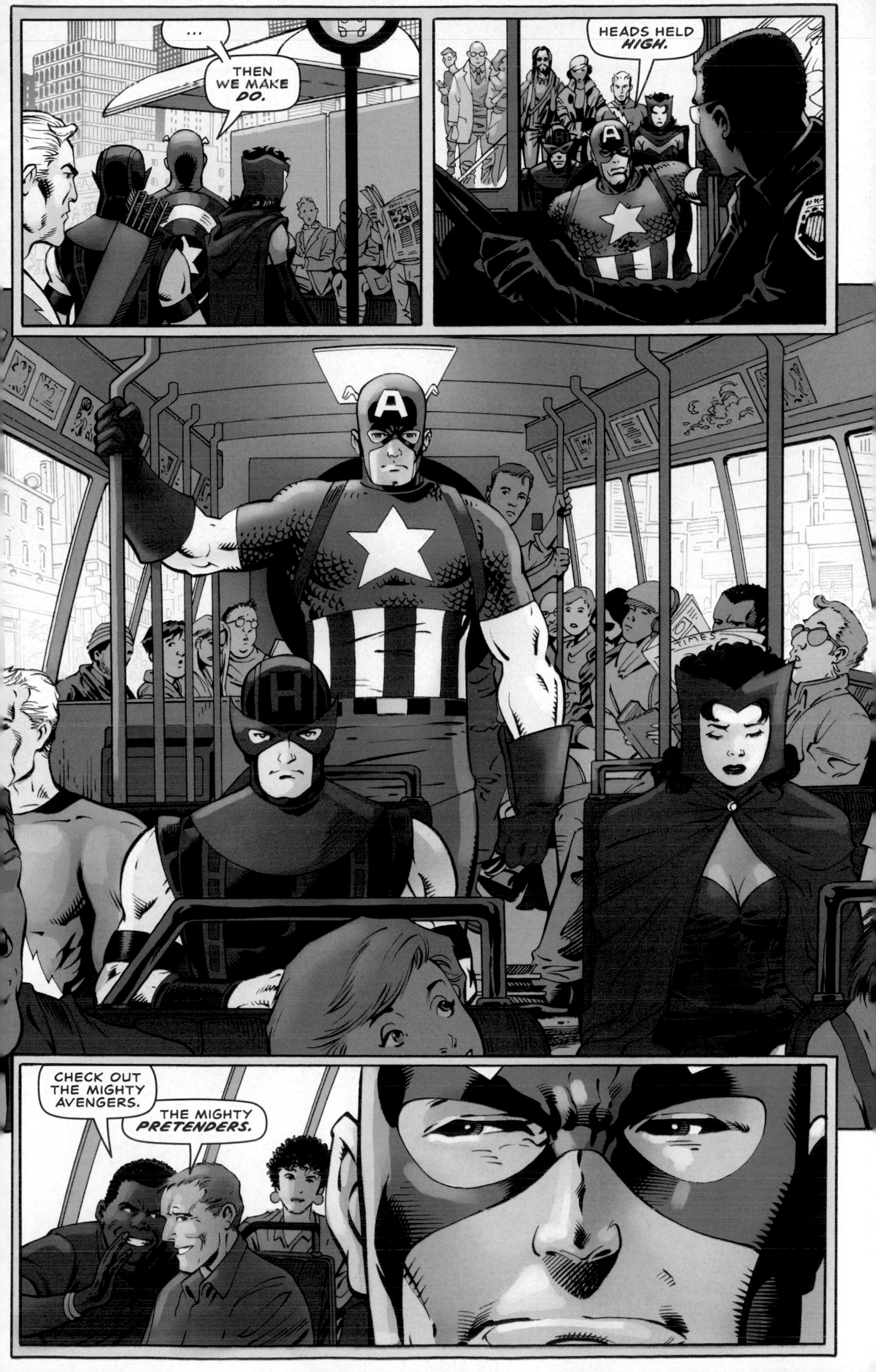
...
THEN WE MAKE *DO.*
HEADS HELD *HIGH.*
TIMES
CHECK OUT THE MIGHTY AVENGERS.
THE MIGHTY *PRETENDERS.*

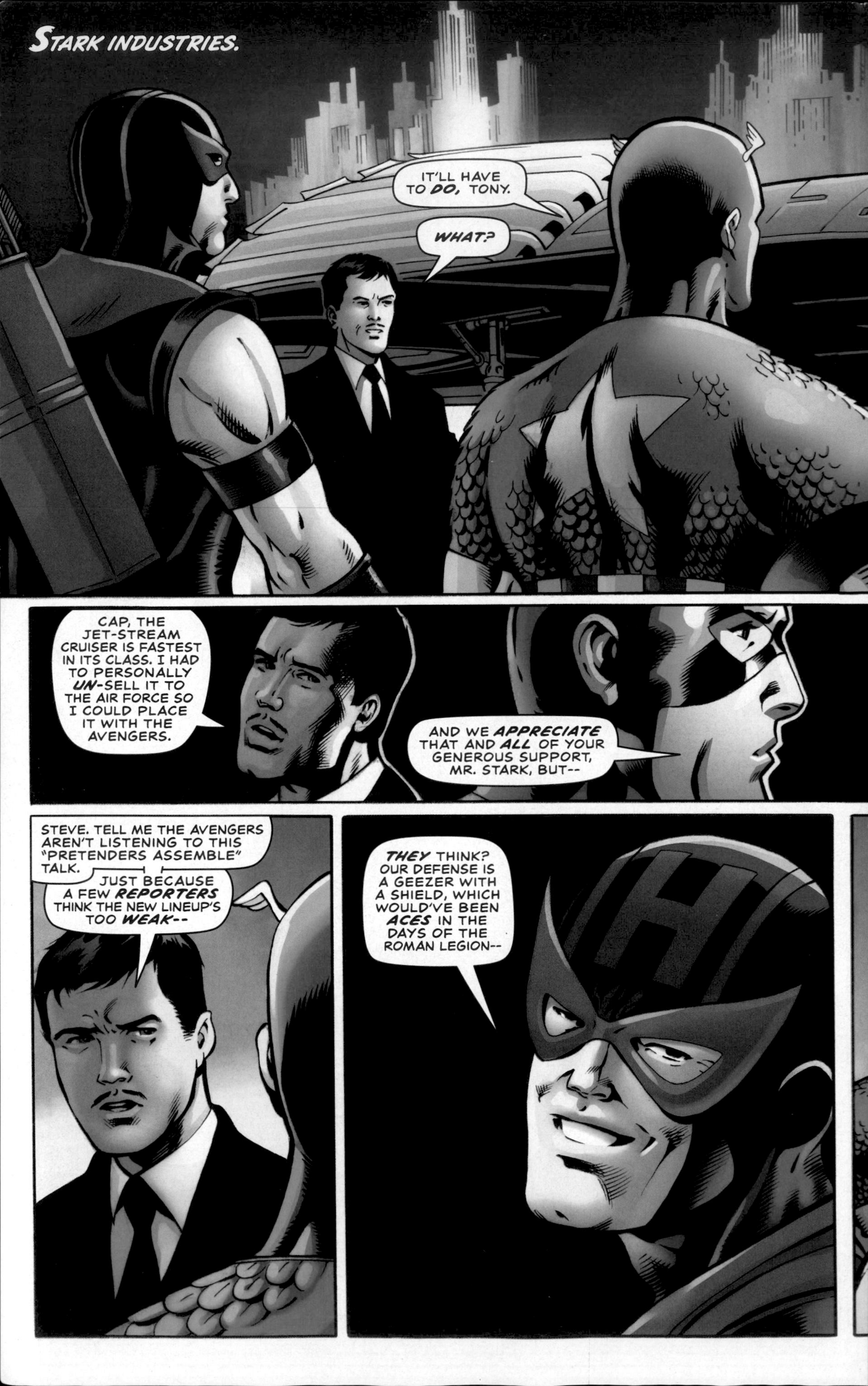
STARK INDUSTRIES.
IT'LL HAVE TO DO, TONY.
WHAT?
CAP, THE JET-STREAM CRUISER IS FASTEST IN ITS CLASS. I HAD TO PERSONALLY UN-SELL IT TO THE AIR FORCE SO I COULD PLACE IT WITH THE AVENGERS.
AND WE APPRECIATE THAT AND ALL OF YOUR GENEROUS SUPPORT, MR. STARK, BUT--
STEVE. TELL ME THE AVENGERS AREN'T LISTENING TO THIS "PRETENDERS ASSEMBLE" TALK.
JUST BECAUSE A FEW REPORTERS THINK THE NEW LINEUP'S TOO WEAK--
THEY THINK? OUR DEFENSE IS A GEEZER WITH A SHIELD, WHICH WOULD'VE BEEN ACES IN THE DAYS OF THE ROMAN LEGION--

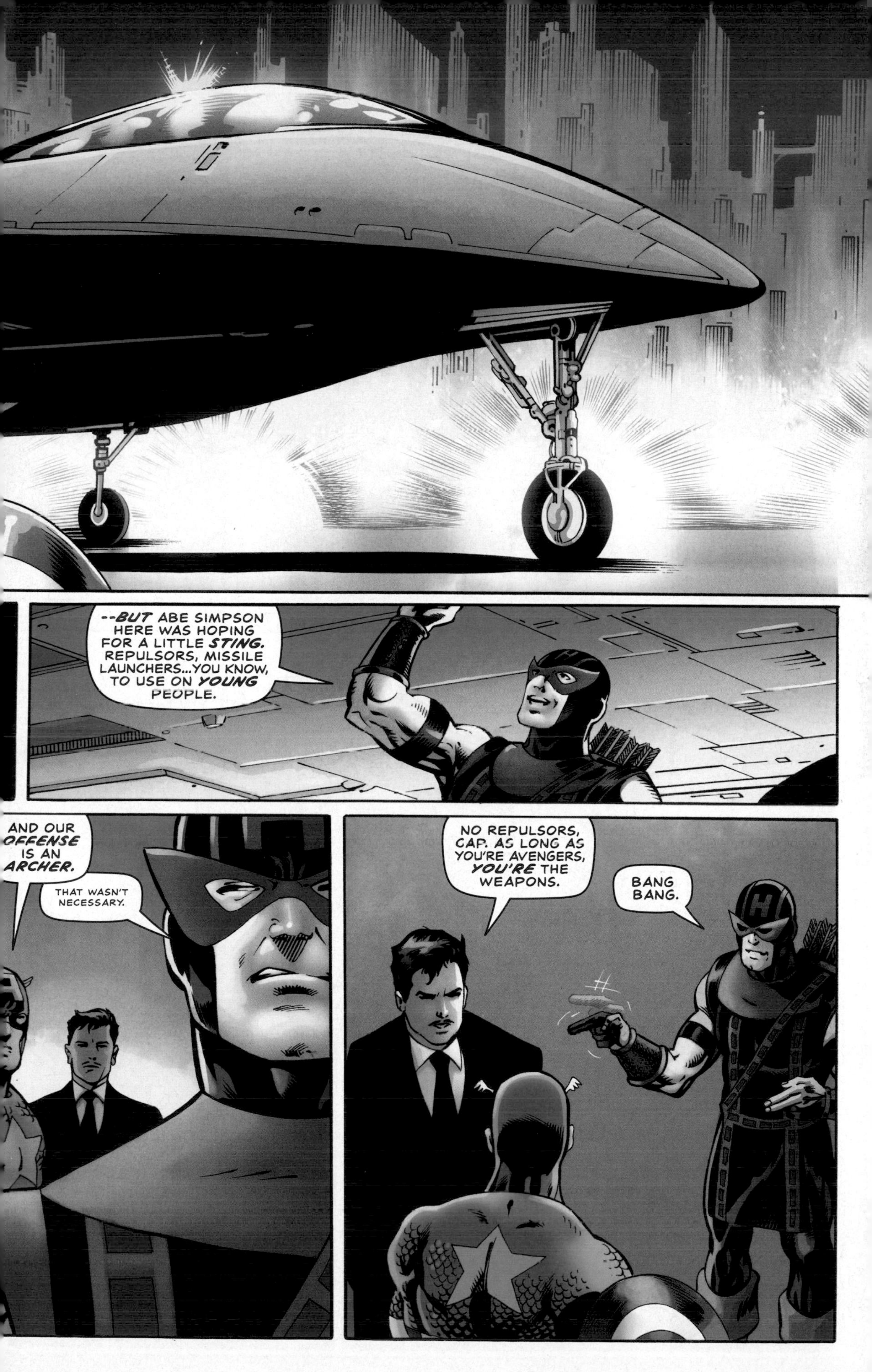
--BUT ABE SIMPSON HERE WAS HOPING FOR A LITTLE STING. REPULSORS, MISSILE LAUNCHERS...YOU KNOW, TO USE ON YOUNG PEOPLE.
AND OUR OFFENSE IS AN ARCHER.
THAT WASN'T NECESSARY.
NO REPULSORS, CAP. AS LONG AS YOU'RE AVENGERS, YOU'RE THE WEAPONS.
BANG BANG.

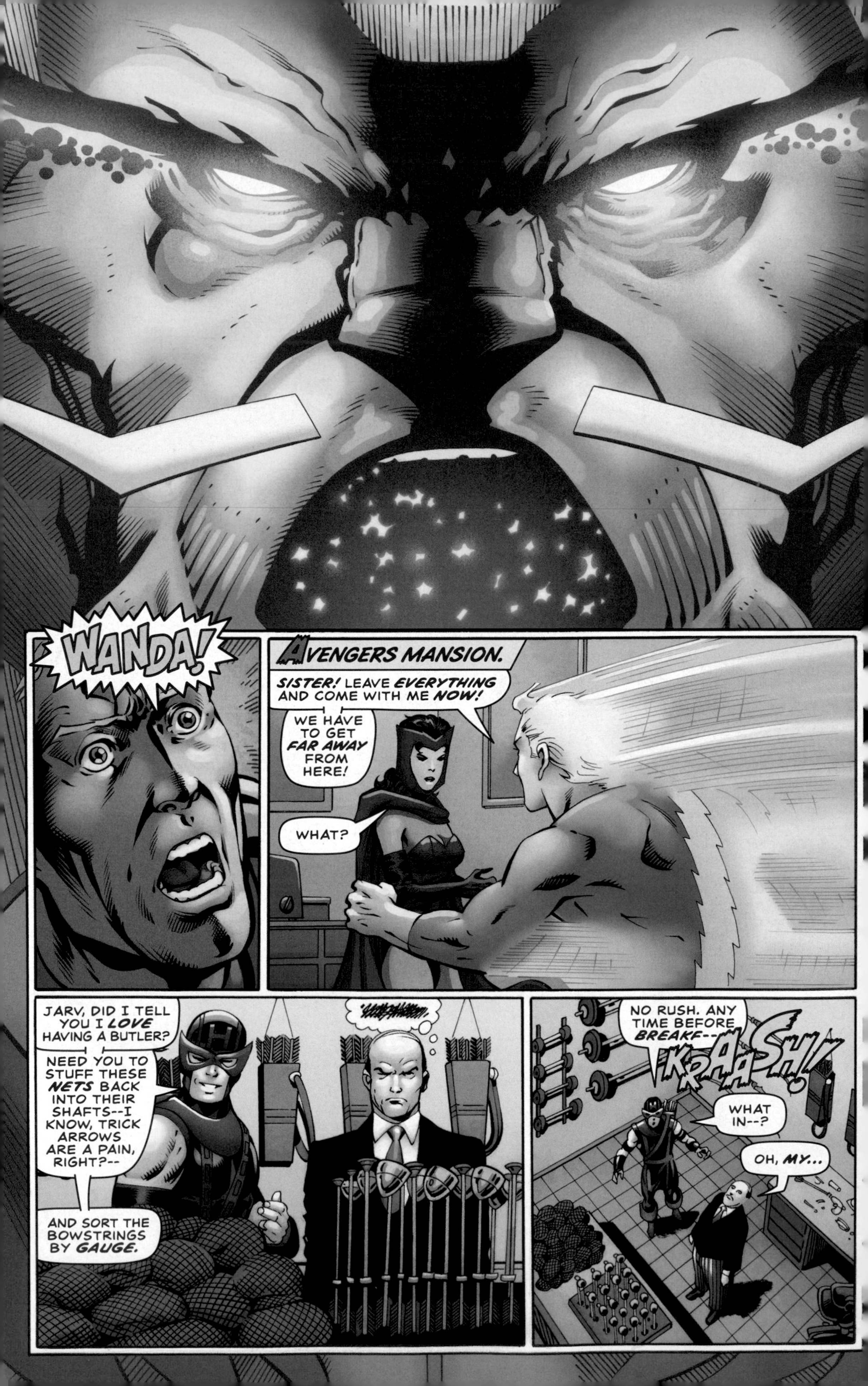
WANDA!
AVENGERS MANSION.
SISTER! LEAVE EVERYTHING AND COME WITH ME NOW!
WE HAVE TO GET FAR AWAY FROM HERE!
WHAT?
JARV, DID I TELL YOU I LOVE HAVING A BUTLER?
NEED YOU TO STUFF THESE NETS BACK INTO THEIR SHAFTS--I KNOW, TRICK ARROWS ARE A PAIN, RIGHT?--
AND SORT THE BOWSTRINGS BY GAUGE.
NO RUSH. ANY TIME BEFORE BREAKF--
KRAASH!
WHAT IN--?
OH, MY...

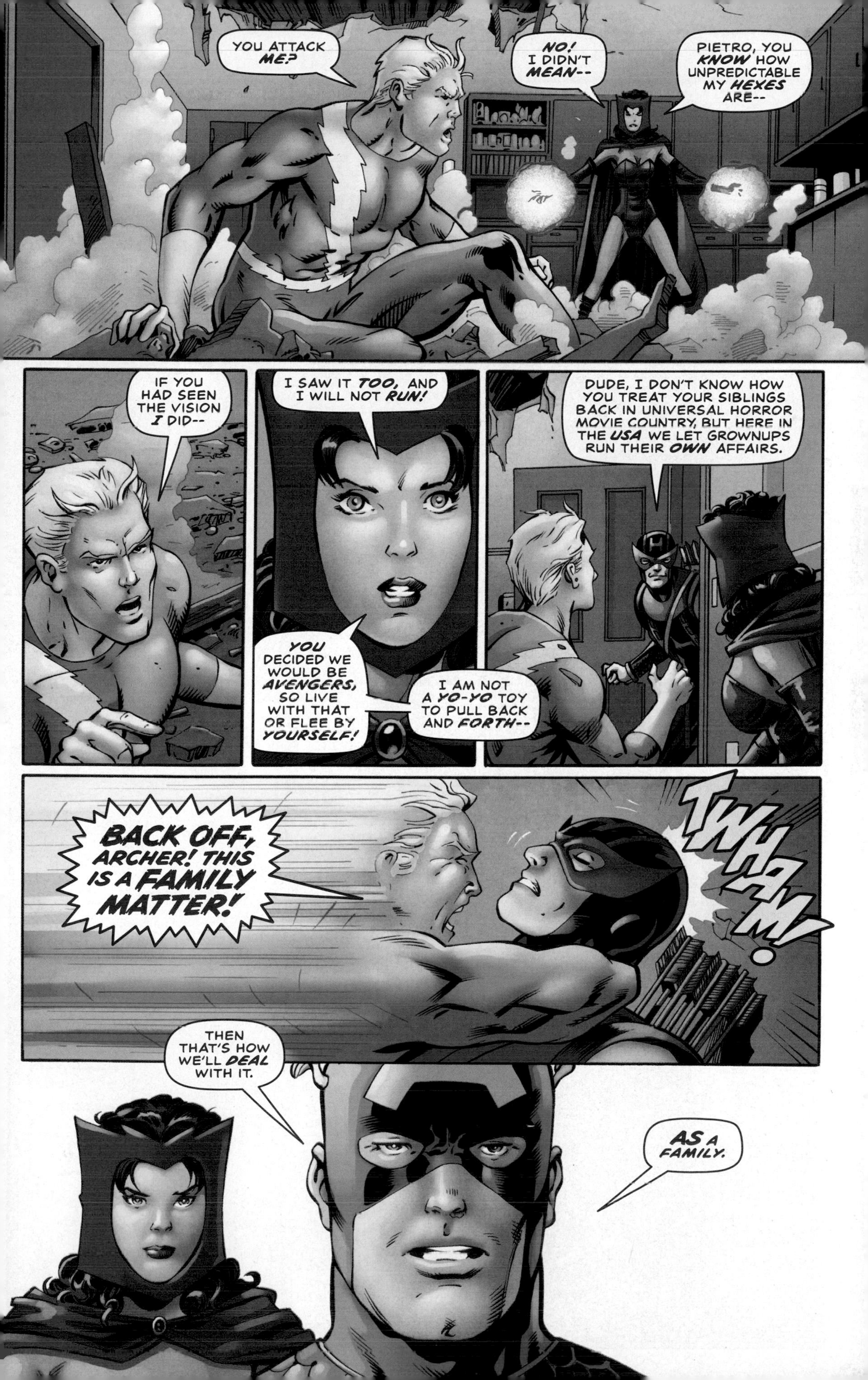

YOU ATTACK ME?
NO! I DIDN'T MEAN--
PIETRO, YOU KNOW HOW UNPREDICTABLE MY HEXES ARE--
IF YOU HAD SEEN THE VISION I DID--
I SAW IT TOO, AND I WILL NOT RUN!
YOU DECIDED WE WOULD BE AVENGERS, SO LIVE WITH THAT OR FLEE BY YOURSELF!
I AM NOT A YO-YO TOY TO PULL BACK AND FORTH--
DUDE, I DON'T KNOW HOW YOU TREAT YOUR SIBLINGS BACK IN UNIVERSAL HORROR MOVIE COUNTRY, BUT HERE IN THE USA WE LET GROWNUPS RUN THEIR OWN AFFAIRS.
BACK OFF, ARCHER! THIS IS A FAMILY MATTER!
THWAM!
THEN THAT'S HOW WE'LL DEAL WITH IT.
AS A FAMILY.

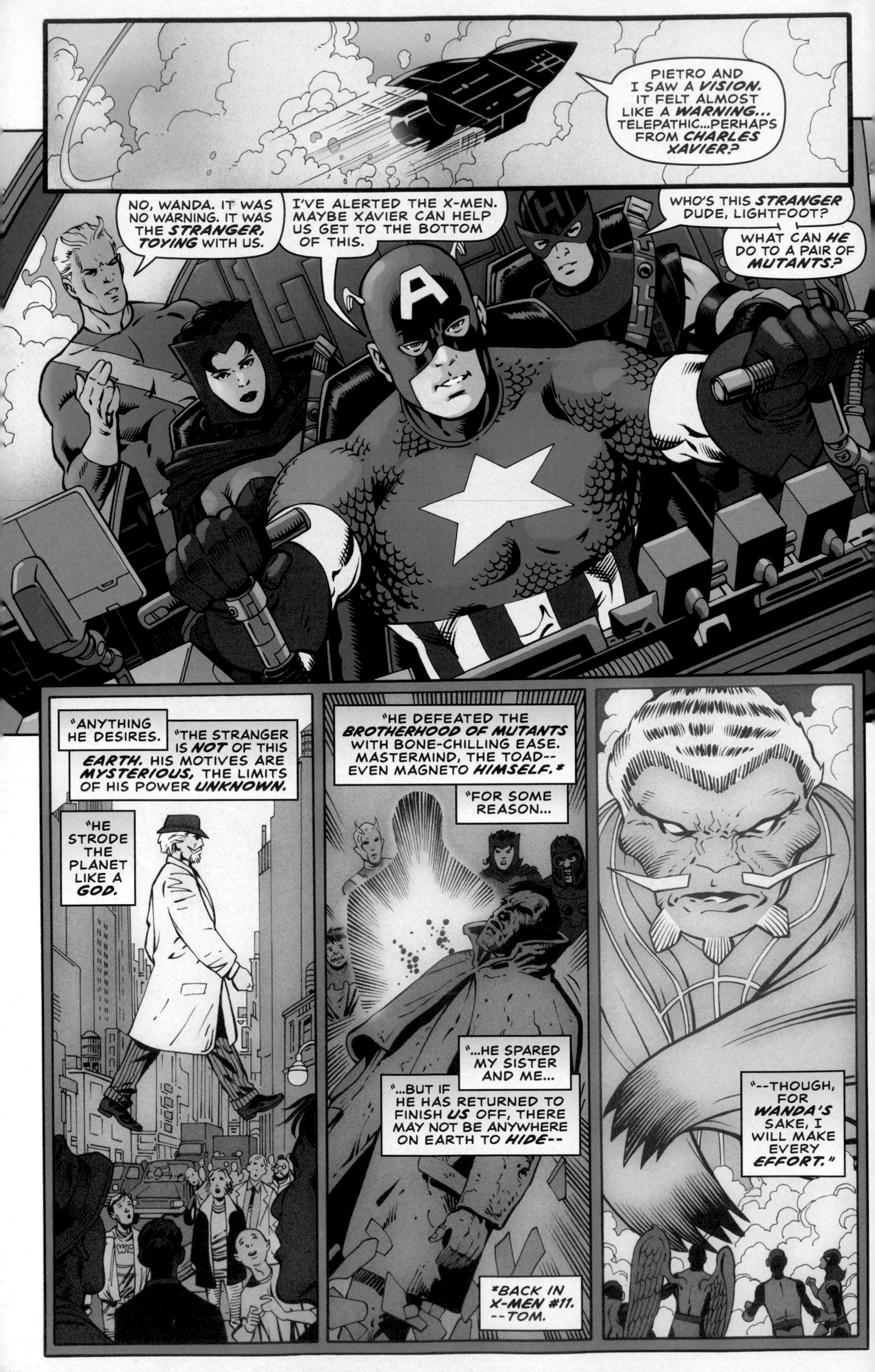
PIETRO AND I SAW A VISION. IT FELT ALMOST LIKE A WARNING... TELEPATHIC...PERHAPS FROM CHARLES XAVIER?
NO, WANDA. IT WAS NO WARNING. IT WAS THE STRANGER, TOYING WITH US.
I'VE ALERTED THE X-MEN. MAYBE XAVIER CAN HELP US GET TO THE BOTTOM OF THIS.
WHO'S THIS STRANGER DUDE, LIGHTFOOT?
WHAT CAN HE DO TO A PAIR OF MUTANTS?
"ANYTHING HE DESIRES.
"THE STRANGER IS NOT OF THIS EARTH. HIS MOTIVES ARE MYSTERIOUS, THE LIMITS OF HIS POWER UNKNOWN.
"HE STRODE THE PLANET LIKE A GOD.
"HE DEFEATED THE BROTHERHOOD OF MUTANTS WITH BONE-CHILLING EASE. MASTERMIND, THE TOAD-- EVEN MAGNETO HIMSELF.*
"FOR SOME REASON...
"...HE SPARED MY SISTER AND ME...
"...BUT IF HE HAS RETURNED TO FINISH US OFF, THERE MAY NOT BE ANYWHERE ON EARTH TO HIDE--
*BACK IN X-MEN #11. --TOM.
"--THOUGH, FOR WANDA'S SAKE, I WILL MAKE EVERY EFFORT."

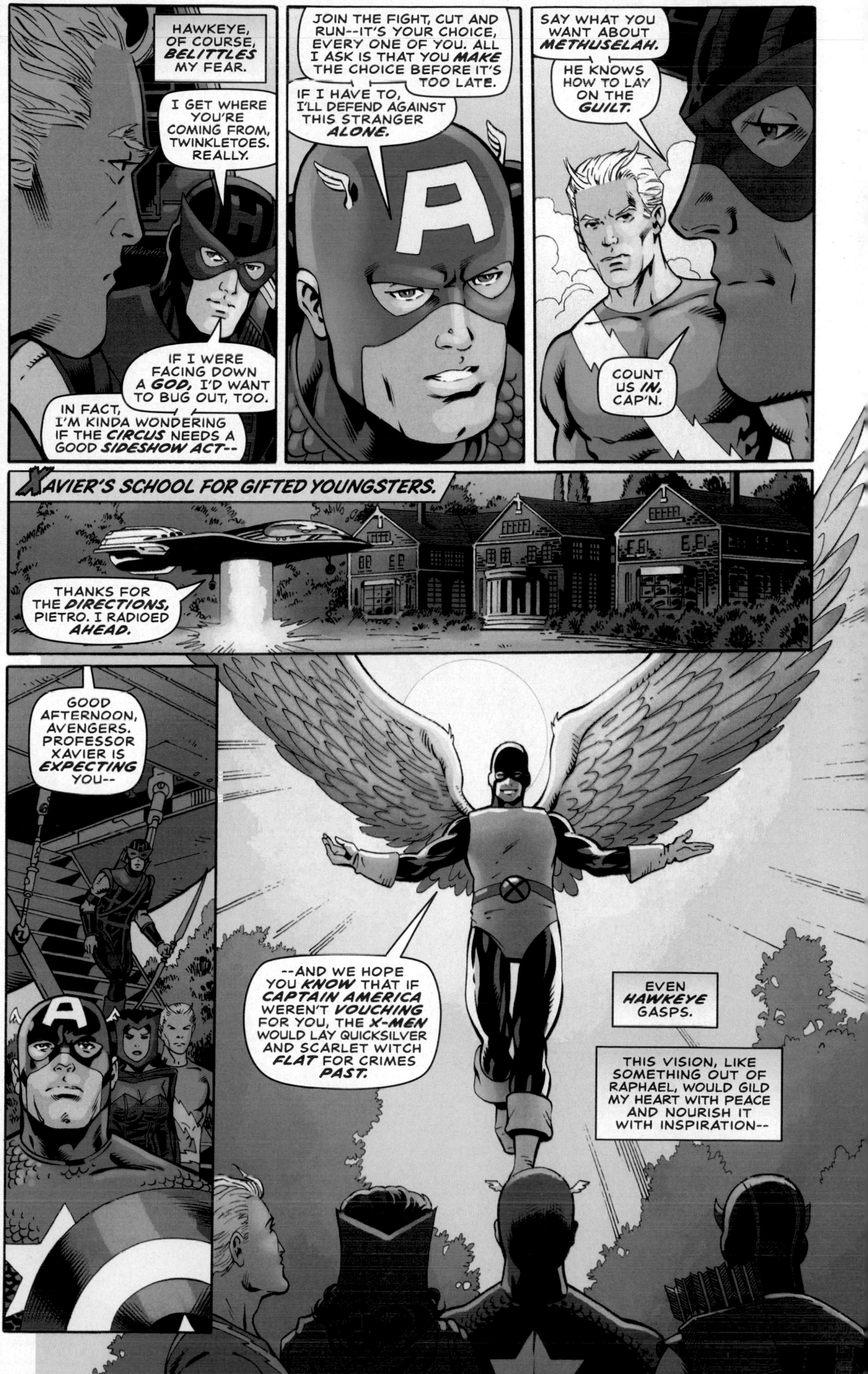
HAWKEYE, OF COURSE, BELITTLES MY FEAR.
I GET WHERE YOU'RE COMING FROM, TWINKLETOES. REALLY.
IF I WERE FACING DOWN A GOD, I'D WANT TO BUG OUT, TOO.
IN FACT, I'M KINDA WONDERING IF THE CIRCUS NEEDS A GOOD SIDESHOW ACT--
JOIN THE FIGHT, CUT AND RUN--IT'S YOUR CHOICE, EVERY ONE OF YOU. ALL I ASK IS THAT YOU MAKE THE CHOICE BEFORE IT'S TOO LATE.
IF I HAVE TO, I'LL DEFEND AGAINST THIS STRANGER ALONE.
SAY WHAT YOU WANT ABOUT METHUSELAH.
HE KNOWS HOW TO LAY ON THE GUILT.
COUNT US IN, CAP'N.
XAVIER'S SCHOOL FOR GIFTED YOUNGSTERS.
THANKS FOR THE DIRECTIONS, PIETRO. I RADIOED AHEAD.
GOOD AFTERNOON, AVENGERS. PROFESSOR XAVIER IS EXPECTING YOU--
--AND WE HOPE YOU KNOW THAT IF CAPTAIN AMERICA WEREN'T VOUCHING FOR YOU, THE X-MEN WOULD LAY QUICKSILVER AND SCARLET WITCH FLAT FOR CRIMES PAST.
EVEN HAWKEYE GASPS.
THIS VISION, LIKE SOMETHING OUT OF RAPHAEL, WOULD GILD MY HEART WITH PEACE AND NOURISH IT WITH INSPIRATION--

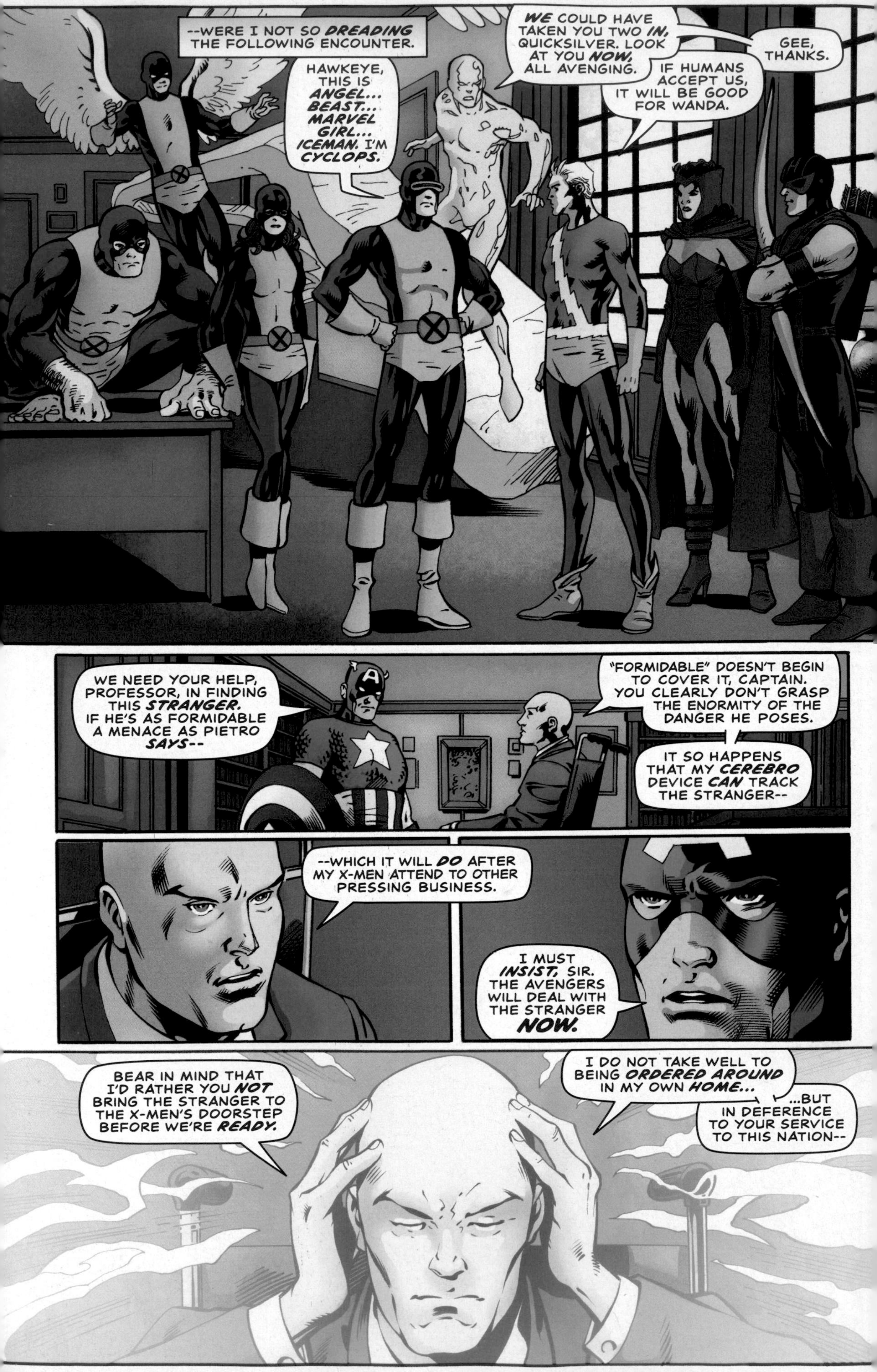
--WERE I NOT SO DREADING THE FOLLOWING ENCOUNTER.
HAWKEYE, THIS IS ANGEL... BEAST... MARVEL GIRL... ICEMAN. I'M CYCLOPS.
WE COULD HAVE TAKEN YOU TWO IN, QUICKSILVER. LOOK AT YOU NOW, ALL AVENGING.
GEE, THANKS.
IF HUMANS ACCEPT US, IT WILL BE GOOD FOR WANDA.
WE NEED YOUR HELP, PROFESSOR, IN FINDING THIS STRANGER. IF HE'S AS FORMIDABLE A MENACE AS PIETRO SAYS--
"FORMIDABLE" DOESN'T BEGIN TO COVER IT, CAPTAIN. YOU CLEARLY DON'T GRASP THE ENORMITY OF THE DANGER HE POSES.
IT SO HAPPENS THAT MY CEREBRO DEVICE CAN TRACK THE STRANGER--
--WHICH IT WILL DO AFTER MY X-MEN ATTEND TO OTHER PRESSING BUSINESS.
I MUST INSIST, SIR. THE AVENGERS WILL DEAL WITH THE STRANGER NOW.
I DO NOT TAKE WELL TO BEING ORDERED AROUND IN MY OWN HOME...
...BUT IN DEFERENCE TO YOUR SERVICE TO THIS NATION--
BEAR IN MIND THAT I'D RATHER YOU NOT BRING THE STRANGER TO THE X-MEN'S DOORSTEP BEFORE WE'RE READY.

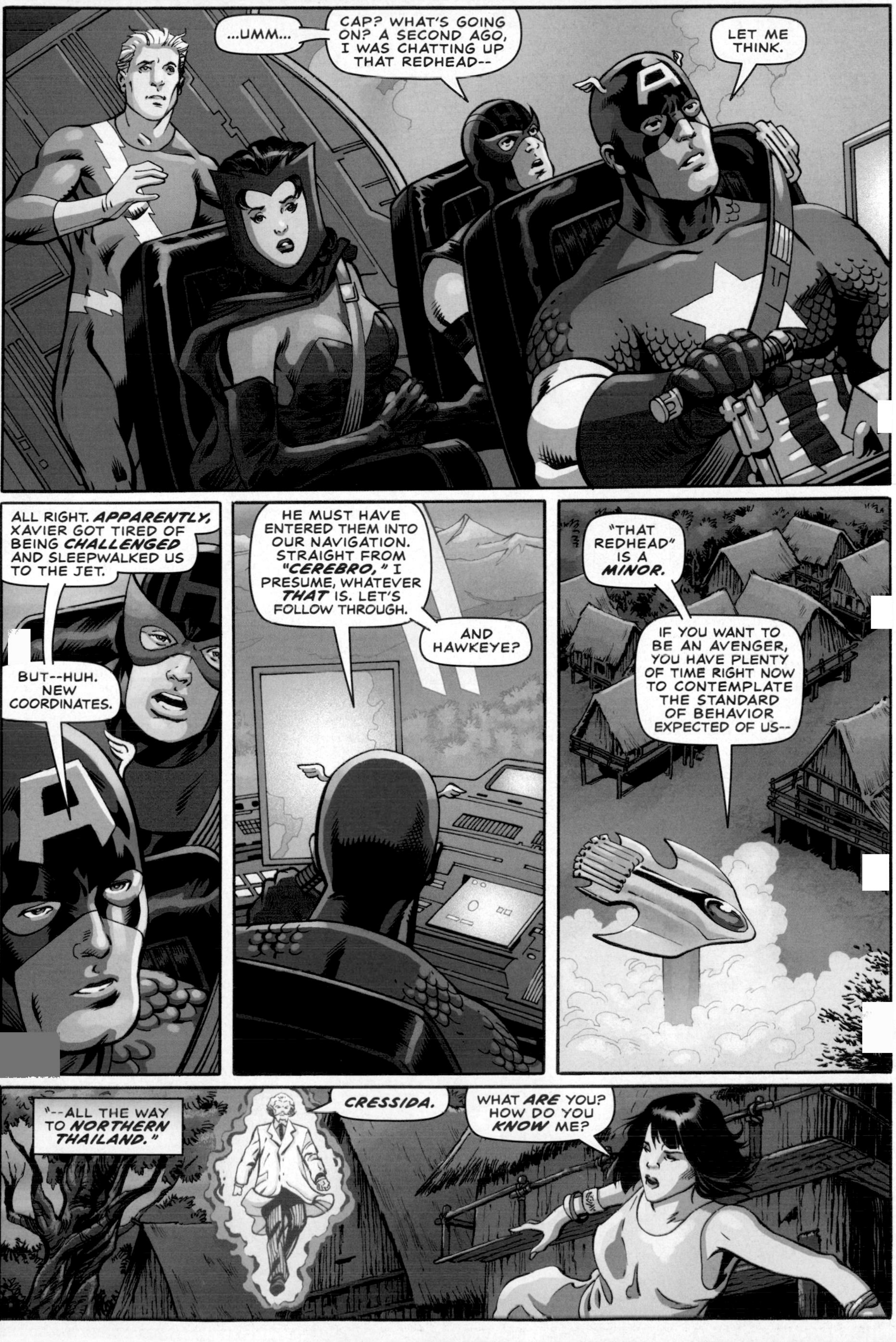

...UMM...
CAP? WHAT'S GOING ON? A SECOND AGO, I WAS CHATTING UP THAT REDHEAD--
LET ME THINK.
ALL RIGHT. APPARENTLY, XAVIER GOT TIRED OF BEING CHALLENGED AND SLEEPWALKED US TO THE JET.
BUT--HUH. NEW COORDINATES.
HE MUST HAVE ENTERED THEM INTO OUR NAVIGATION. STRAIGHT FROM "CEREBRO," I PRESUME, WHATEVER THAT IS. LET'S FOLLOW THROUGH.
AND HAWKEYE?
"THAT REDHEAD" IS A MINOR.
IF YOU WANT TO BE AN AVENGER, YOU HAVE PLENTY OF TIME RIGHT NOW TO CONTEMPLATE THE STANDARD OF BEHAVIOR EXPECTED OF US--
"--ALL THE WAY TO NORTHERN THAILAND."
CRESSIDA.
WHAT ARE YOU? HOW DO YOU KNOW ME?

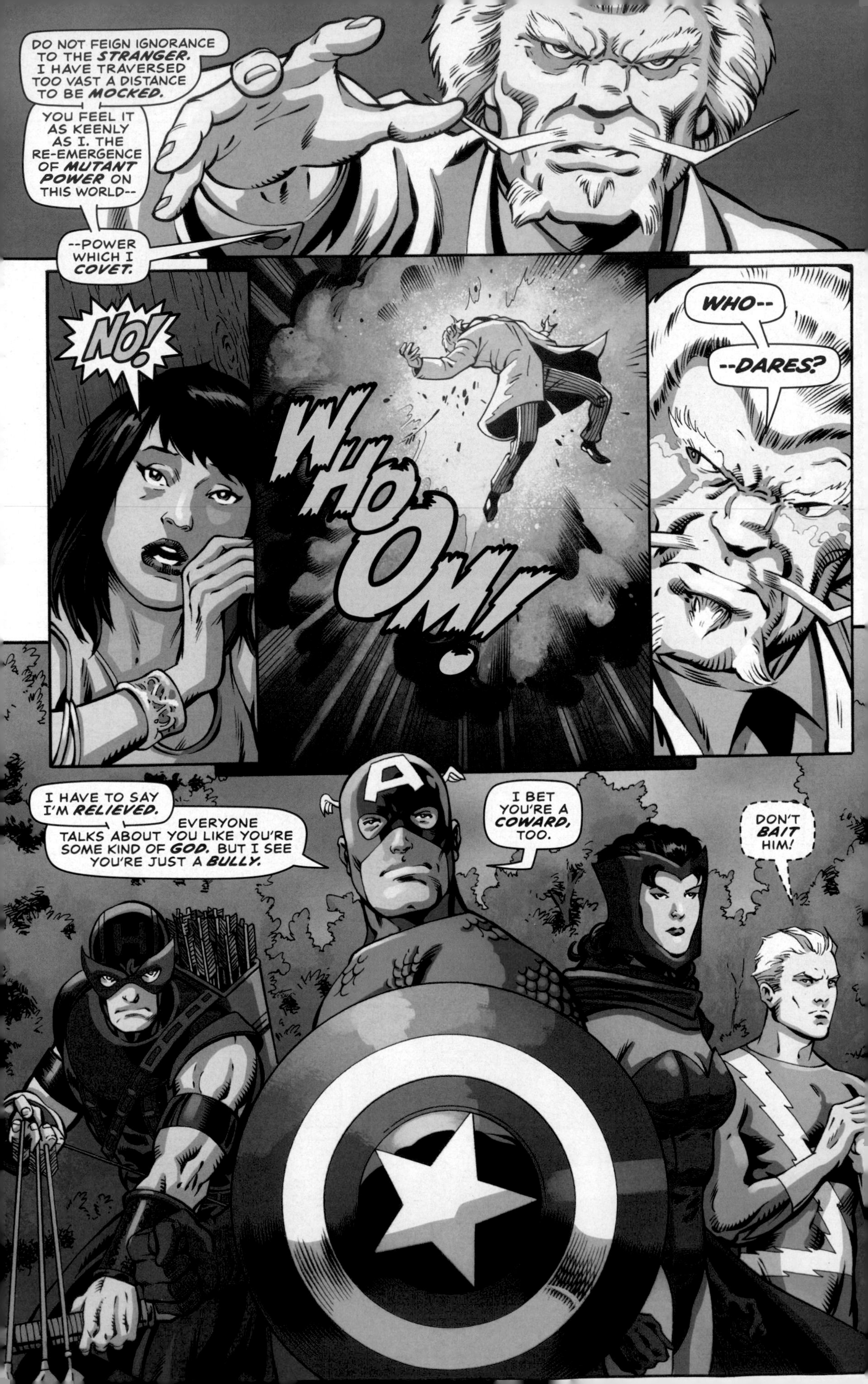
DO NOT FEIGN IGNORANCE TO THE STRANGER. I HAVE TRAVERSED TOO VAST A DISTANCE TO BE MOCKED.
YOU FEEL IT AS KEENLY AS I. THE RE-EMERGENCE OF MUTANT POWER ON THIS WORLD--
--POWER WHICH I COVET.
NO!
WHOOM!
WHO--
--DARES?
I HAVE TO SAY I'M RELIEVED.
EVERYONE TALKS ABOUT YOU LIKE YOU'RE SOME KIND OF GOD. BUT I SEE YOU'RE JUST A BULLY.
I BET YOU'RE A COWARD, TOO.
DON'T BAIT HIM!

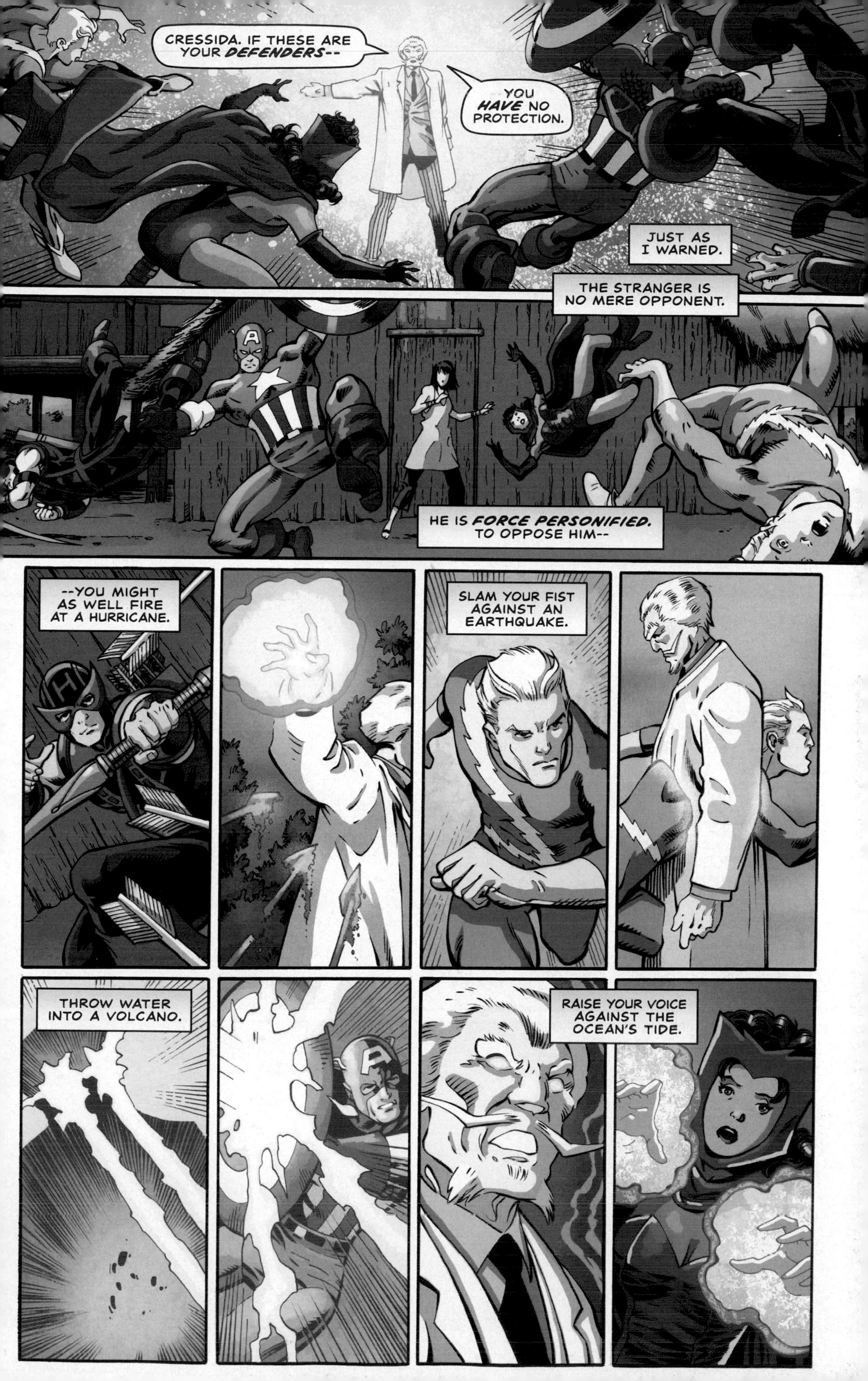
CRESSIDA. IF THESE ARE YOUR DEFENDERS--
YOU HAVE NO PROTECTION.
JUST AS I WARNED.
THE STRANGER IS NO MERE OPPONENT.
HE IS FORCE PERSONIFIED. TO OPPOSE HIM--
--YOU MIGHT AS WELL FIRE AT A HURRICANE.
SLAM YOUR FIST AGAINST AN EARTHQUAKE.
THROW WATER INTO A VOLCANO.
RAISE YOUR VOICE AGAINST THE OCEAN'S TIDE.

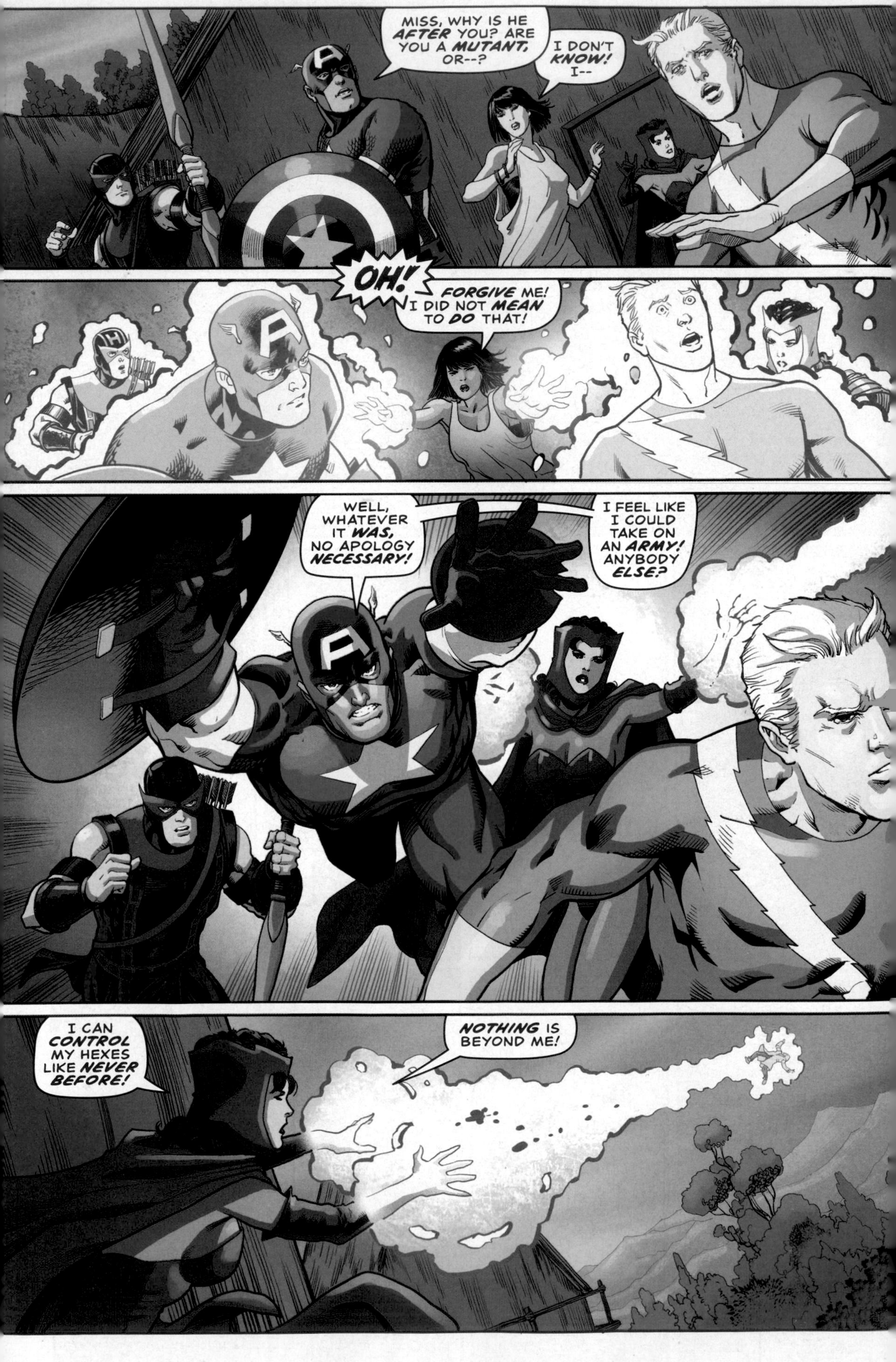
MISS, WHY IS HE *AFTER* YOU? ARE YOU A *MUTANT,* OR--?
I DON'T *KNOW!* I--
OH!
FORGIVE ME! I DID NOT *MEAN* TO *DO* THAT!
WELL, WHATEVER IT *WAS,* NO APOLOGY *NECESSARY!*
I FEEL LIKE I COULD TAKE ON AN *ARMY!* ANYBODY *ELSE?*
I CAN *CONTROL* MY HEXES LIKE *NEVER BEFORE!*
NOTHING IS BEYOND ME!

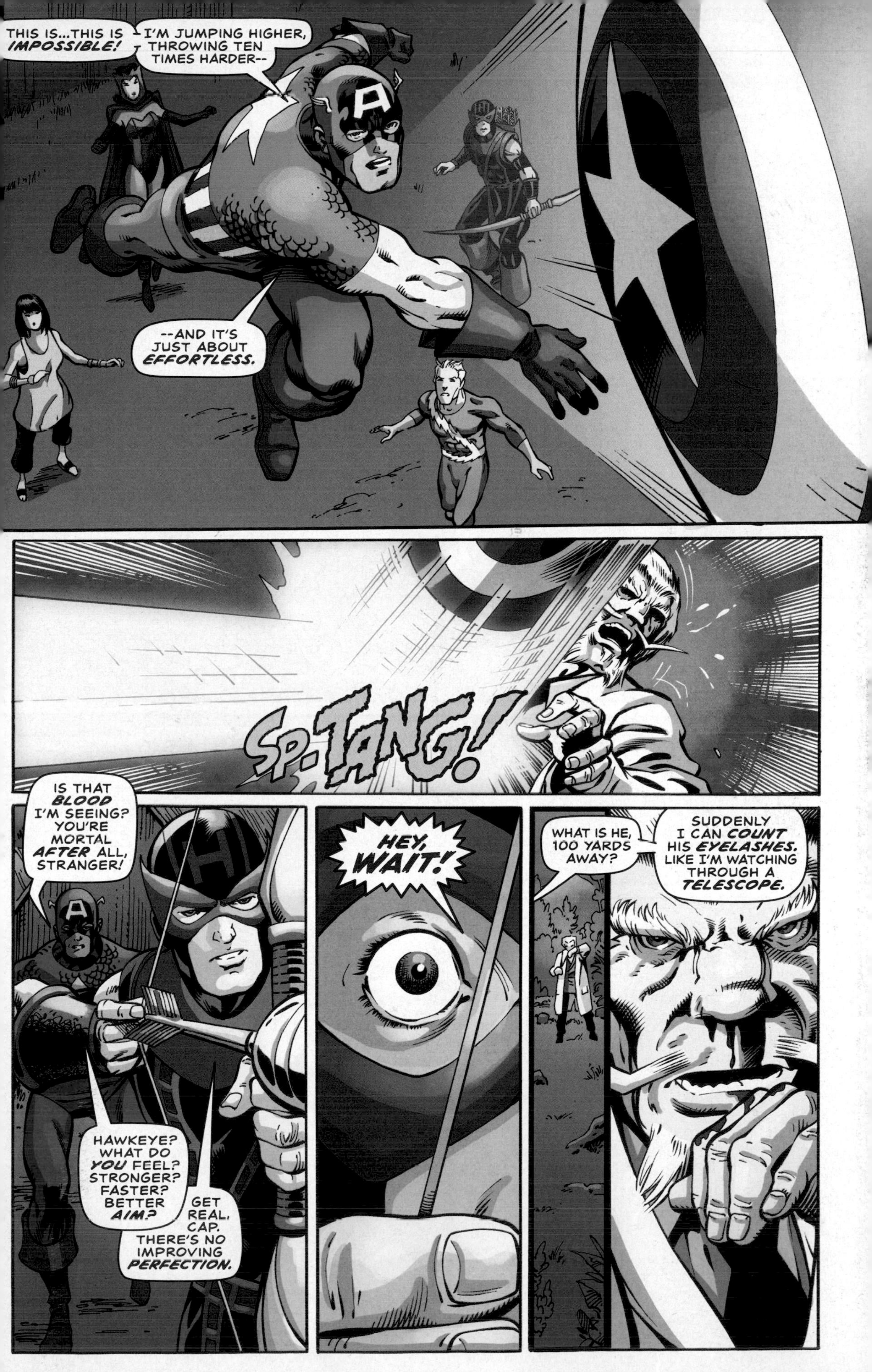
THIS IS...THIS IS IMPOSSIBLE!
I'M JUMPING HIGHER, THROWING TEN TIMES HARDER--
--AND IT'S JUST ABOUT EFFORTLESS.
SP-TANG!
IS THAT BLOOD I'M SEEING? YOU'RE MORTAL AFTER ALL, STRANGER!
HAWKEYE? WHAT DO YOU FEEL? STRONGER? FASTER? BETTER AIM?
GET REAL, CAP. THERE'S NO IMPROVING PERFECTION.
HEY, WAIT!
WHAT IS HE, 100 YARDS AWAY?
SUDDENLY I CAN COUNT HIS EYELASHES. LIKE I'M WATCHING THROUGH A TELESCOPE.

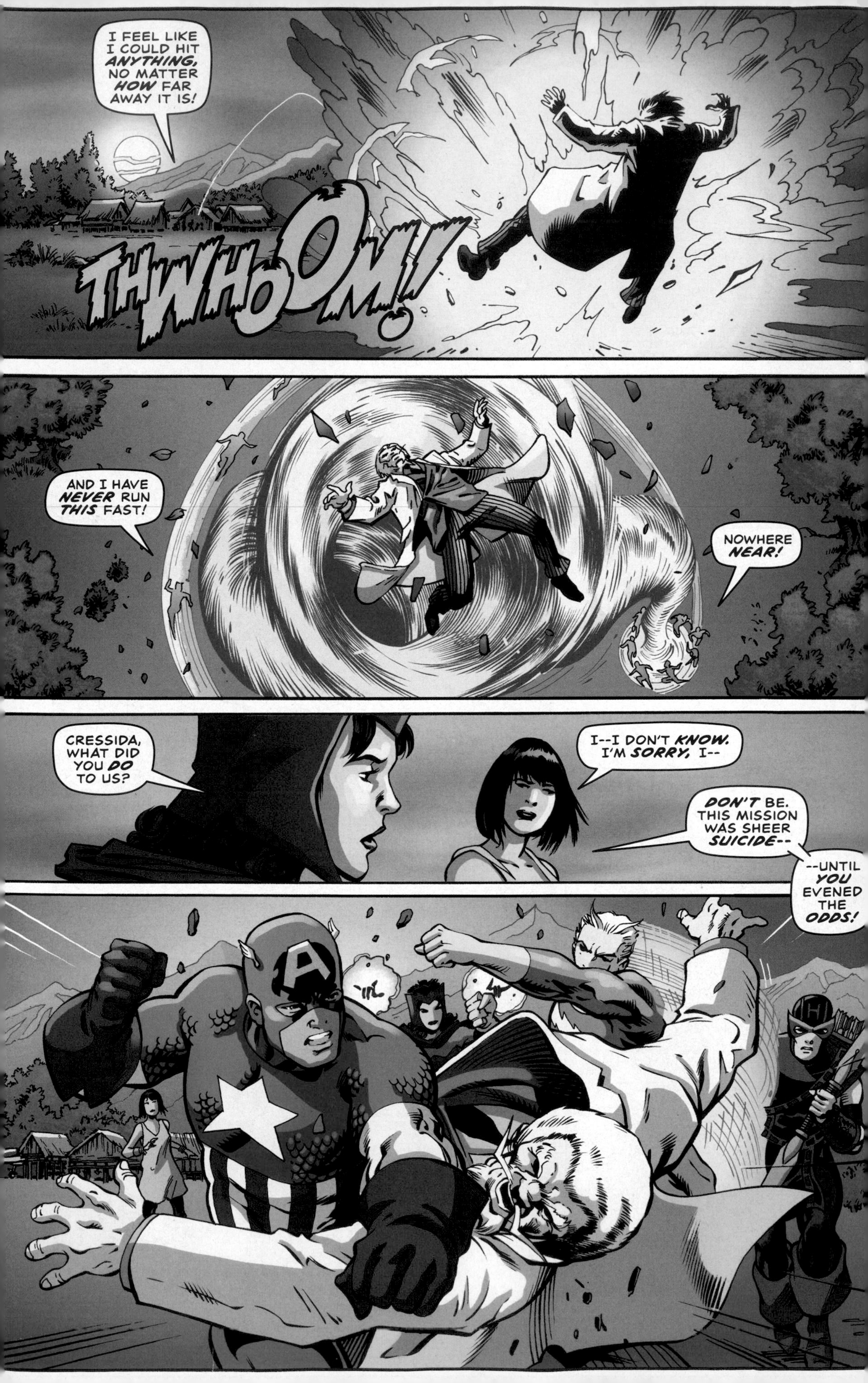
I FEEL LIKE I COULD HIT ANYTHING, NO MATTER HOW FAR AWAY IT IS!
THWHOOM!!
AND I HAVE NEVER RUN THIS FAST!
NOWHERE NEAR!
CRESSIDA, WHAT DID YOU DO TO US?
I--I DON'T KNOW. I'M SORRY, I--
DON'T BE. THIS MISSION WAS SHEER SUICIDE--
--UNTIL YOU EVENED THE ODDS!

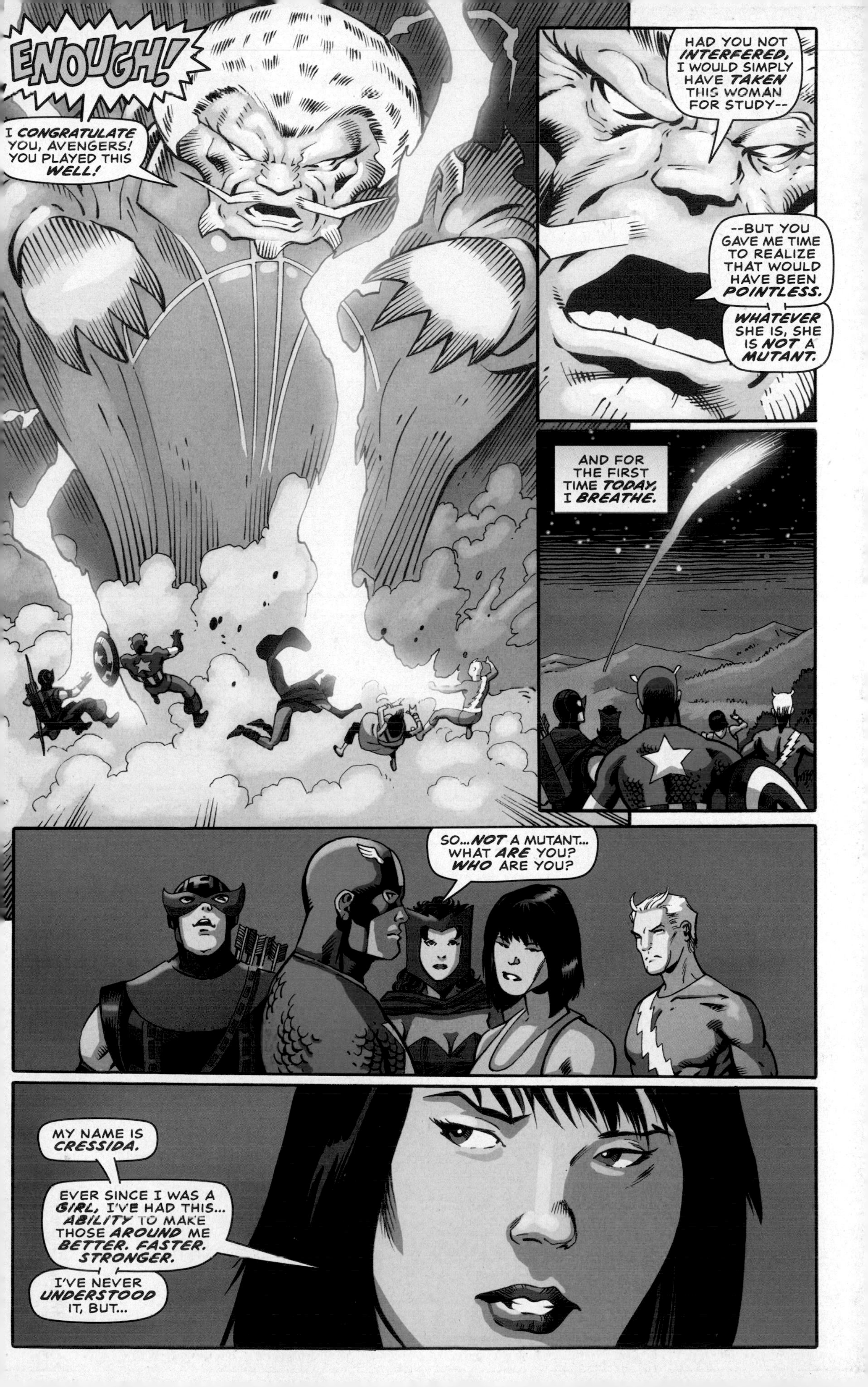
ENOUGH!
I CONGRATULATE YOU, AVENGERS! YOU PLAYED THIS WELL!
HAD YOU NOT INTERFERED, I WOULD SIMPLY HAVE TAKEN THIS WOMAN FOR STUDY--
--BUT YOU GAVE ME TIME TO REALIZE THAT WOULD HAVE BEEN POINTLESS.
WHATEVER SHE IS, SHE IS NOT A MUTANT.
AND FOR THE FIRST TIME TODAY, I BREATHE.
SO...NOT A MUTANT... WHAT ARE YOU? WHO ARE YOU?
MY NAME IS CRESSIDA.
EVER SINCE I WAS A GIRL, I'VE HAD THIS... ABILITY TO MAKE THOSE AROUND ME BETTER. FASTER. STRONGER.
I'VE NEVER UNDERSTOOD IT, BUT...

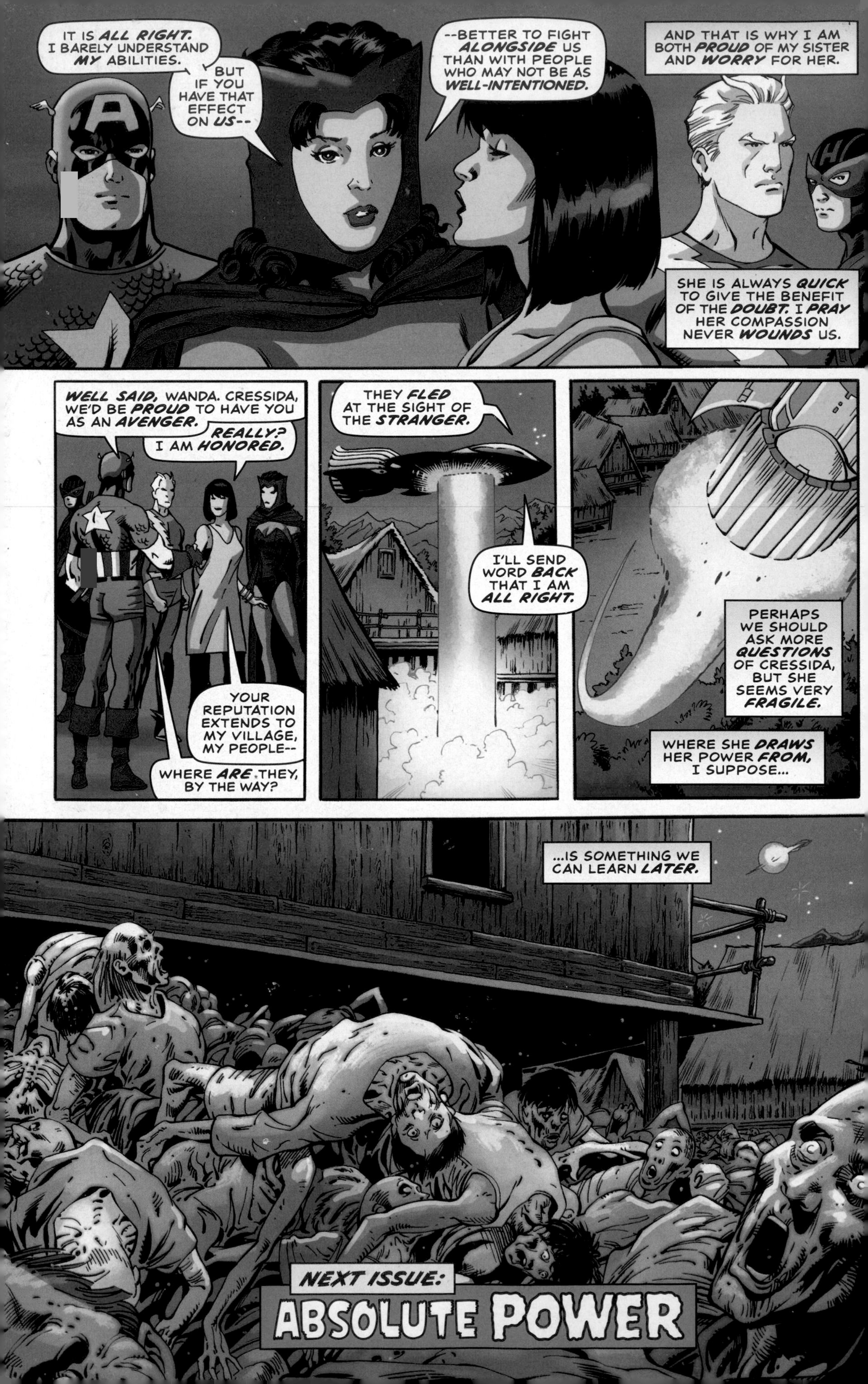
IT IS ALL RIGHT. I BARELY UNDERSTAND MY ABILITIES.
BUT IF YOU HAVE THAT EFFECT ON US--
--BETTER TO FIGHT ALONGSIDE US THAN WITH PEOPLE WHO MAY NOT BE AS WELL-INTENTIONED.
AND THAT IS WHY I AM BOTH PROUD OF MY SISTER AND WORRY FOR HER.
SHE IS ALWAYS QUICK TO GIVE THE BENEFIT OF THE DOUBT. I PRAY HER COMPASSION NEVER WOUNDS US.
WELL SAID, WANDA. CRESSIDA, WE'D BE PROUD TO HAVE YOU AS AN AVENGER.
REALLY? I AM HONORED.
YOUR REPUTATION EXTENDS TO MY VILLAGE, MY PEOPLE--
WHERE ARE THEY, BY THE WAY?
THEY FLED AT THE SIGHT OF THE STRANGER.
I'LL SEND WORD BACK THAT I AM ALL RIGHT.
PERHAPS WE SHOULD ASK MORE QUESTIONS OF CRESSIDA, BUT SHE SEEMS VERY FRAGILE.
WHERE SHE DRAWS HER POWER FROM, I SUPPOSE...
...IS SOMETHING WE CAN LEARN LATER.
NEXT ISSUE:
ABSOLUTE POWER

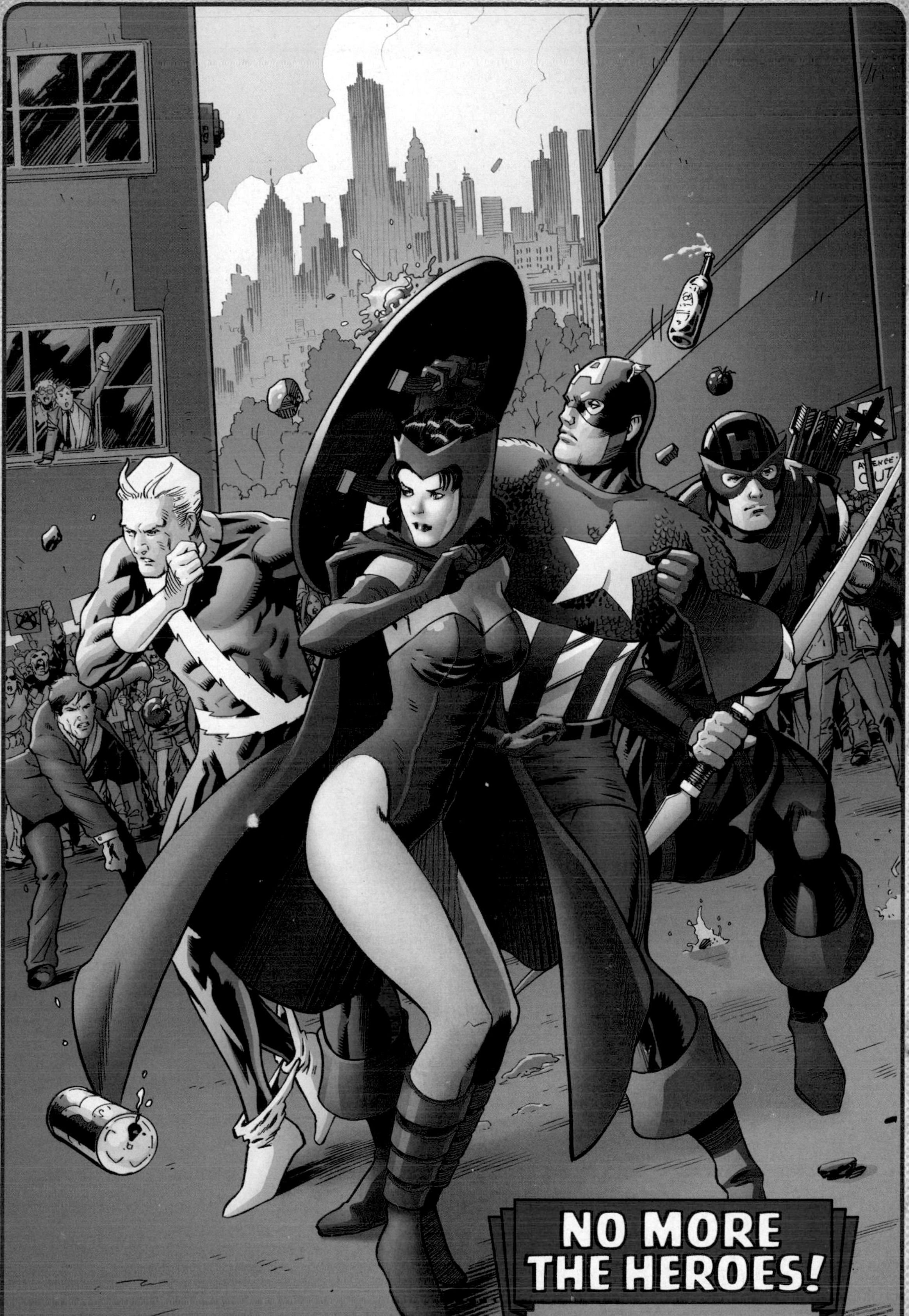
NO MORE
THE HEROES!

...TONIGHT, OUR SPOTLIGHT FALLS ON *CAPTAIN AMERICA*, *HAWKEYE*, *QUICKSILVER* AND THE *SCARLET WITCH*...

...THE TEAM NEW YORKERS HAVE TAKEN TO CALLING *"EARTH'S MIGHTIEST PRETENDERS."*

WITH ME TONIGHT TO *DISCUSS* THE AVENGERS ARE...

...CITY COUNCILMAN *CHARLES OLIVETTI* AND SOCIOLOGIST *BETTE CANFORD.*

ALWAYS A PLEASURE, BETTE.

LET'S DIVE IN. HUGH, CAN WE CUT TO YOUR FIELD REPORTER FOR A MOMENT?

HUGH, WE'VE BEEN ROVING MANHATTAN TO GET SOME CANDID REACTIONS TO THE NEW AVENGERS:

THOR? HE COULD PUT OUT A *THREE-ALARMER* WITH A WAVE OF THAT *HAMMER.*

WHERE'S *HE?*

ROOKIES, MOST OF 'EM. NO *POWER.*

I LOVE *CAP,* BUT THE *OTHER* THREE...

ALL I CAN TELL YOU IS THAT WE AT COUNTY GENERAL *PRAY* THAT THOSE FOUR DON'T HAVE TO HANDLE ANYTHING *BIG.*

AND LIVE WITH A CROWD OF *PROTESTERS...*

HI MOM

AVENGERS? I DON'T THINK SO

EX-CONVICTS NOT AVENGERS

NY DOESN'T NEED THE AVEN

AVE GE

AWKEYE EALLY?

MIGHTY PRETENDERS O THANKS

...WELL, THEY SEEM *ADAMANT* THAT IF THE AVENGERS CAN'T *PROTECT* OUR CITY, THEY SHOULD *LEAVE* IT.

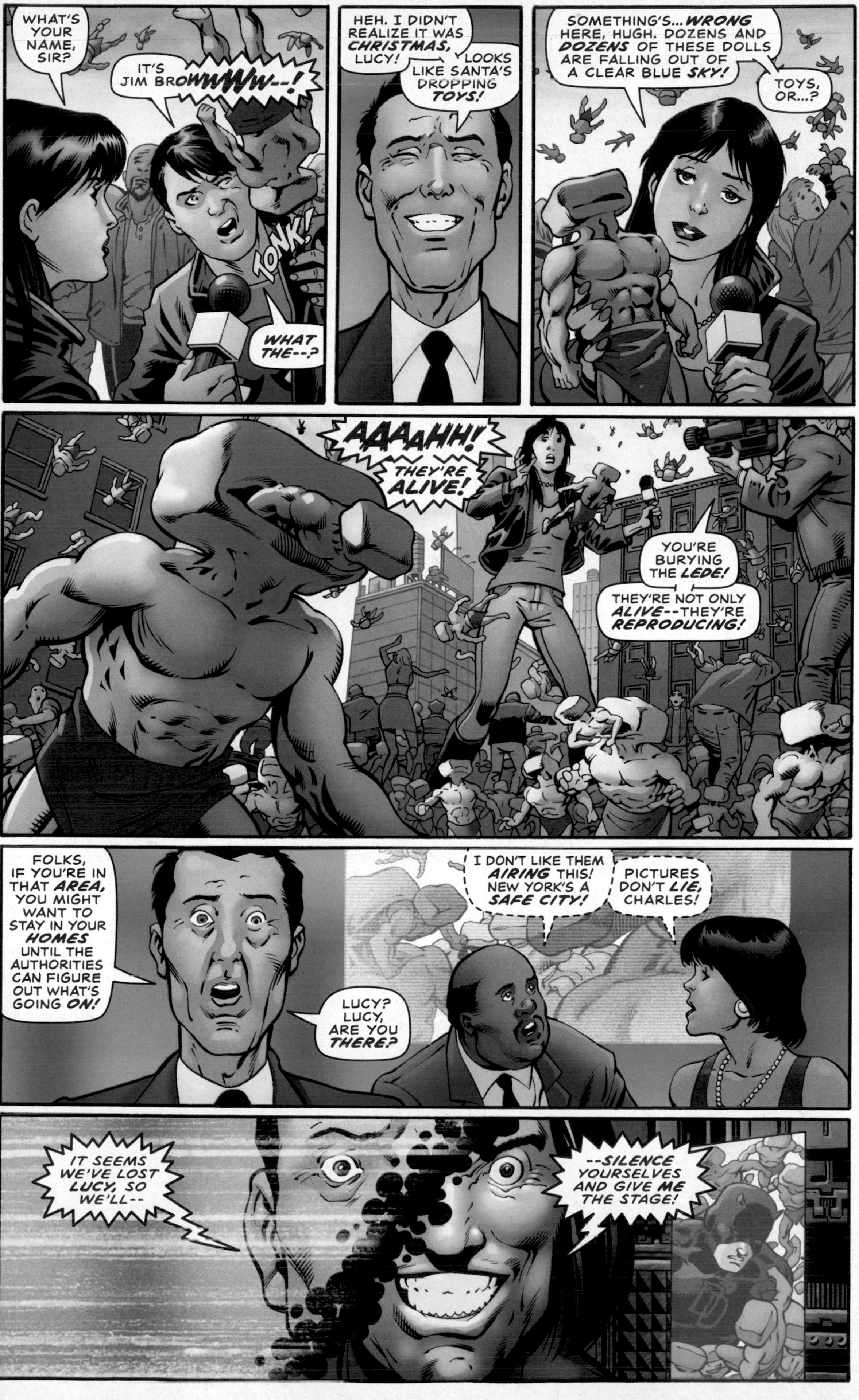
WHAT'S YOUR NAME, SIR?
IT'S JIM BROWWWW--!
TONK!
WHAT THE--?
HEH. I DIDN'T REALIZE IT WAS CHRISTMAS, LUCY!
LOOKS LIKE SANTA'S DROPPING TOYS!
SOMETHING'S...WRONG HERE, HUGH. DOZENS AND DOZENS OF THESE DOLLS ARE FALLING OUT OF A CLEAR BLUE SKY!
TOYS, OR...?
AAAAHH! THEY'RE ALIVE!
YOU'RE BURYING THE LEDE!
THEY'RE NOT ONLY ALIVE--THEY'RE REPRODUCING!
FOLKS, IF YOU'RE IN THAT AREA, YOU MIGHT WANT TO STAY IN YOUR HOMES UNTIL THE AUTHORITIES CAN FIGURE OUT WHAT'S GOING ON!
LUCY? LUCY, ARE YOU THERE?
I DON'T LIKE THEM AIRING THIS! NEW YORK'S A SAFE CITY!
PICTURES DON'T LIE, CHARLES!
IT SEEMS WE'VE LOST LUCY, SO WE'LL--
--SILENCE YOURSELVES AND GIVE ME THE STAGE!

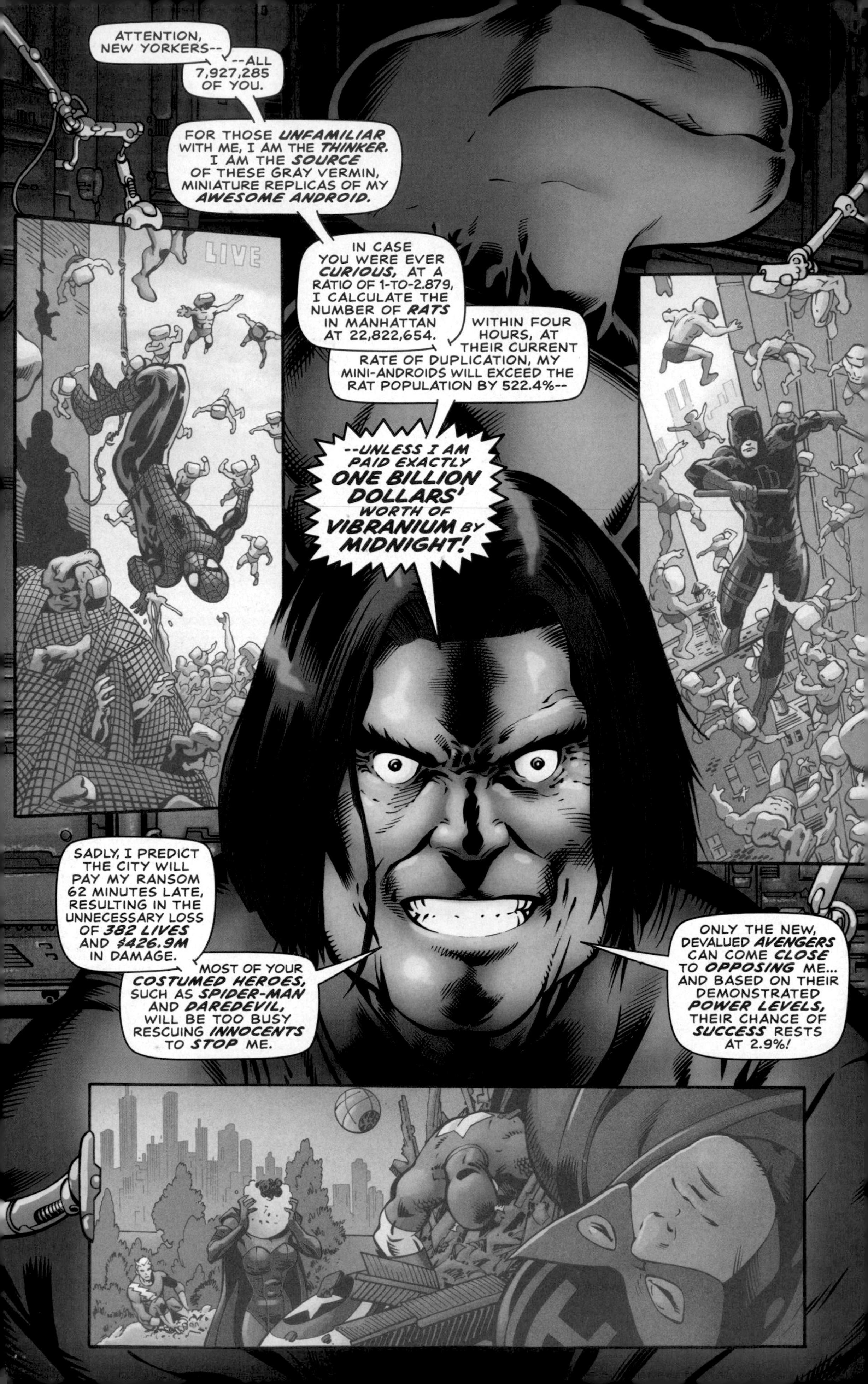
ATTENTION, NEW YORKERS--
--ALL 7,927,285 OF YOU.
FOR THOSE UNFAMILIAR WITH ME, I AM THE THINKER. I AM THE SOURCE OF THESE GRAY VERMIN, MINIATURE REPLICAS OF MY AWESOME ANDROID.
LIVE
IN CASE YOU WERE EVER CURIOUS, AT A RATIO OF 1-TO-2.879, I CALCULATE THE NUMBER OF RATS IN MANHATTAN AT 22,822,654.
WITHIN FOUR HOURS, AT THEIR CURRENT RATE OF DUPLICATION, MY MINI-ANDROIDS WILL EXCEED THE RAT POPULATION BY 522.4%--
--UNLESS I AM PAID EXACTLY ONE BILLION DOLLARS' WORTH OF VIBRANIUM BY MIDNIGHT!
SADLY, I PREDICT THE CITY WILL PAY MY RANSOM 62 MINUTES LATE, RESULTING IN THE UNNECESSARY LOSS OF 382 LIVES AND $426.9M IN DAMAGE.
MOST OF YOUR COSTUMED HEROES, SUCH AS SPIDER-MAN AND DAREDEVIL, WILL BE TOO BUSY RESCUING INNOCENTS TO STOP ME.
ONLY THE NEW, DEVALUED AVENGERS CAN COME CLOSE TO OPPOSING ME... AND BASED ON THEIR DEMONSTRATED POWER LEVELS, THEIR CHANCE OF SUCCESS RESTS AT 2.9%!

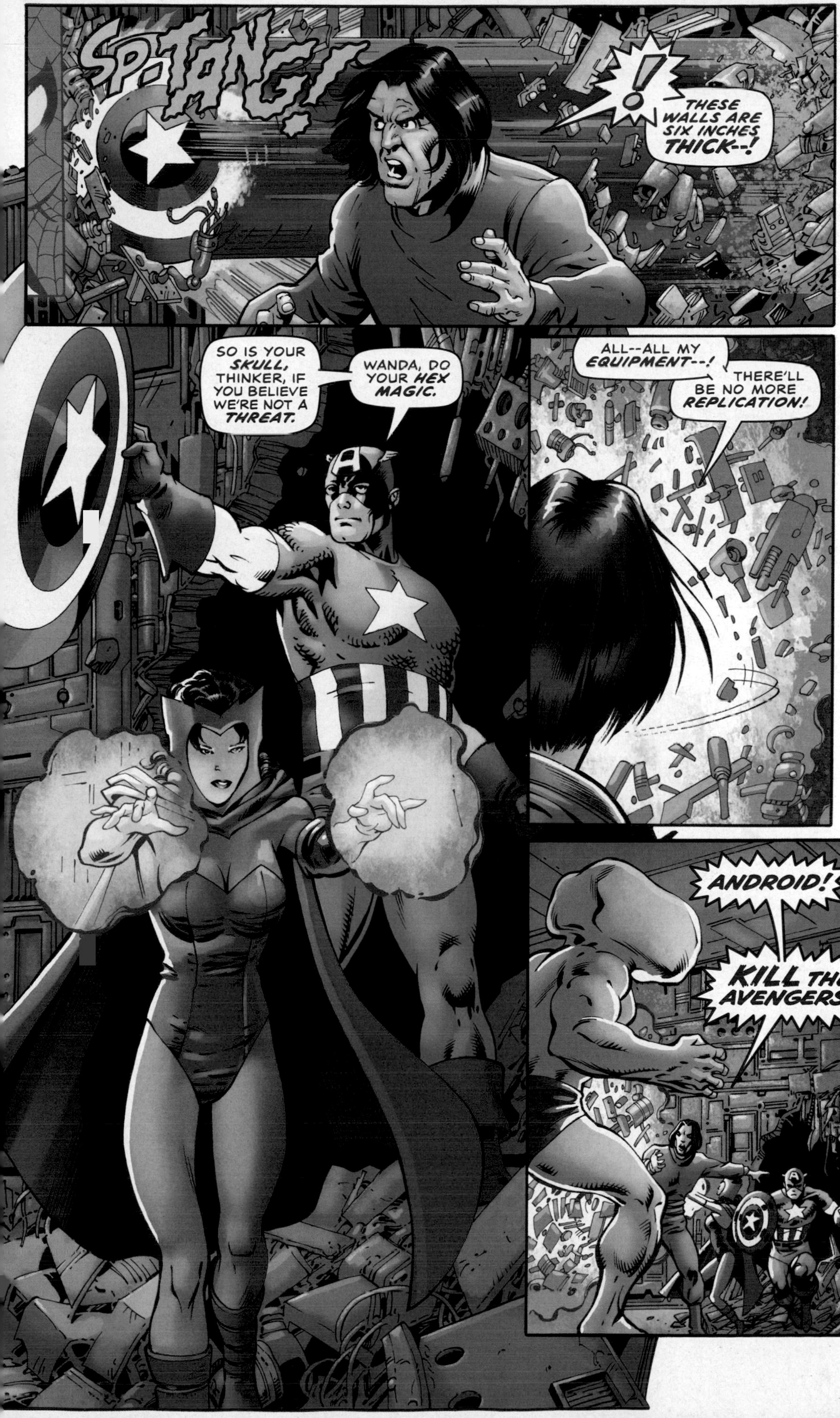
SP-TANG!
!
THESE WALLS ARE SIX INCHES THICK--!
SO IS YOUR SKULL, THINKER, IF YOU BELIEVE WE'RE NOT A THREAT.
WANDA, DO YOUR HEX MAGIC.
ALL--ALL MY EQUIPMENT--!
THERE'LL BE NO MORE REPLICATION!
ANDROID!
KILL THE AVENGERS!

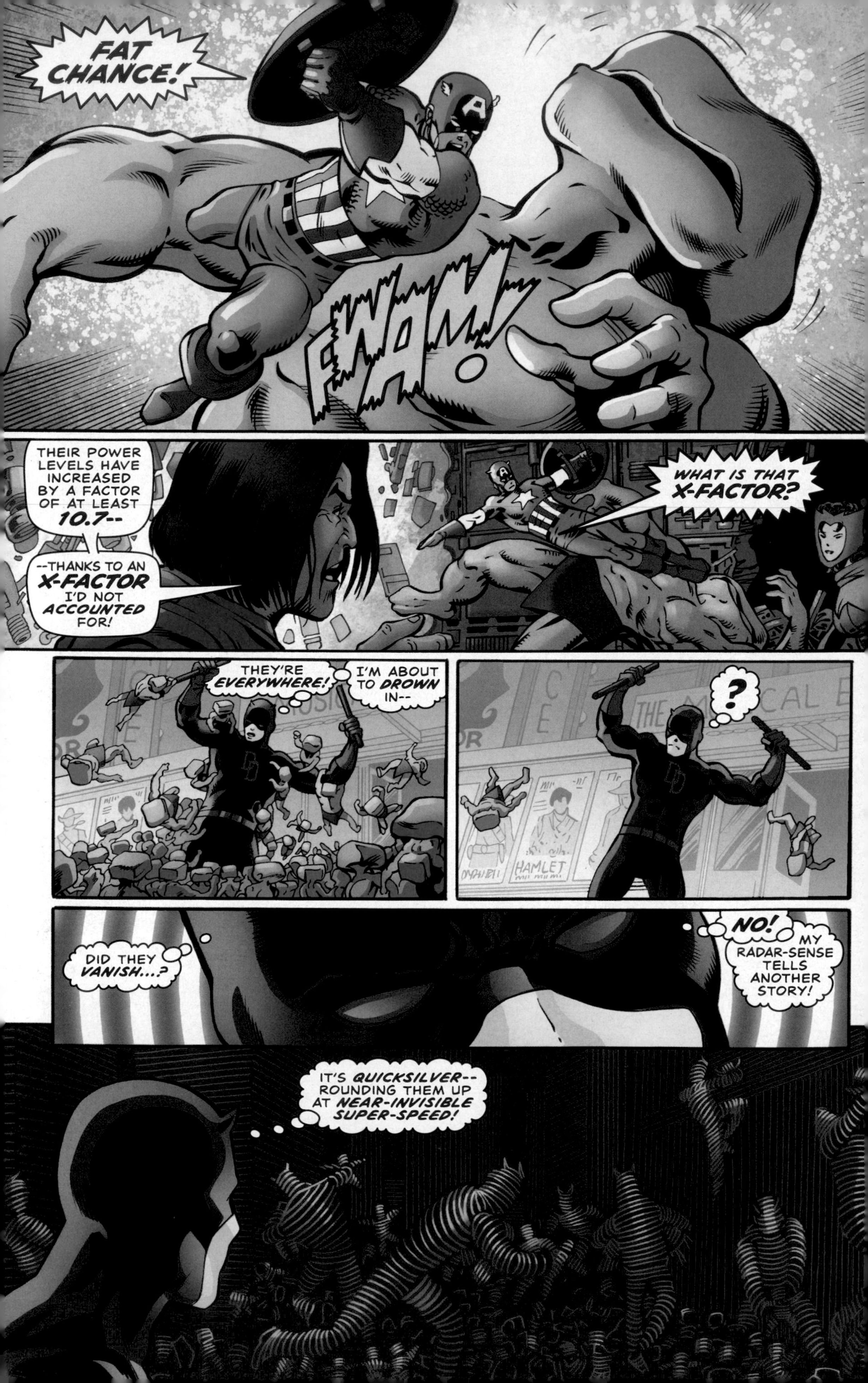
FAT CHANCE!
FWAM!
THEIR POWER LEVELS HAVE INCREASED BY A FACTOR OF AT LEAST 10.7--
--THANKS TO AN X-FACTOR I'D NOT ACCOUNTED FOR!
WHAT IS THAT X-FACTOR?
THEY'RE EVERYWHERE!
I'M ABOUT TO DROWN IN--
?
THE
HAMLET
DID THEY VANISH...?
NO! MY RADAR-SENSE TELLS ANOTHER STORY!
IT'S QUICKSILVER-- ROUNDING THEM UP AT NEAR-INVISIBLE SUPER-SPEED!

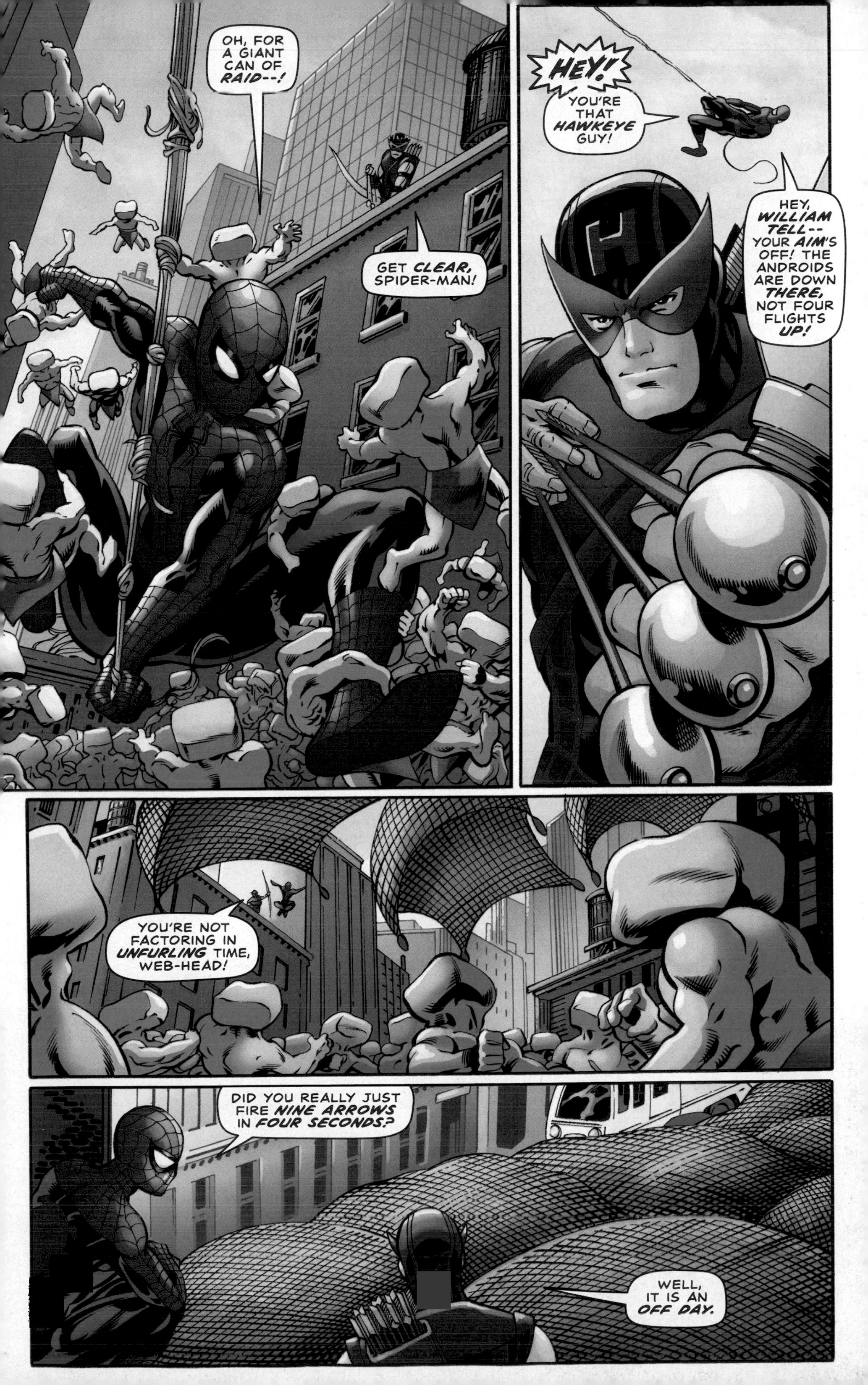
OH, FOR A GIANT CAN OF RAID--!
GET CLEAR, SPIDER-MAN!
HEY!
YOU'RE THAT HAWKEYE GUY!
HEY, WILLIAM TELL-- YOUR AIM'S OFF! THE ANDROIDS ARE DOWN THERE, NOT FOUR FLIGHTS UP!
YOU'RE NOT FACTORING IN UNFURLING TIME, WEB-HEAD!
DID YOU REALLY JUST FIRE NINE ARROWS IN FOUR SECONDS?
WELL, IT IS AN OFF DAY.

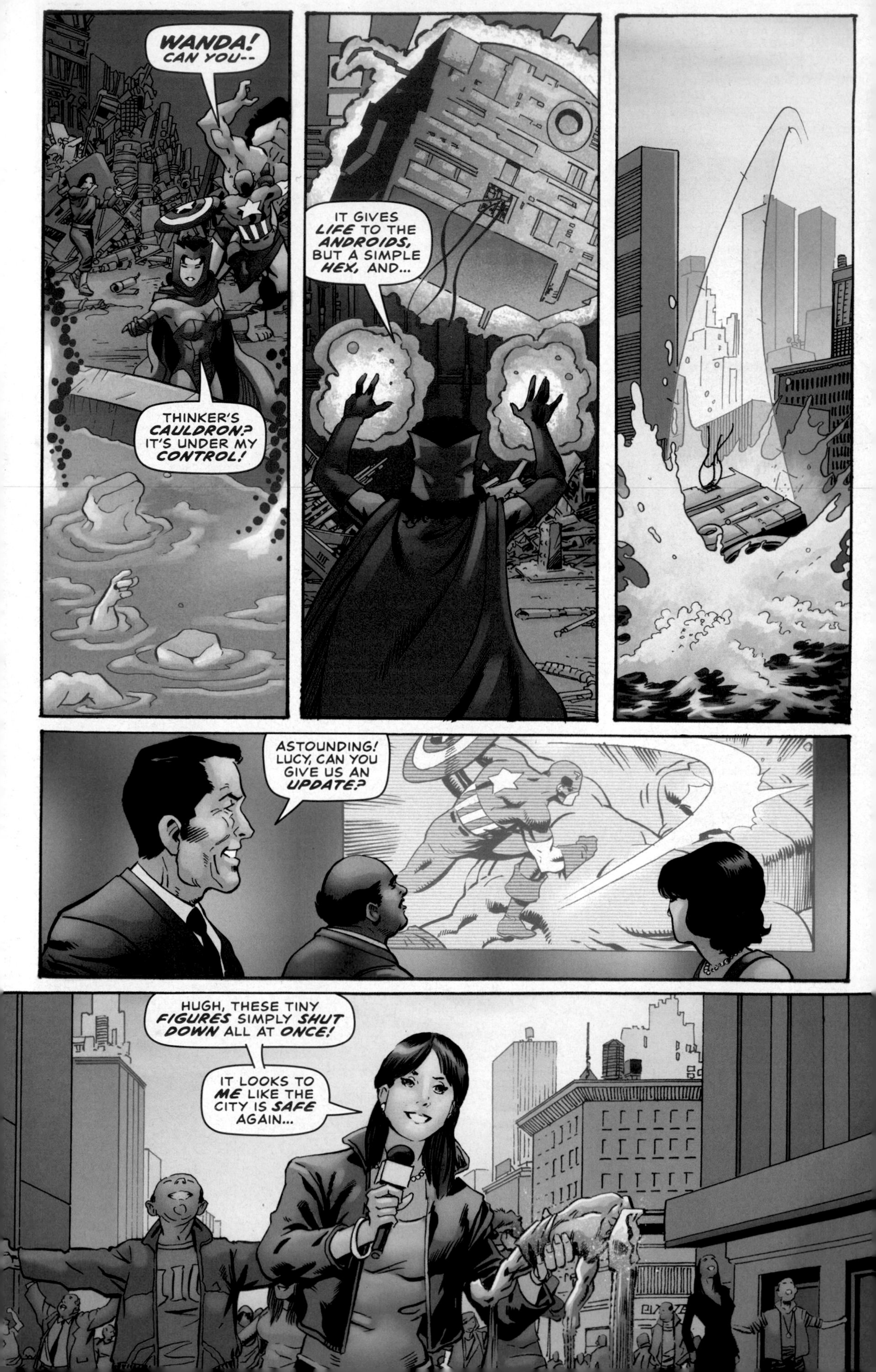
WANDA! CAN YOU--
THINKER'S CAULDRON? IT'S UNDER MY CONTROL!
IT GIVES LIFE TO THE ANDROIDS, BUT A SIMPLE HEX, AND...
ASTOUNDING! LUCY, CAN YOU GIVE US AN UPDATE?
HUGH, THESE TINY FIGURES SIMPLY SHUT DOWN ALL AT ONCE!
IT LOOKS TO ME LIKE THE CITY IS SAFE AGAIN...

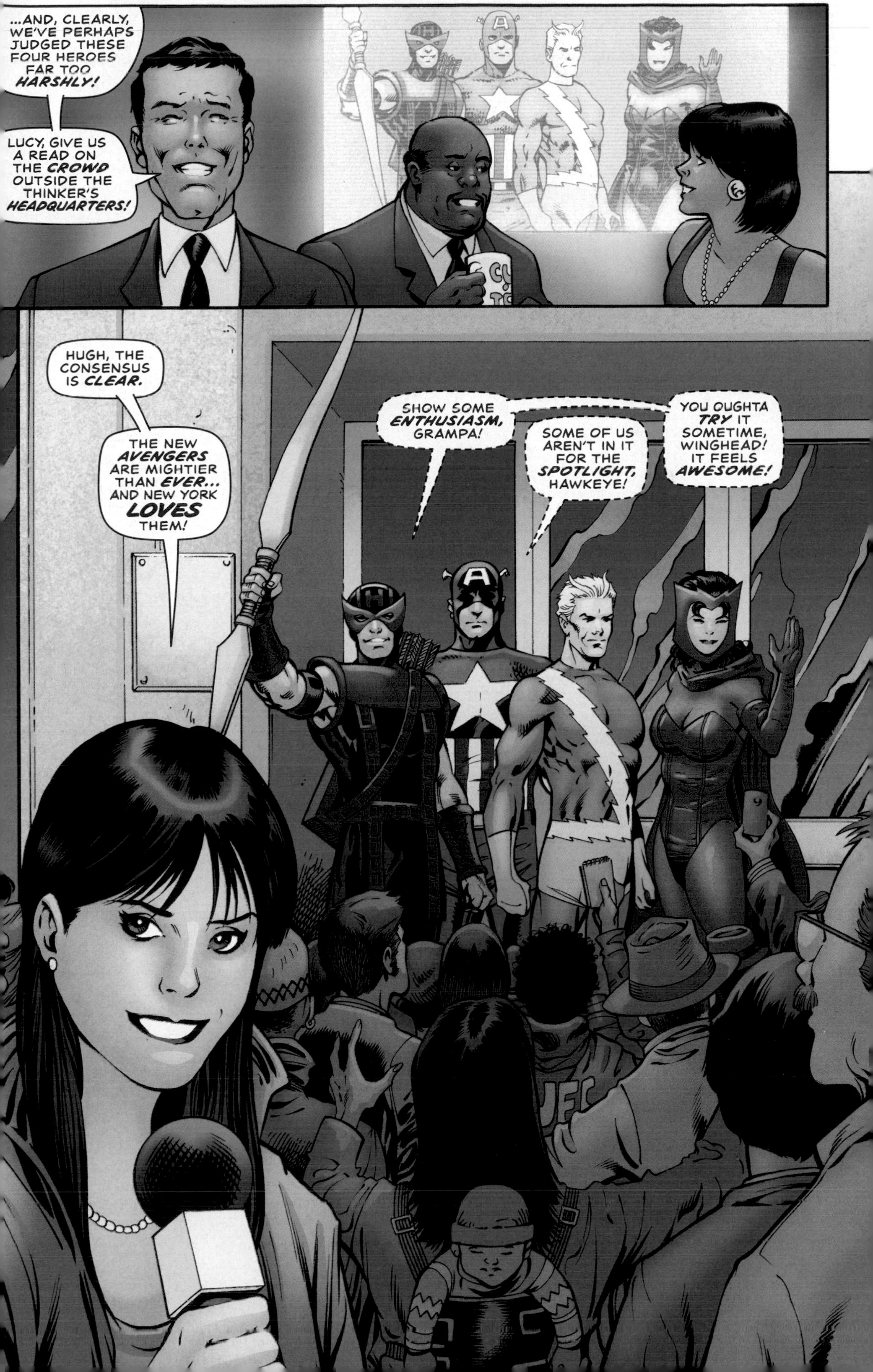
...AND, CLEARLY, WE'VE PERHAPS JUDGED THESE FOUR HEROES FAR TOO HARSHLY!
LUCY, GIVE US A READ ON THE CROWD OUTSIDE THE THINKER'S HEADQUARTERS!
HUGH, THE CONSENSUS IS CLEAR.
THE NEW AVENGERS ARE MIGHTIER THAN EVER... AND NEW YORK LOVES THEM!
SHOW SOME ENTHUSIASM, GRAMPA!
SOME OF US AREN'T IN IT FOR THE SPOTLIGHT, HAWKEYE!
YOU OUGHTA TRY IT SOMETIME, WINGHEAD! IT FEELS AWESOME!

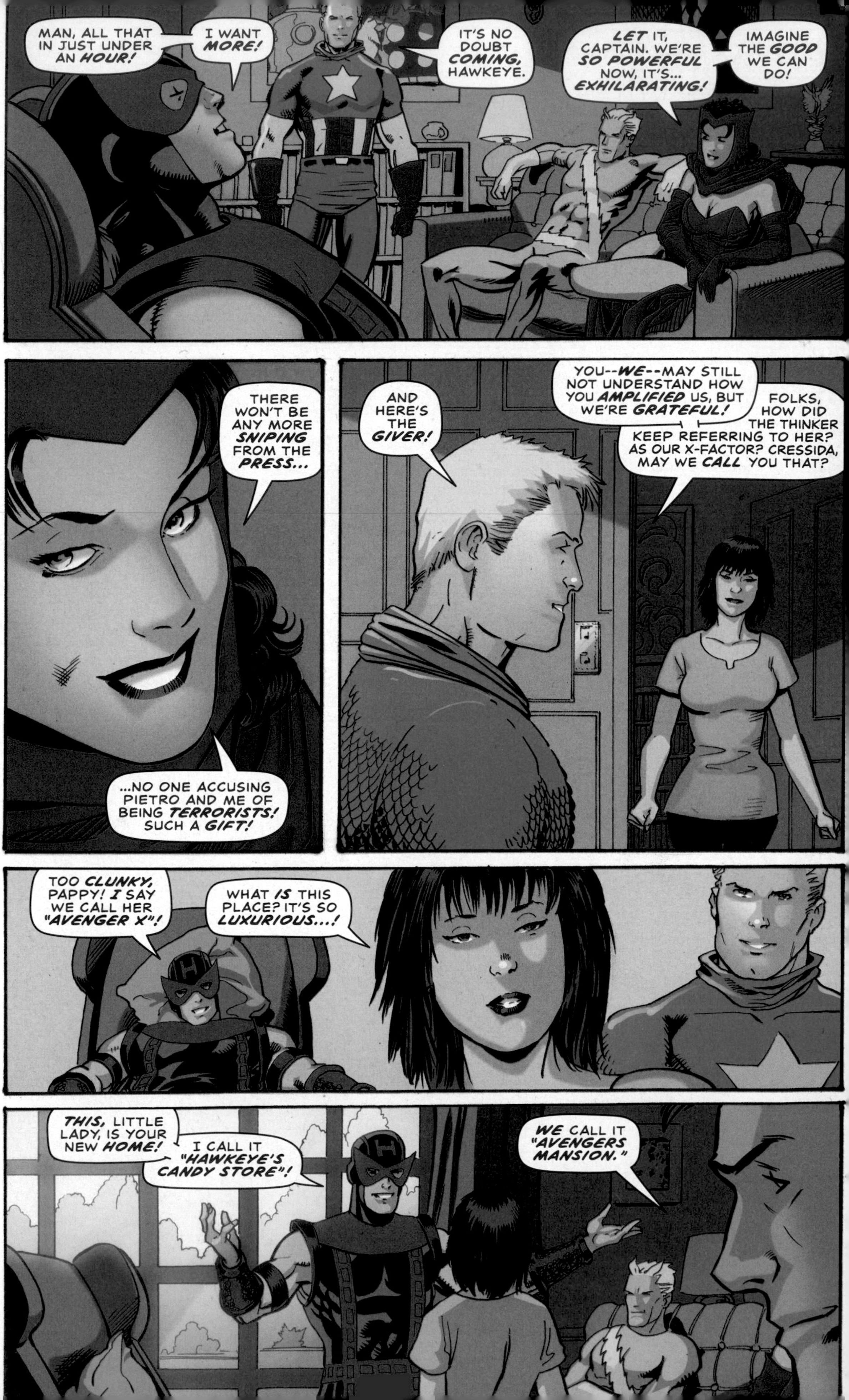
MAN, ALL THAT IN JUST UNDER AN HOUR!
I WANT MORE!
IT'S NO DOUBT COMING, HAWKEYE.
LET IT, CAPTAIN. WE'RE SO POWERFUL NOW, IT'S... EXHILARATING!
IMAGINE THE GOOD WE CAN DO!
THERE WON'T BE ANY MORE SNIPING FROM THE PRESS...
...NO ONE ACCUSING PIETRO AND ME OF BEING TERRORISTS! SUCH A GIFT!
AND HERE'S THE GIVER!
YOU--WE--MAY STILL NOT UNDERSTAND HOW YOU AMPLIFIED US, BUT WE'RE GRATEFUL!
FOLKS, HOW DID THE THINKER KEEP REFERRING TO HER? AS OUR X-FACTOR? CRESSIDA, MAY WE CALL YOU THAT?
TOO CLUNKY, PAPPY! I SAY WE CALL HER "AVENGER X"!
WHAT IS THIS PLACE? IT'S SO LUXURIOUS...!
THIS, LITTLE LADY, IS YOUR NEW HOME!
I CALL IT "HAWKEYE'S CANDY STORE"!
WE CALL IT "AVENGERS MANSION."

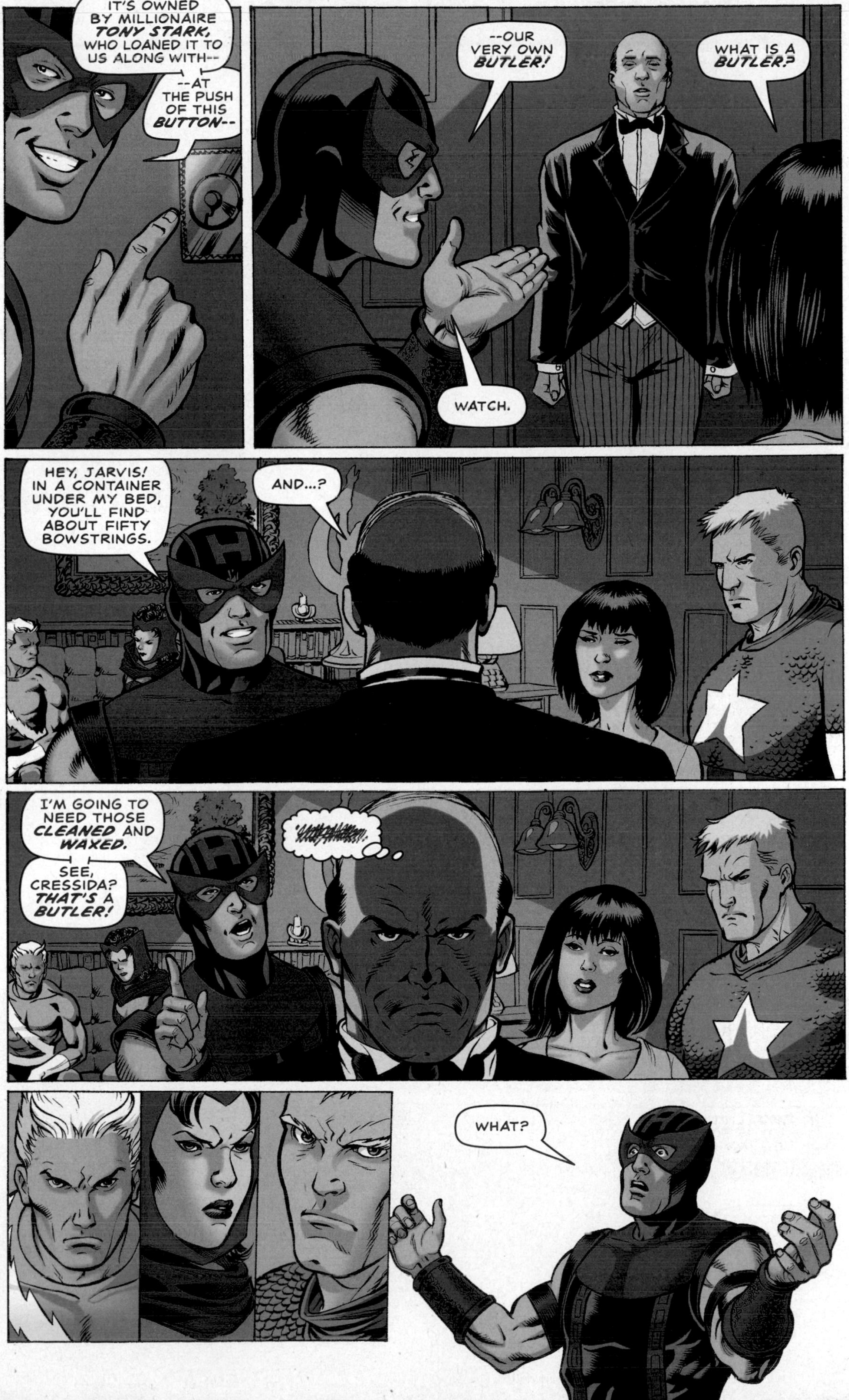
IT'S OWNED BY MILLIONAIRE TONY STARK, WHO LOANED IT TO US ALONG WITH--
--AT THE PUSH OF THIS BUTTON--
--OUR VERY OWN BUTLER!
WHAT IS A BUTLER?
WATCH.
HEY, JARVIS! IN A CONTAINER UNDER MY BED, YOU'LL FIND ABOUT FIFTY BOWSTRINGS.
AND...?
I'M GOING TO NEED THOSE CLEANED AND WAXED.
SEE, CRESSIDA? THAT'S A BUTLER!
WHAT?

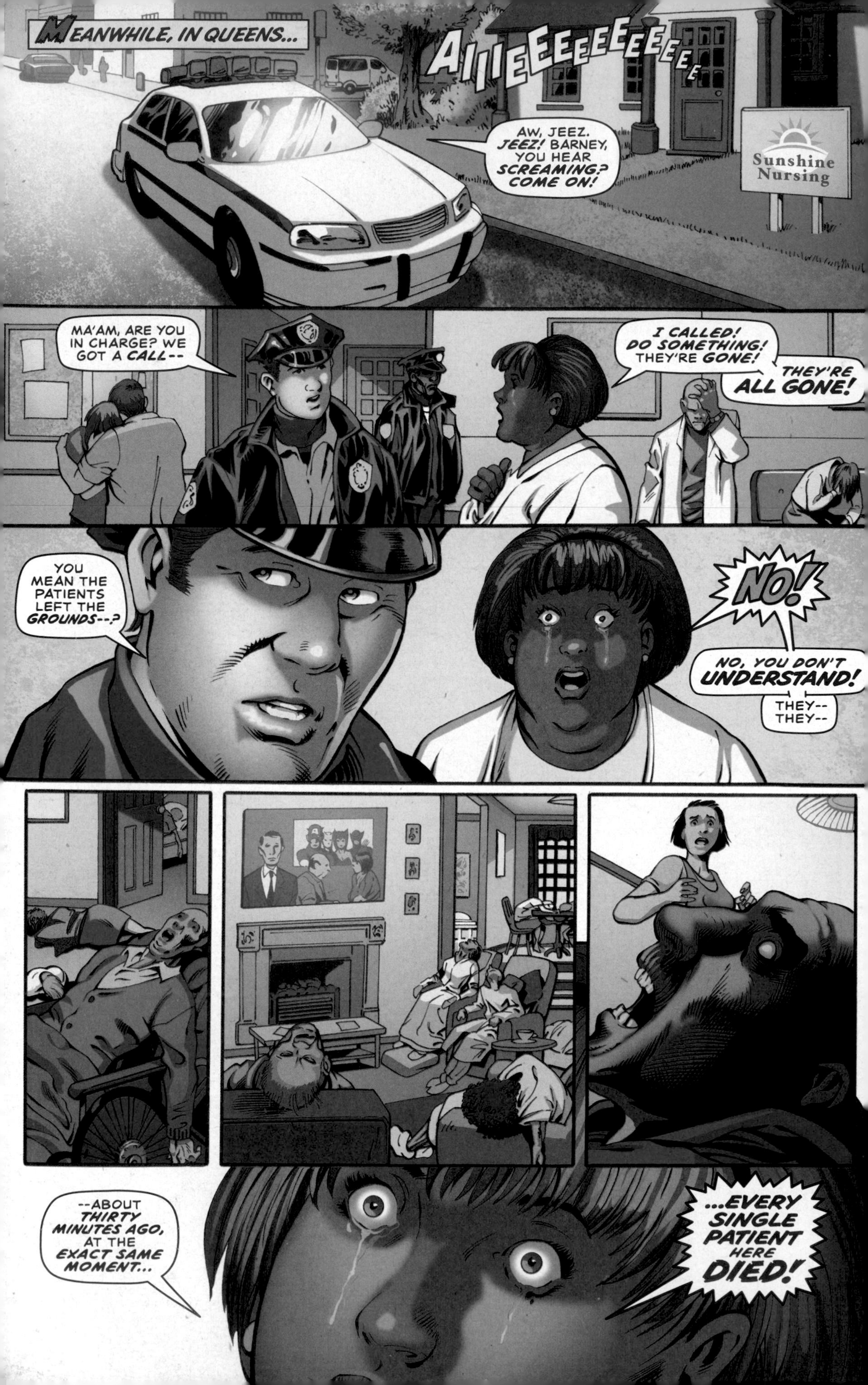
MEANWHILE, IN QUEENS...
AIIIEEEEEEEEEE
AW, JEEZ. JEEZ! BARNEY, YOU HEAR SCREAMING? COME ON!
Sunshine Nursing
MA'AM, ARE YOU IN CHARGE? WE GOT A CALL--
I CALLED! DO SOMETHING! THEY'RE GONE!
THEY'RE ALL GONE!
YOU MEAN THE PATIENTS LEFT THE GROUNDS--?
NO!
NO, YOU DON'T UNDERSTAND!
THEY-- THEY--
--ABOUT THIRTY MINUTES AGO, AT THE EXACT SAME MOMENT...
...EVERY SINGLE PATIENT HERE DIED!

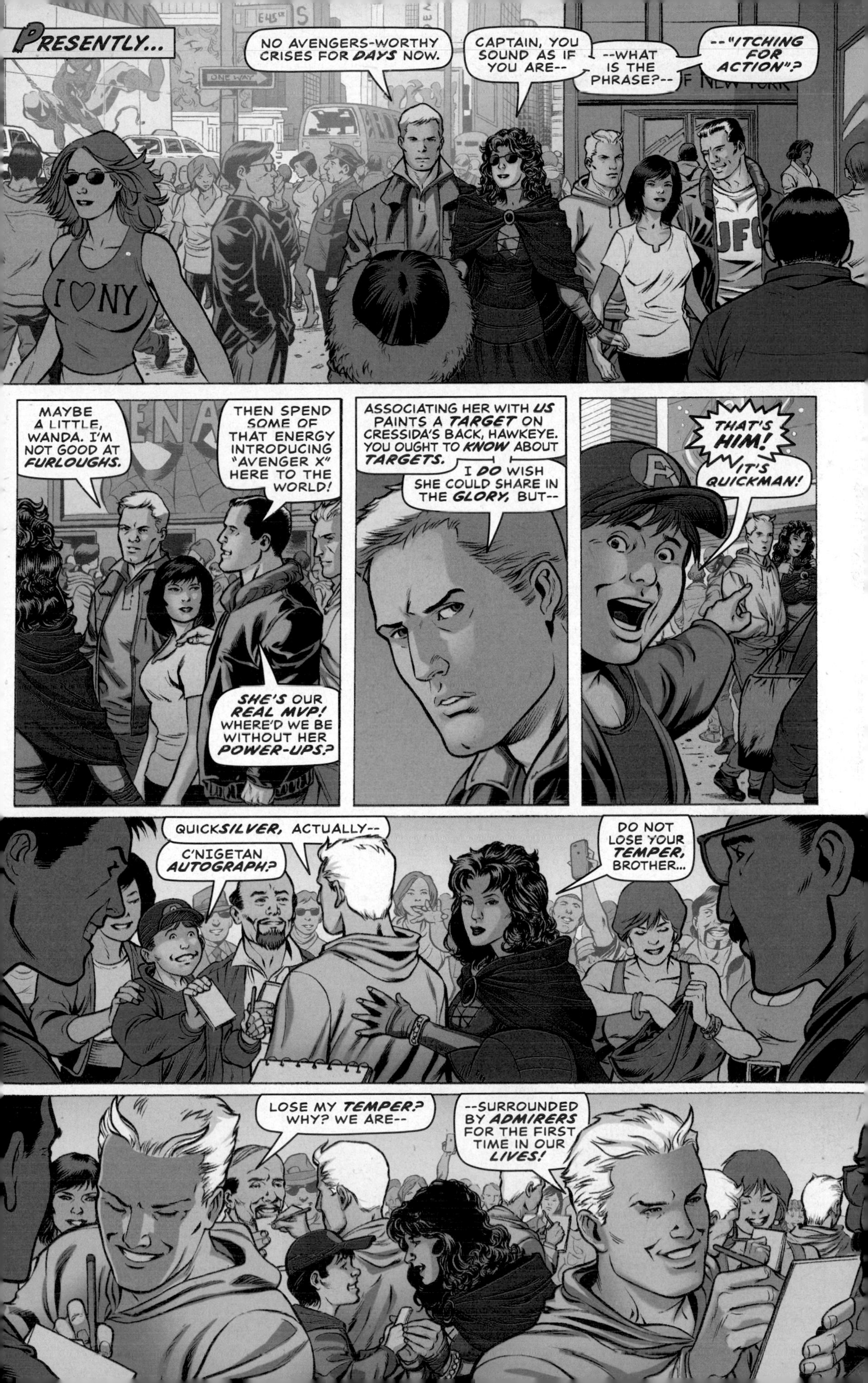
PRESENTLY...
NO AVENGERS-WORTHY CRISES FOR DAYS NOW.
CAPTAIN, YOU SOUND AS IF YOU ARE--
--WHAT IS THE PHRASE?--
--"ITCHING FOR ACTION"?
I ♡ NY
MAYBE A LITTLE, WANDA. I'M NOT GOOD AT FURLOUGHS.
THEN SPEND SOME OF THAT ENERGY INTRODUCING "AVENGER X" HERE TO THE WORLD!
SHE'S OUR REAL MVP! WHERE'D WE BE WITHOUT HER POWER-UPS?
ASSOCIATING HER WITH US PAINTS A TARGET ON CRESSIDA'S BACK, HAWKEYE. YOU OUGHT TO KNOW ABOUT TARGETS.
I DO WISH SHE COULD SHARE IN THE GLORY, BUT--
THAT'S HIM!
IT'S QUICKMAN!
QUICKSILVER, ACTUALLY--
C'NIGETAN AUTOGRAPH?
DO NOT LOSE YOUR TEMPER, BROTHER...
LOSE MY TEMPER? WHY? WE ARE--
--SURROUNDED BY ADMIRERS FOR THE FIRST TIME IN OUR LIVES!

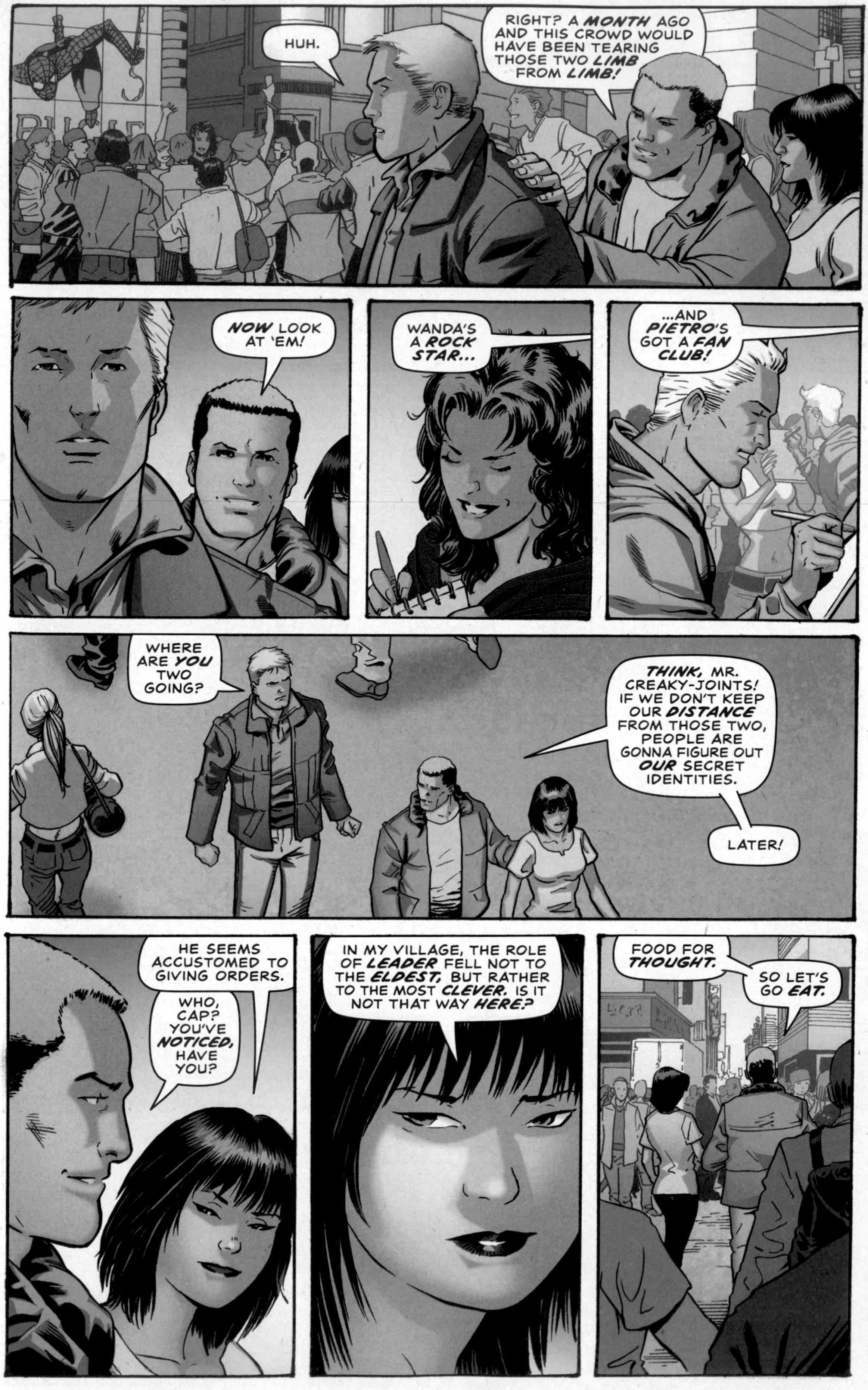
HUH.
RIGHT? A MONTH AGO AND THIS CROWD WOULD HAVE BEEN TEARING THOSE TWO LIMB FROM LIMB!
NOW LOOK AT 'EM!
WANDA'S A ROCK STAR...
...AND PIETRO'S GOT A FAN CLUB!
WHERE ARE YOU TWO GOING?
THINK, MR. CREAKY-JOINTS! IF WE DON'T KEEP OUR DISTANCE FROM THOSE TWO, PEOPLE ARE GONNA FIGURE OUT OUR SECRET IDENTITIES.
LATER!
HE SEEMS ACCUSTOMED TO GIVING ORDERS.
WHO, CAP? YOU'VE NOTICED, HAVE YOU?
IN MY VILLAGE, THE ROLE OF LEADER FELL NOT TO THE ELDEST, BUT RATHER TO THE MOST CLEVER. IS IT NOT THAT WAY HERE?
FOOD FOR THOUGHT.
SO LET'S GO EAT.

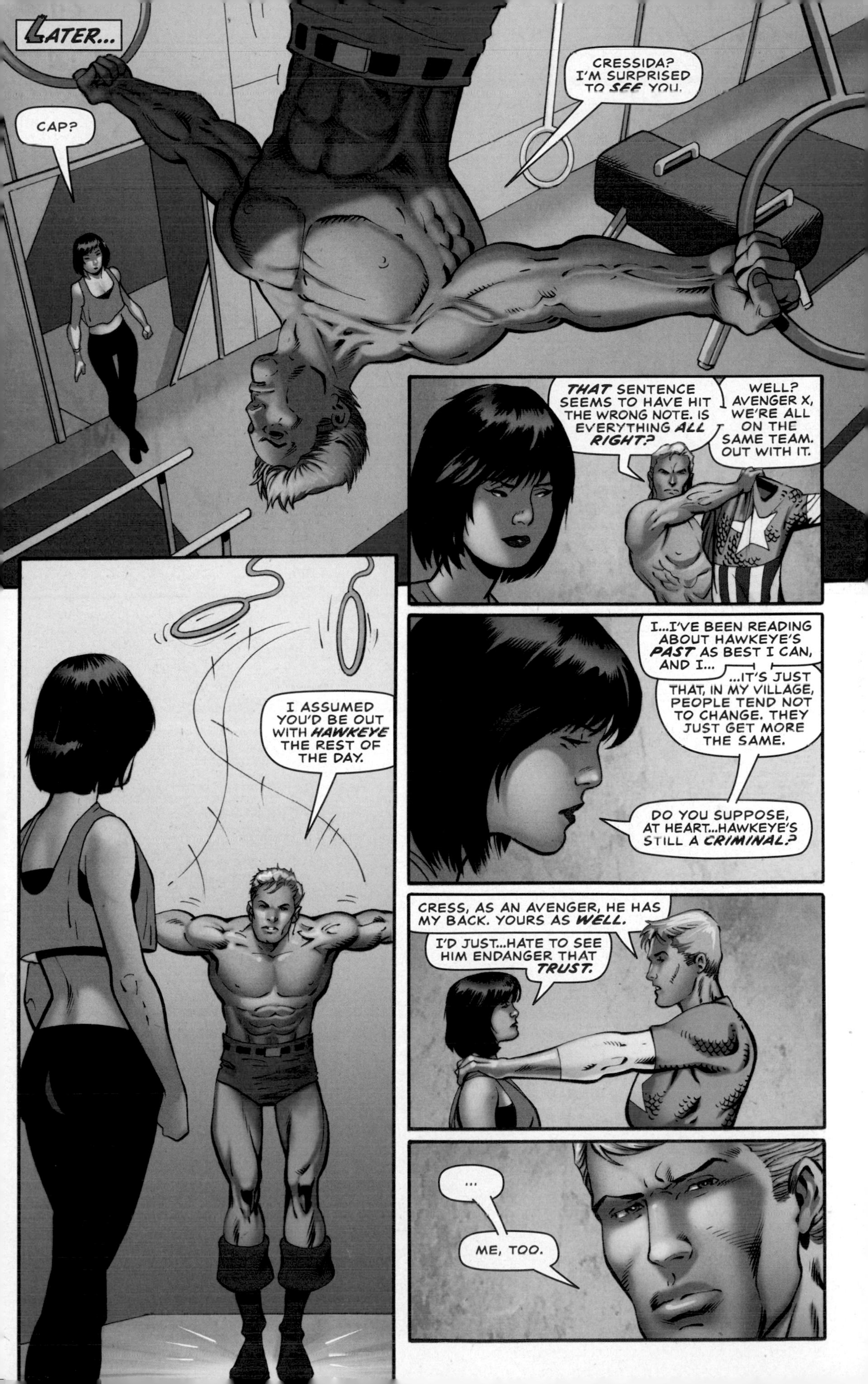
LATER...
CAP?
CRESSIDA? I'M SURPRISED TO SEE YOU.
THAT SENTENCE SEEMS TO HAVE HIT THE WRONG NOTE. IS EVERYTHING ALL RIGHT?
WELL? AVENGER X, WE'RE ALL ON THE SAME TEAM. OUT WITH IT.
I ASSUMED YOU'D BE OUT WITH HAWKEYE THE REST OF THE DAY.
I...I'VE BEEN READING ABOUT HAWKEYE'S PAST AS BEST I CAN, AND I...
...IT'S JUST THAT, IN MY VILLAGE, PEOPLE TEND NOT TO CHANGE. THEY JUST GET MORE THE SAME.
DO YOU SUPPOSE, AT HEART...HAWKEYE'S STILL A CRIMINAL?
CRESS, AS AN AVENGER, HE HAS MY BACK. YOURS AS WELL.
I'D JUST...HATE TO SEE HIM ENDANGER THAT TRUST.
...
ME, TOO.

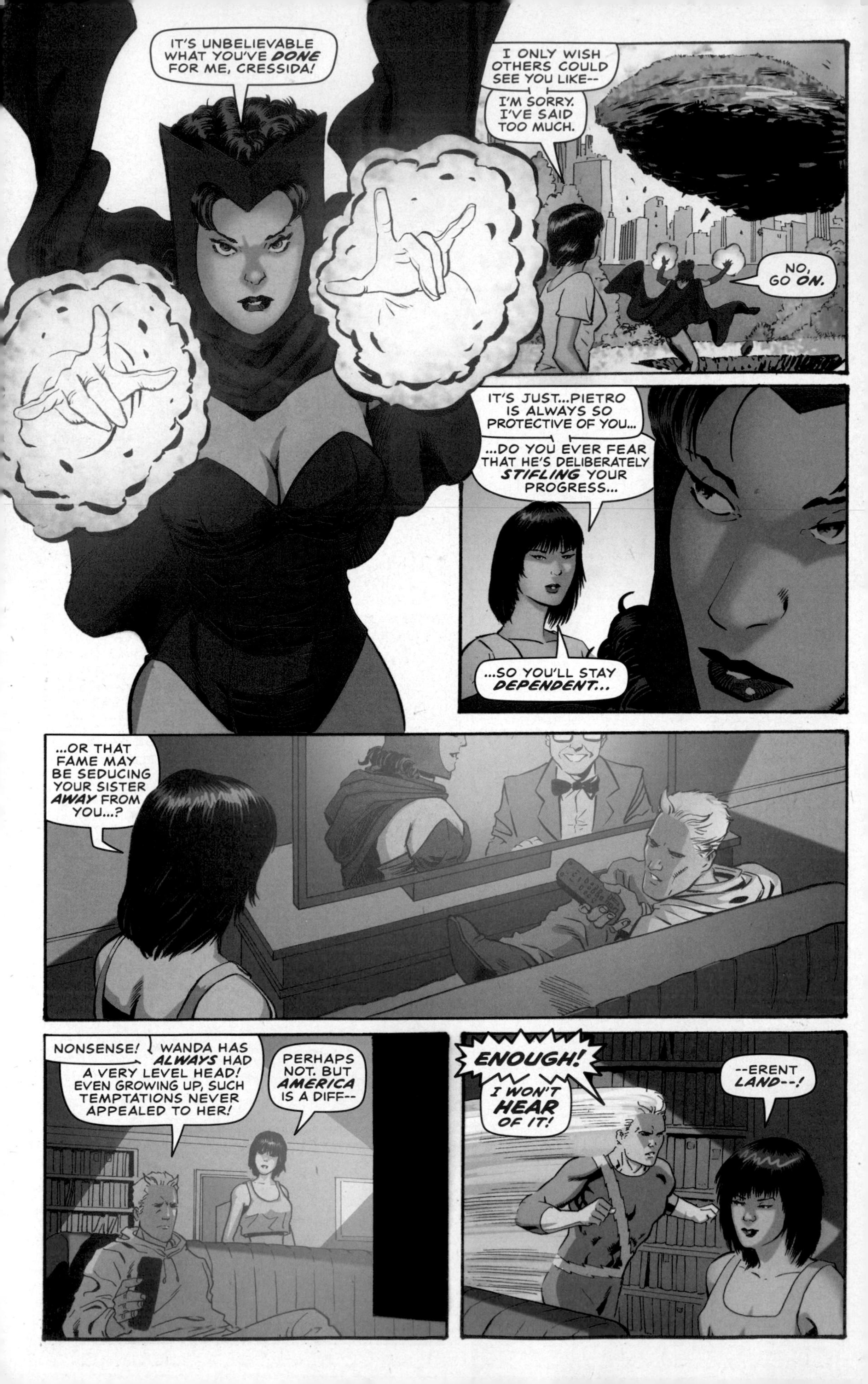
IT'S UNBELIEVABLE WHAT YOU'VE DONE FOR ME, CRESSIDA!
I ONLY WISH OTHERS COULD SEE YOU LIKE--
I'M SORRY. I'VE SAID TOO MUCH.
NO, GO ON.
IT'S JUST...PIETRO IS ALWAYS SO PROTECTIVE OF YOU...
...DO YOU EVER FEAR THAT HE'S DELIBERATELY STIFLING YOUR PROGRESS...
...SO YOU'LL STAY DEPENDENT...
...OR THAT FAME MAY BE SEDUCING YOUR SISTER AWAY FROM YOU...?
NONSENSE!
WANDA HAS ALWAYS HAD A VERY LEVEL HEAD! EVEN GROWING UP, SUCH TEMPTATIONS NEVER APPEALED TO HER!
PERHAPS NOT. BUT AMERICA IS A DIFF--
ENOUGH!
I WON'T HEAR OF IT!
--ERENT LAND--!

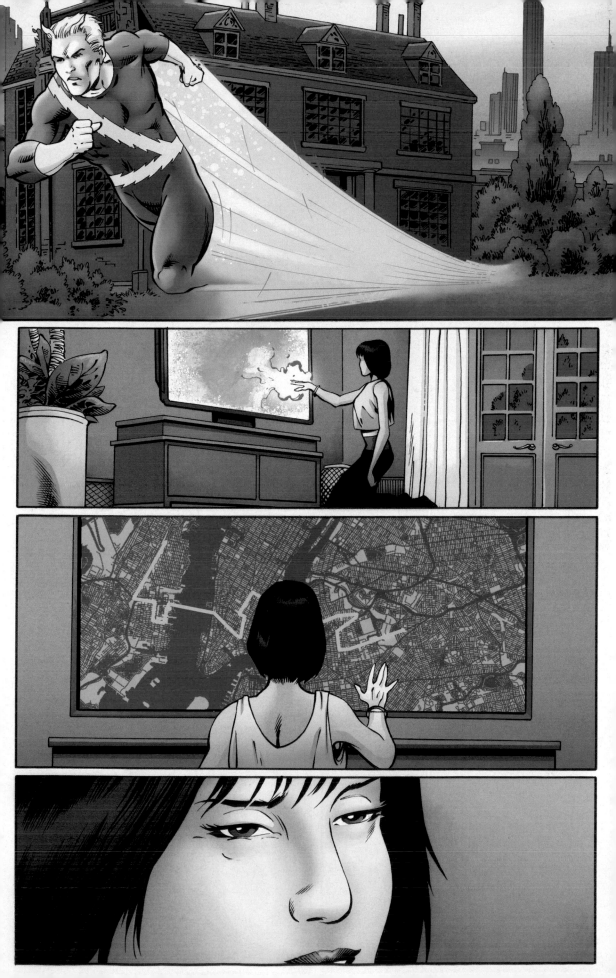

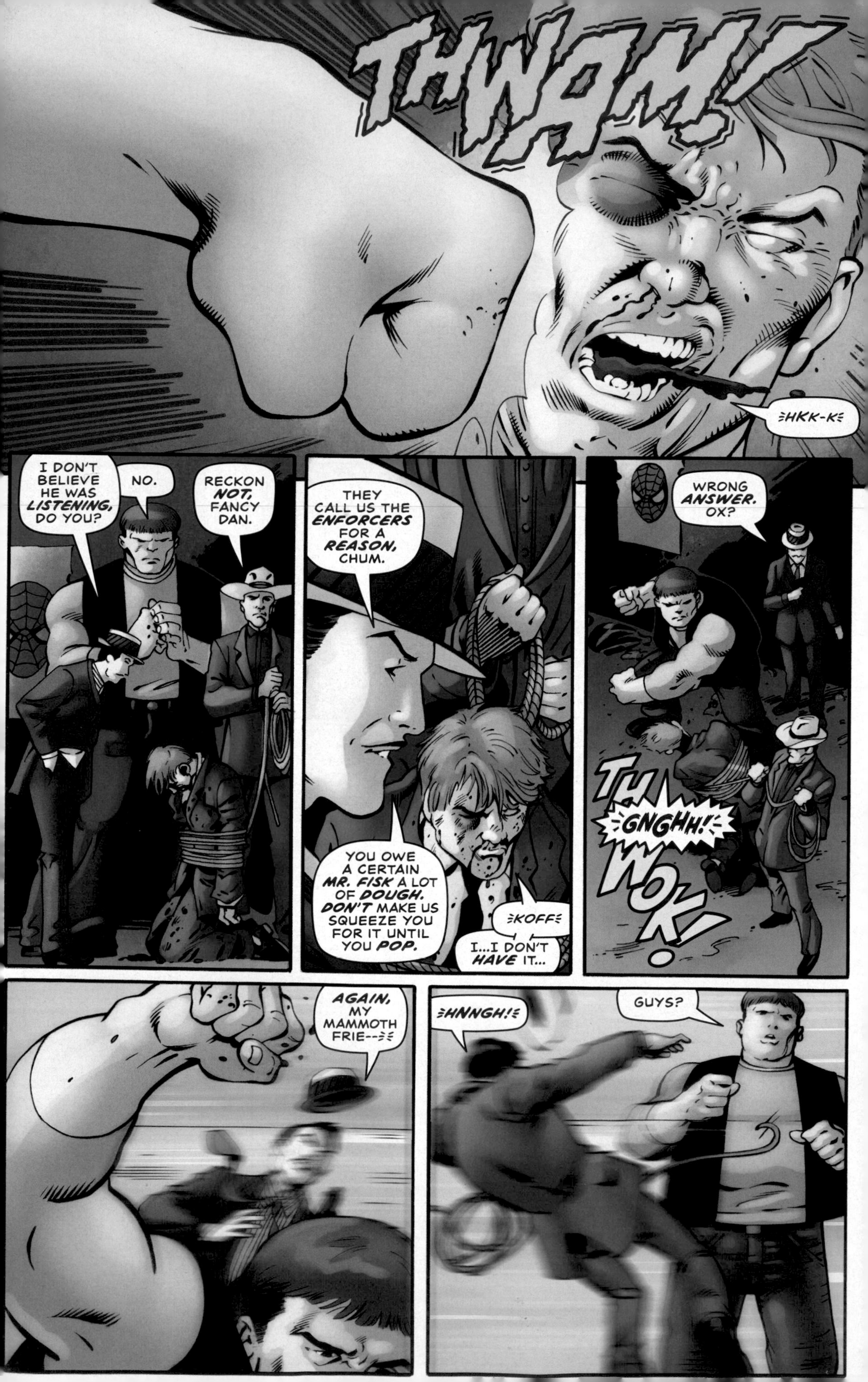
THWAM!
HKK-K
I DON'T BELIEVE HE WAS LISTENING, DO YOU?
NO.
RECKON NOT, FANCY DAN.
THEY CALL US THE ENFORCERS FOR A REASON, CHUM.
YOU OWE A CERTAIN MR. FISK A LOT OF DOUGH. DON'T MAKE US SQUEEZE YOU FOR IT UNTIL YOU POP.
KOFF
I...I DON'T HAVE IT...
WRONG ANSWER. OX?
THWOK!
GNGHH!
AGAIN, MY MAMMOTH FRIE--
HNNGH!
GUYS?

NONE OF YOU WILL BE *BRUTALIZING* ANYONE AGAIN ANYTIME *SOON!*

OH, NO...?

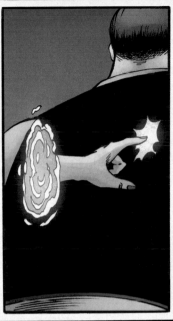

SEE HOW

IT *FEELS*

YOU LUMBERING

BEHEMOTH!

HEH.

-*UNGHH!*-

FWWOM!

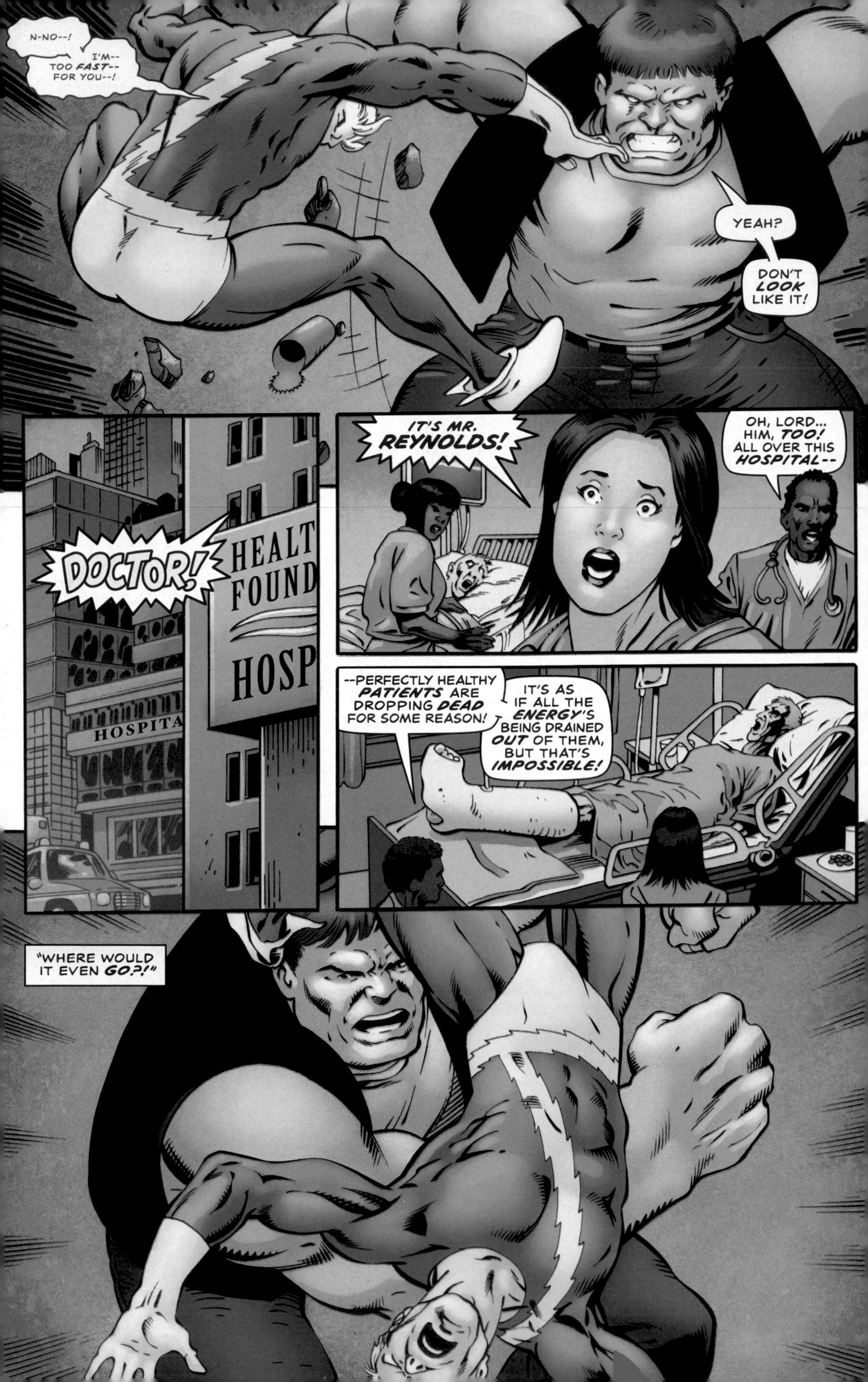

N-NO--!
I'M-- TOO FAST-- FOR YOU--!
YEAH?
DON'T LOOK LIKE IT!
DOCTOR!
HEALT
FOUND
HOSP
HOSPITA
IT'S MR. REYNOLDS!
OH, LORD... HIM, TOO! ALL OVER THIS HOSPITAL--
--PERFECTLY HEALTHY PATIENTS ARE DROPPING DEAD FOR SOME REASON!
IT'S AS IF ALL THE ENERGY'S BEING DRAINED OUT OF THEM, BUT THAT'S IMPOSSIBLE!
"WHERE WOULD IT EVEN GO?!"

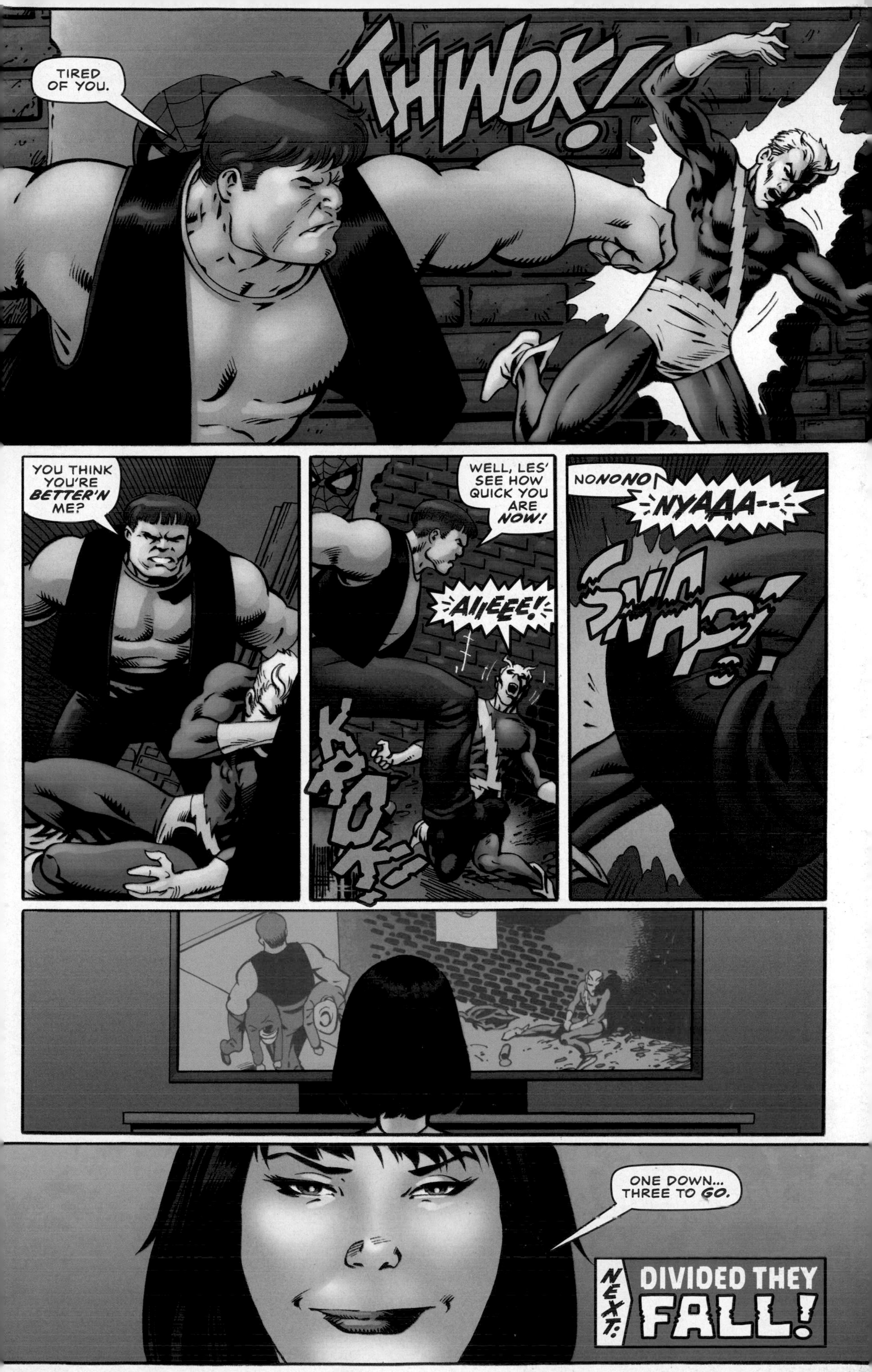
TIRED OF YOU.
THWOK!
YOU THINK YOU'RE *BETTER'N* ME?
WELL, LES' SEE HOW QUICK YOU ARE *NOW!*
AIIEEE!
KROK!
NONONO
NYAAA--
SNAP!
ONE DOWN... THREE TO *GO.*
NEXT: DIVIDED THEY FALL!

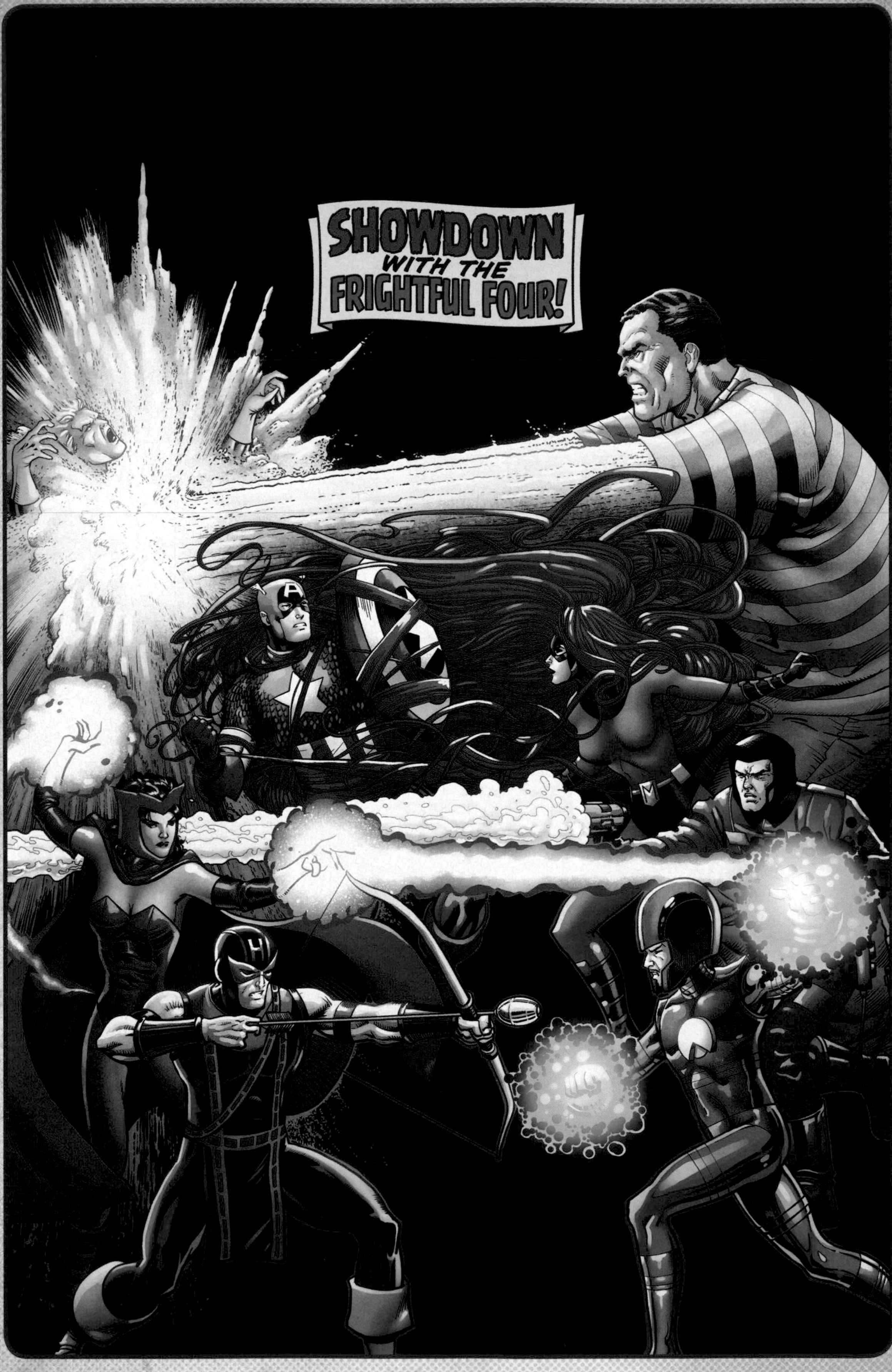
SHOWDOWN WITH THE FRIGHTFUL FOUR!

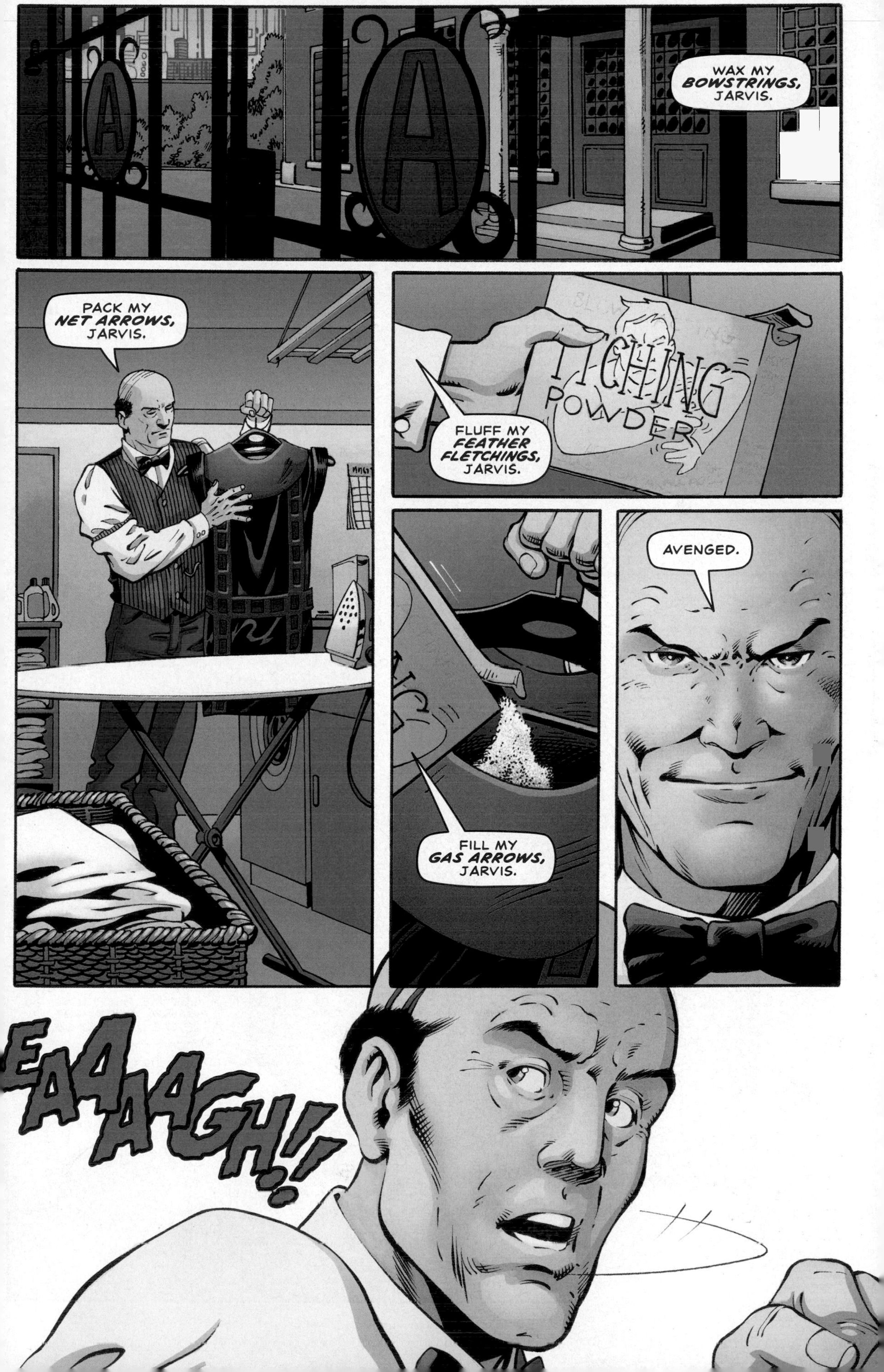
WAX MY BOWSTRINGS, JARVIS.
PACK MY NET ARROWS, JARVIS.
ITCHING POWDER
FLUFF MY FEATHER FLETCHINGS, JARVIS.
FILL MY GAS ARROWS, JARVIS.
AVENGED.
EAAAAGH!!

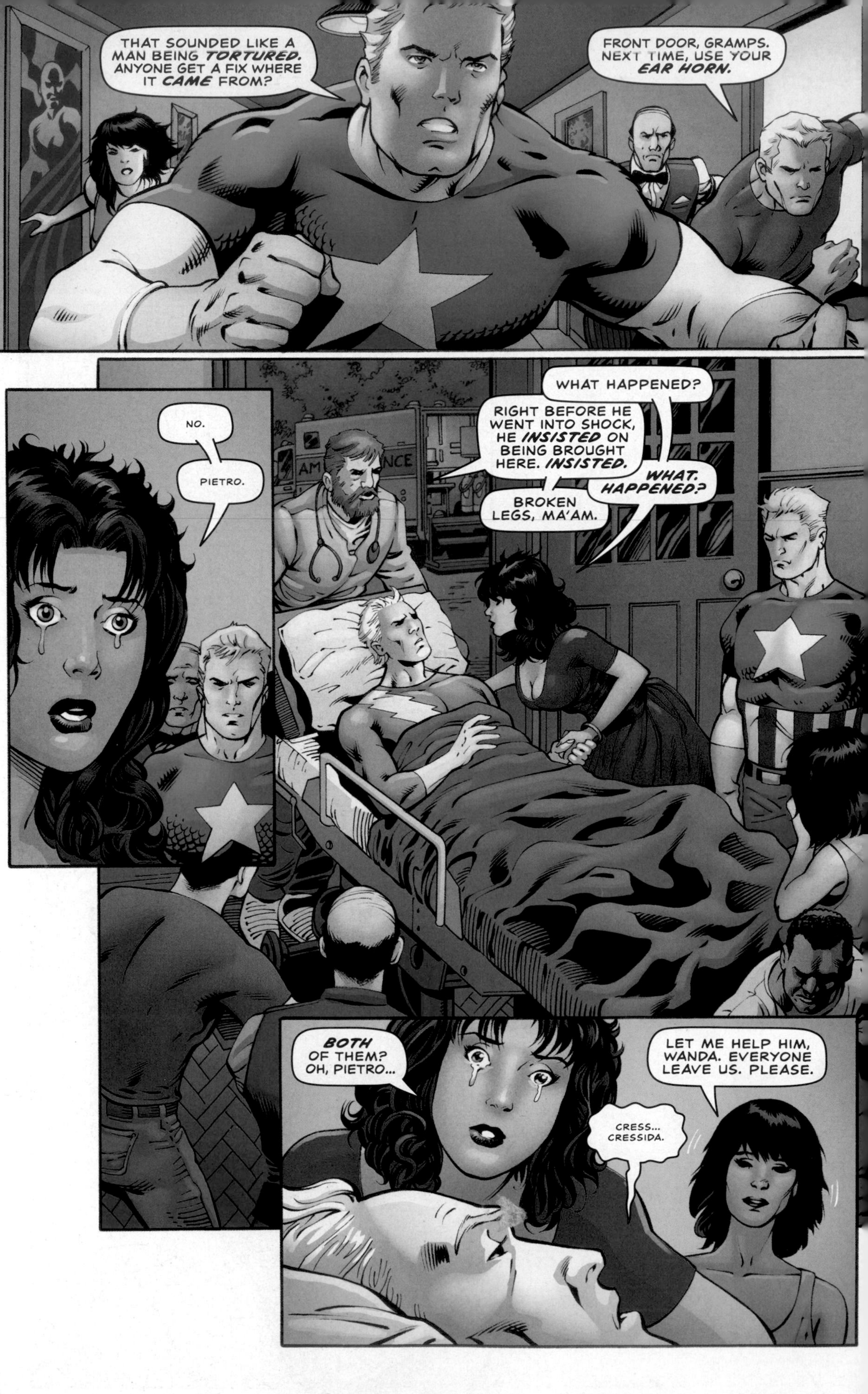
THAT SOUNDED LIKE A MAN BEING TORTURED. ANYONE GET A FIX WHERE IT CAME FROM?
FRONT DOOR, GRAMPS. NEXT TIME, USE YOUR EAR HORN.
WHAT HAPPENED?
RIGHT BEFORE HE WENT INTO SHOCK, HE INSISTED ON BEING BROUGHT HERE. INSISTED.
BROKEN LEGS, MA'AM.
WHAT. HAPPENED?
NO.
PIETRO.
BOTH OF THEM? OH, PIETRO...
LET ME HELP HIM, WANDA. EVERYONE LEAVE US. PLEASE.
CRESS... CRESSIDA.

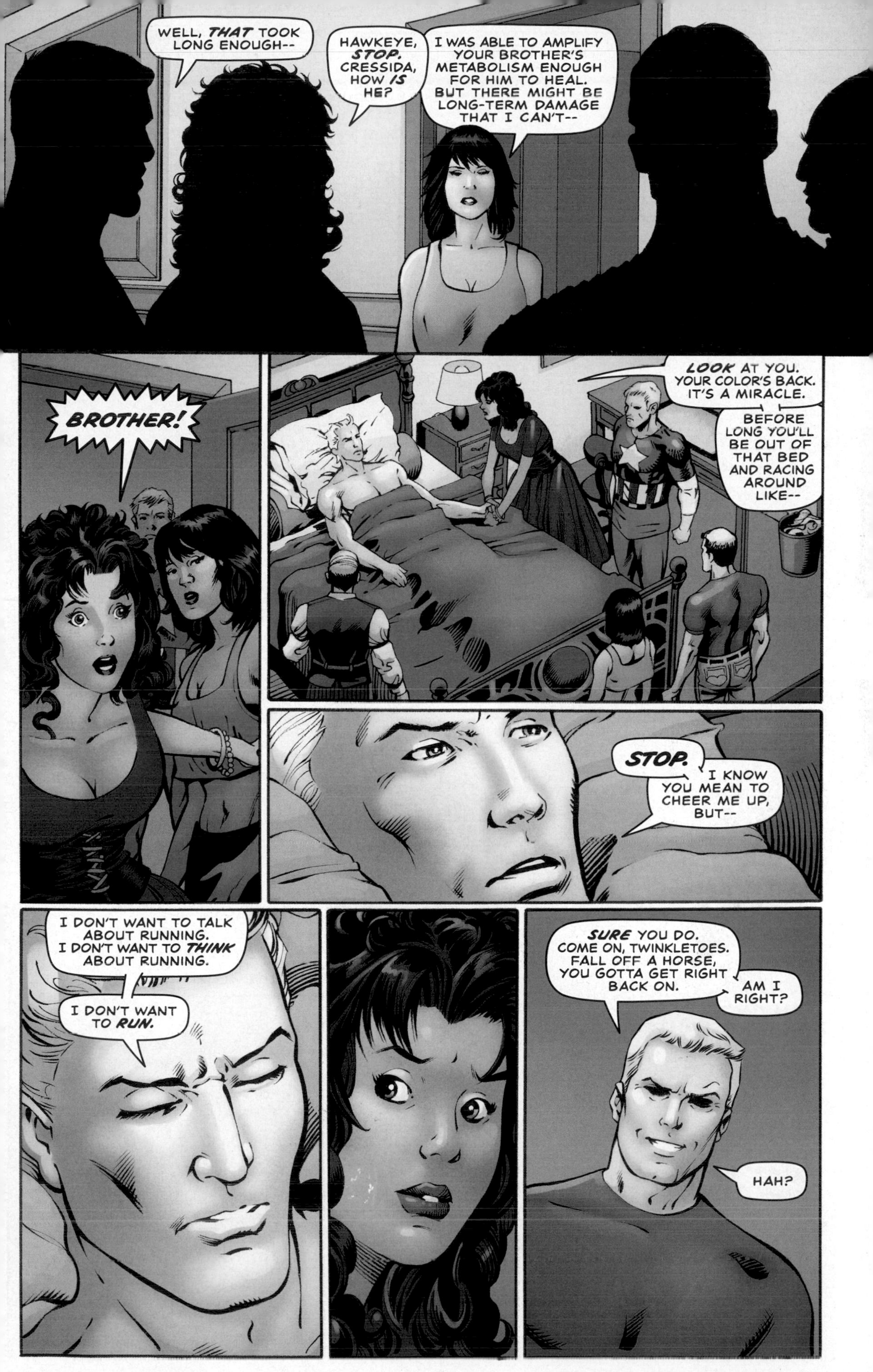
WELL, *THAT* TOOK LONG ENOUGH--
HAWKEYE, *STOP.* CRESSIDA, HOW *IS* HE?
I WAS ABLE TO AMPLIFY YOUR BROTHER'S METABOLISM ENOUGH FOR HIM TO HEAL. BUT THERE MIGHT BE LONG-TERM DAMAGE THAT I CAN'T--
BROTHER!
LOOK AT YOU. YOUR COLOR'S BACK. IT'S A MIRACLE.
BEFORE LONG YOU'LL BE OUT OF THAT BED AND RACING AROUND LIKE--
STOP.
I KNOW YOU MEAN TO CHEER ME UP, BUT--
I DON'T WANT TO TALK ABOUT RUNNING. I DON'T WANT TO *THINK* ABOUT RUNNING.
I DON'T WANT TO *RUN.*
SURE YOU DO. COME ON, TWINKLETOES. FALL OFF A HORSE, YOU GOTTA GET RIGHT BACK ON.
AM I RIGHT?
HAH?

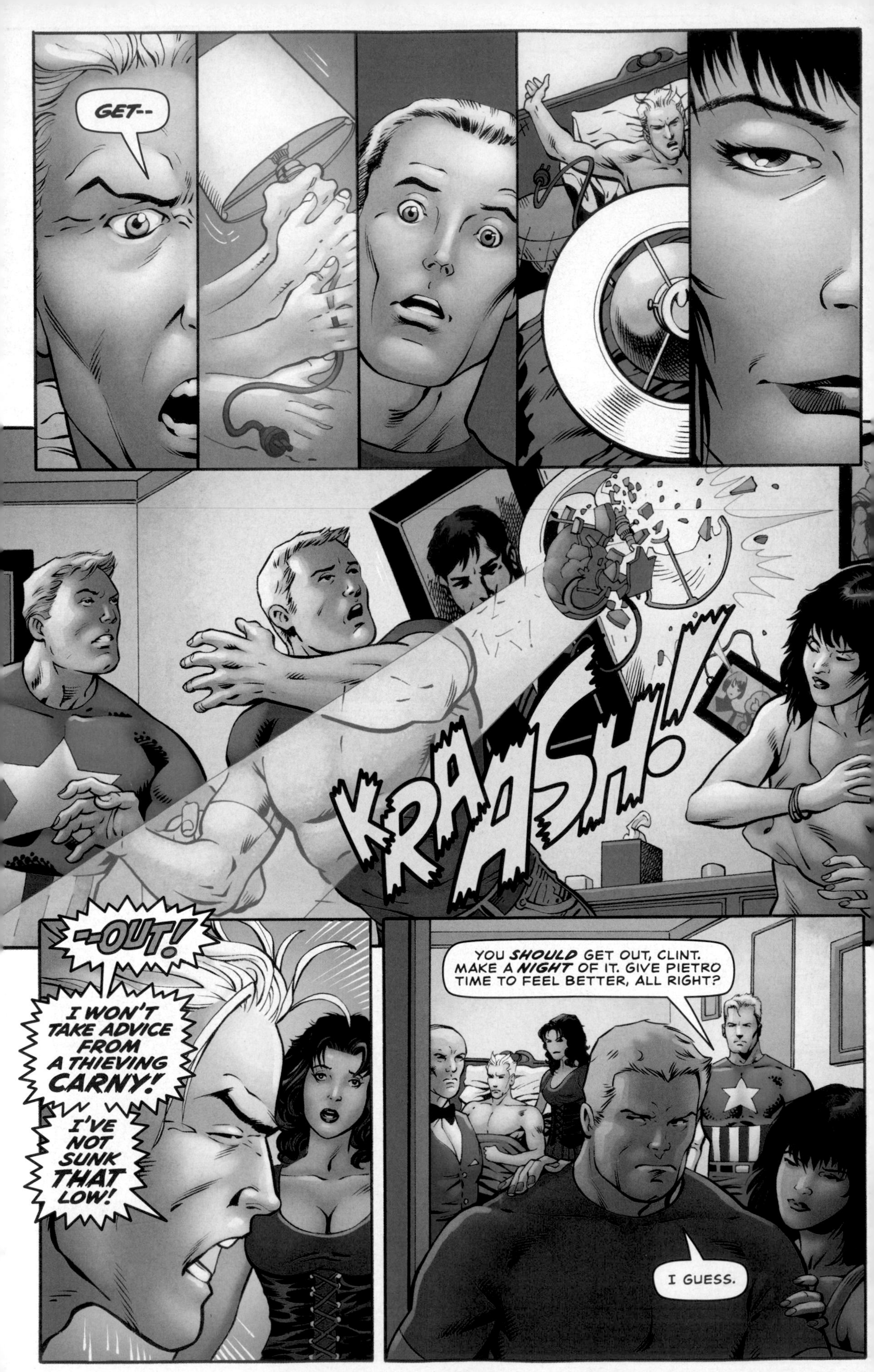
GET--
KRASH!
--OUT!
I WON'T TAKE ADVICE FROM A THIEVING CARNY!
I'VE NOT SUNK THAT LOW!
YOU SHOULD GET OUT, CLINT. MAKE A NIGHT OF IT. GIVE PIETRO TIME TO FEEL BETTER, ALL RIGHT?
I GUESS.

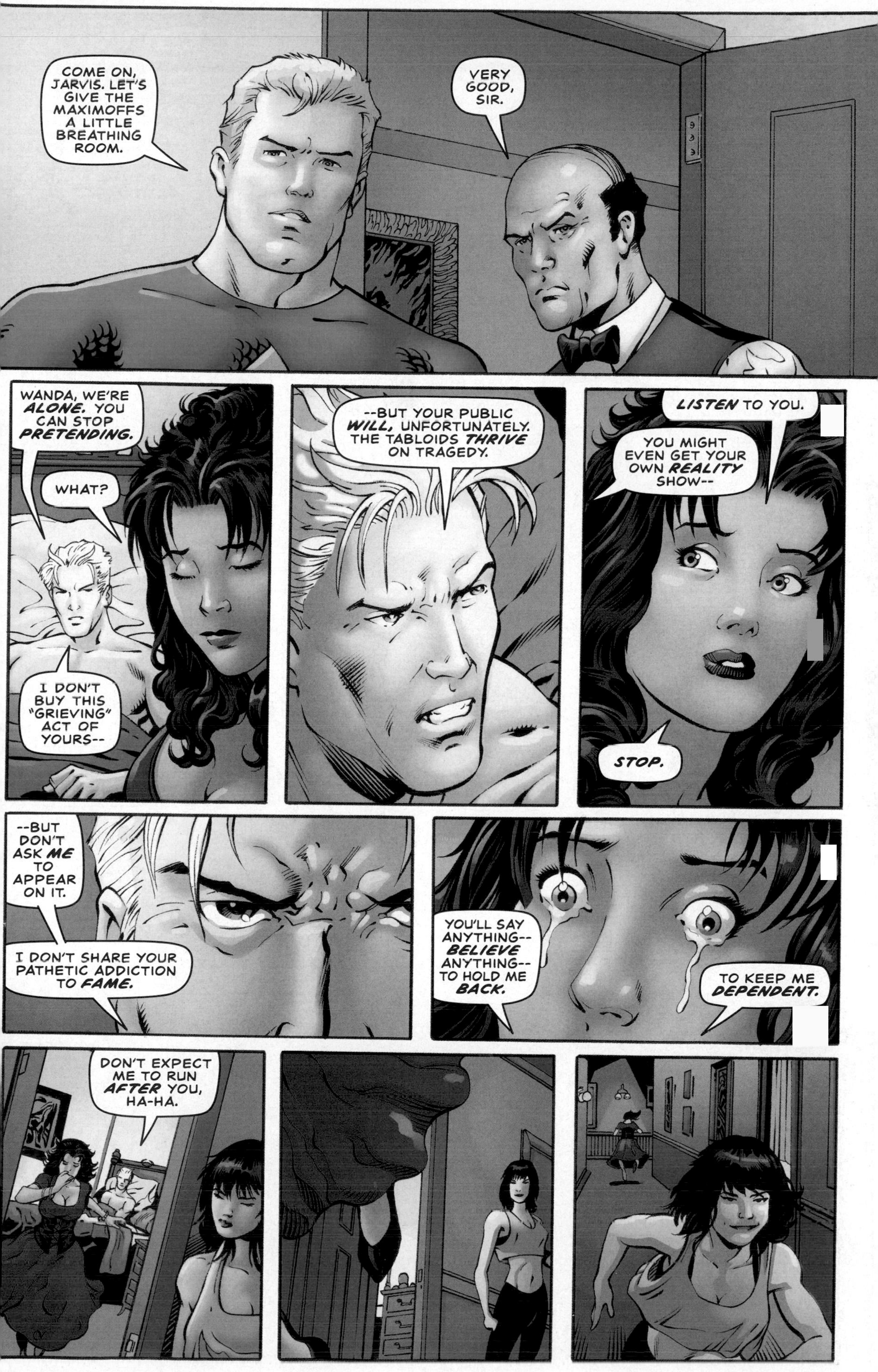
COME ON, JARVIS. LET'S GIVE THE MAXIMOFFS A LITTLE BREATHING ROOM.
VERY GOOD, SIR.
WANDA, WE'RE ALONE. YOU CAN STOP PRETENDING.
WHAT?
I DON'T BUY THIS "GRIEVING" ACT OF YOURS--
--BUT YOUR PUBLIC WILL, UNFORTUNATELY. THE TABLOIDS THRIVE ON TRAGEDY.
LISTEN TO YOU.
YOU MIGHT EVEN GET YOUR OWN REALITY SHOW--
STOP.
--BUT DON'T ASK ME TO APPEAR ON IT.
I DON'T SHARE YOUR PATHETIC ADDICTION TO FAME.
YOU'LL SAY ANYTHING-- BELIEVE ANYTHING-- TO HOLD ME BACK.
TO KEEP ME DEPENDENT.
DON'T EXPECT ME TO RUN AFTER YOU, HA-HA.

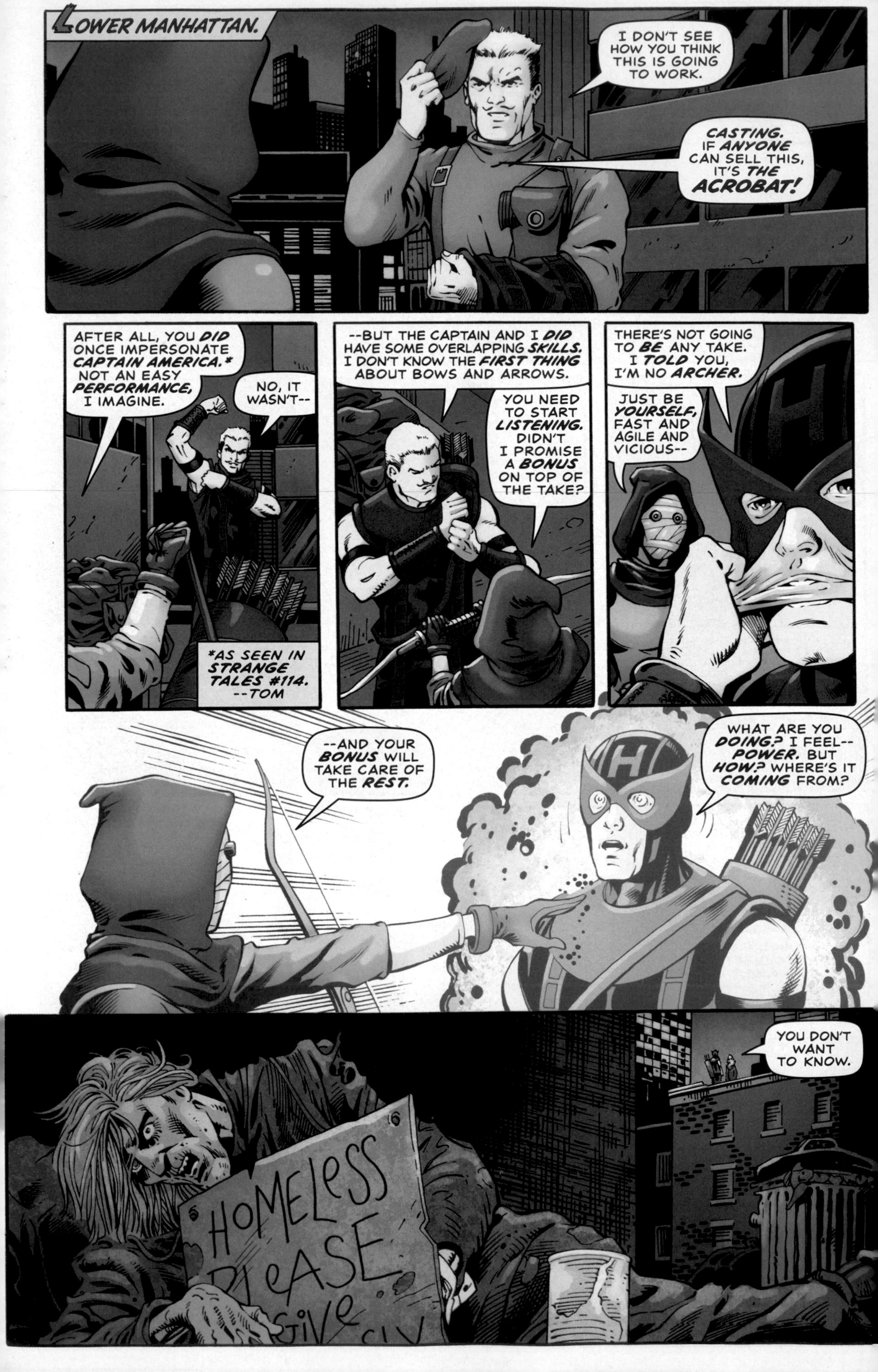
LOWER MANHATTAN.
I DON'T SEE HOW YOU THINK THIS IS GOING TO WORK.
CASTING. IF ANYONE CAN SELL THIS, IT'S THE ACROBAT!
AFTER ALL, YOU DID ONCE IMPERSONATE CAPTAIN AMERICA.* NOT AN EASY PERFORMANCE, I IMAGINE.
NO, IT WASN'T--
*AS SEEN IN STRANGE TALES #114. --TOM
--BUT THE CAPTAIN AND I DID HAVE SOME OVERLAPPING SKILLS. I DON'T KNOW THE FIRST THING ABOUT BOWS AND ARROWS.
YOU NEED TO START LISTENING. DIDN'T I PROMISE A BONUS ON TOP OF THE TAKE?
THERE'S NOT GOING TO BE ANY TAKE. I TOLD YOU, I'M NO ARCHER.
JUST BE YOURSELF, FAST AND AGILE AND VICIOUS--
--AND YOUR BONUS WILL TAKE CARE OF THE REST.
WHAT ARE YOU DOING? I FEEL-- POWER. BUT HOW? WHERE'S IT COMING FROM?
YOU DON'T WANT TO KNOW.
HOMELESS PLEASE GIVE

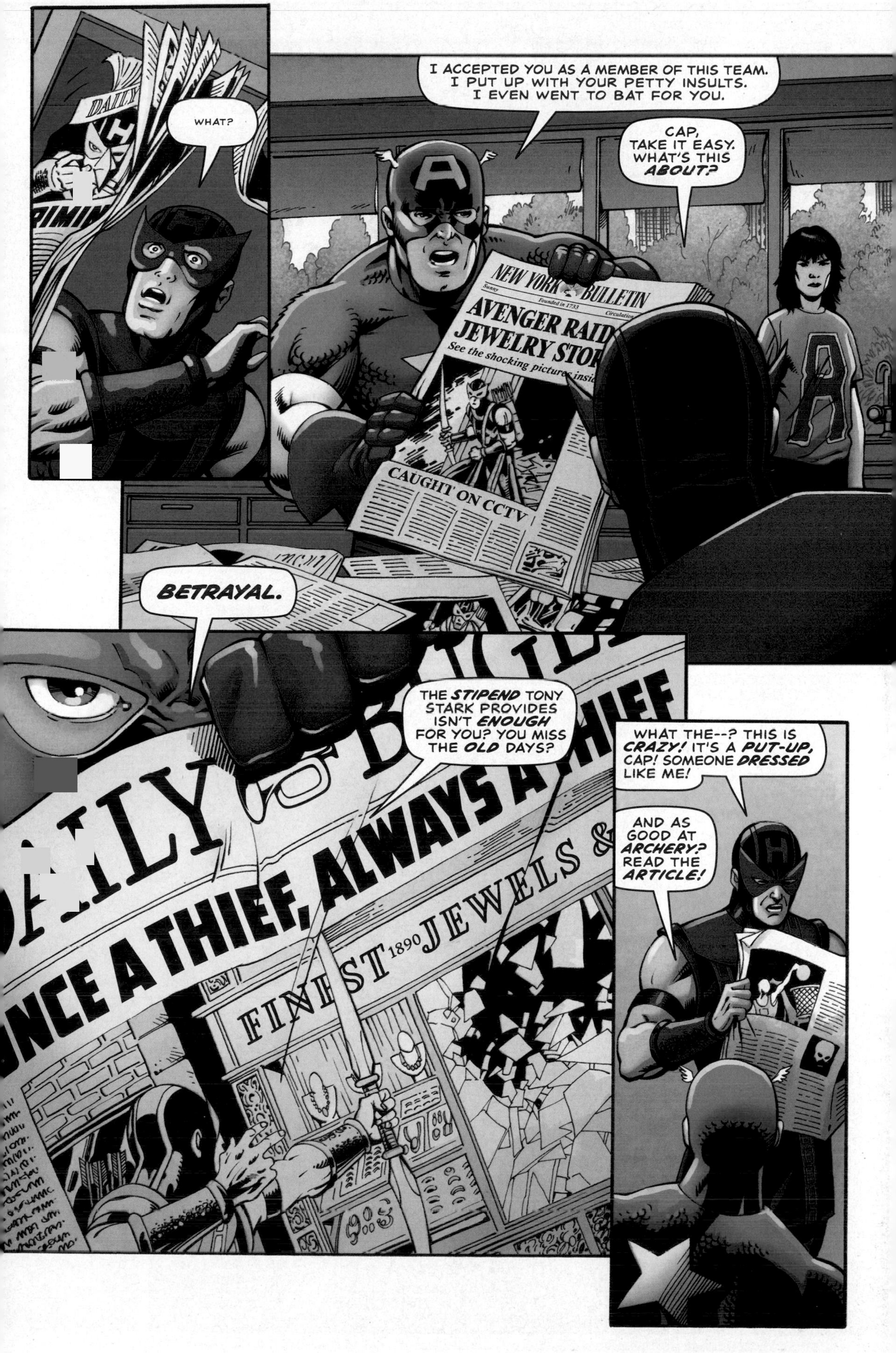

DAILY
WHAT?
I ACCEPTED YOU AS A MEMBER OF THIS TEAM. I PUT UP WITH YOUR PETTY INSULTS. I EVEN WENT TO BAT FOR YOU.
CAP, TAKE IT EASY. WHAT'S THIS ABOUT?
NEW YORK BULLETIN
Founded in 1733
AVENGER RAID JEWELRY STOR
See the shocking pictures insi
CAUGHT ON CCTV
BETRAYAL.
THE STIPEND TONY STARK PROVIDES ISN'T ENOUGH FOR YOU? YOU MISS THE OLD DAYS?
ONCE A THIEF, ALWAYS A THIEF
FINEST 1890 JEWELS &
WHAT THE--? THIS IS CRAZY! IT'S A PUT-UP, CAP! SOMEONE DRESSED LIKE ME!
AND AS GOOD AT ARCHERY? READ THE ARTICLE!

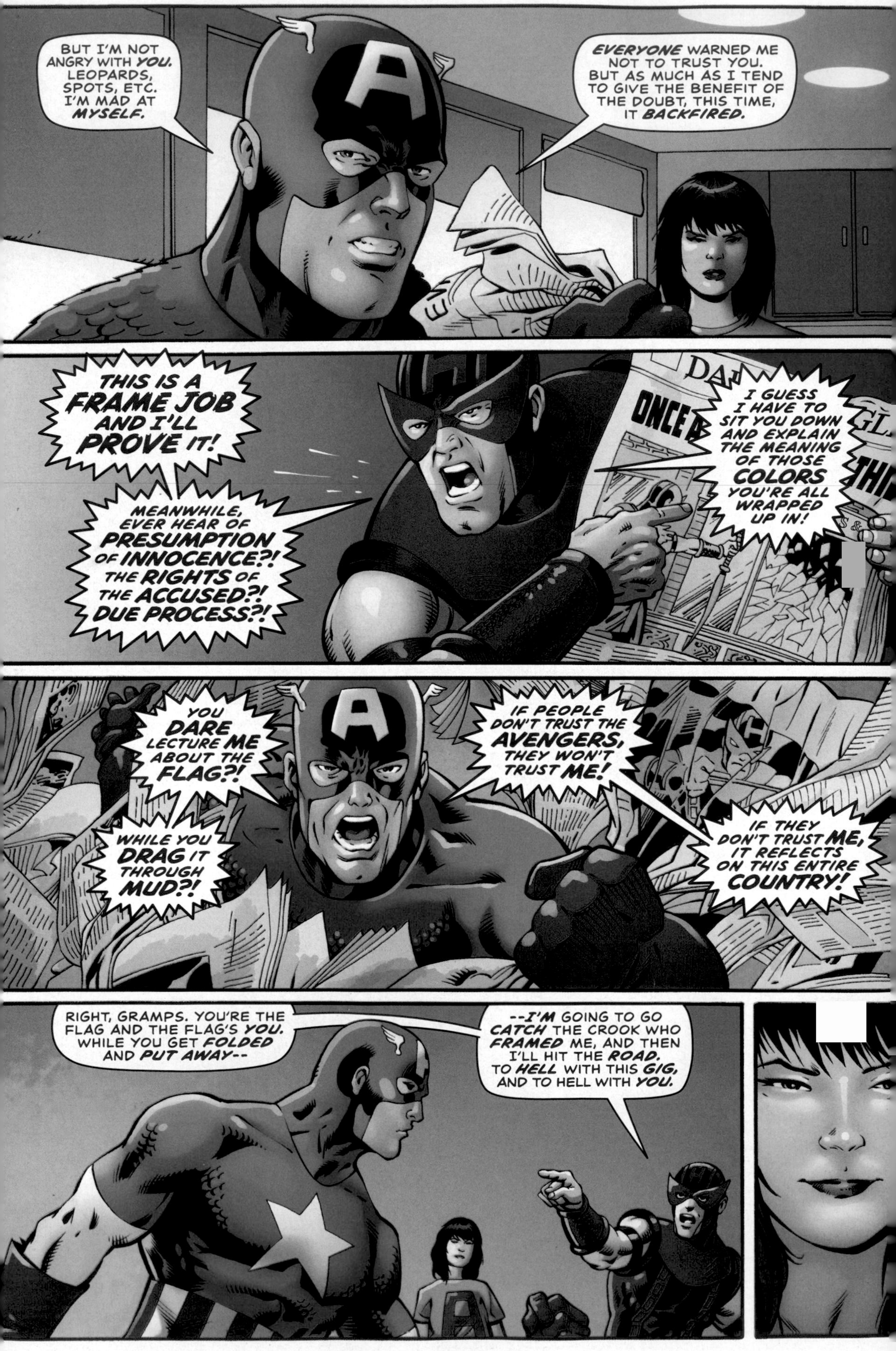
BUT I'M NOT ANGRY WITH YOU. LEOPARDS, SPOTS, ETC. I'M MAD AT MYSELF.
EVERYONE WARNED ME NOT TO TRUST YOU. BUT AS MUCH AS I TEND TO GIVE THE BENEFIT OF THE DOUBT, THIS TIME, IT BACKFIRED.
THIS IS A FRAME JOB AND I'LL PROVE IT!
MEANWHILE, EVER HEAR OF PRESUMPTION OF INNOCENCE?! THE RIGHTS OF THE ACCUSED?! DUE PROCESS?!
I GUESS I HAVE TO SIT YOU DOWN AND EXPLAIN THE MEANING OF THOSE COLORS YOU'RE ALL WRAPPED UP IN!
YOU DARE LECTURE ME ABOUT THE FLAG?!
WHILE YOU DRAG IT THROUGH MUD?!
IF PEOPLE DON'T TRUST THE AVENGERS, THEY WON'T TRUST ME!
IF THEY DON'T TRUST ME, IT REFLECTS ON THIS ENTIRE COUNTRY!
RIGHT, GRAMPS. YOU'RE THE FLAG AND THE FLAG'S YOU. WHILE YOU GET FOLDED AND PUT AWAY--
--I'M GOING TO GO CATCH THE CROOK WHO FRAMED ME, AND THEN I'LL HIT THE ROAD. TO HELL WITH THIS GIG, AND TO HELL WITH YOU.

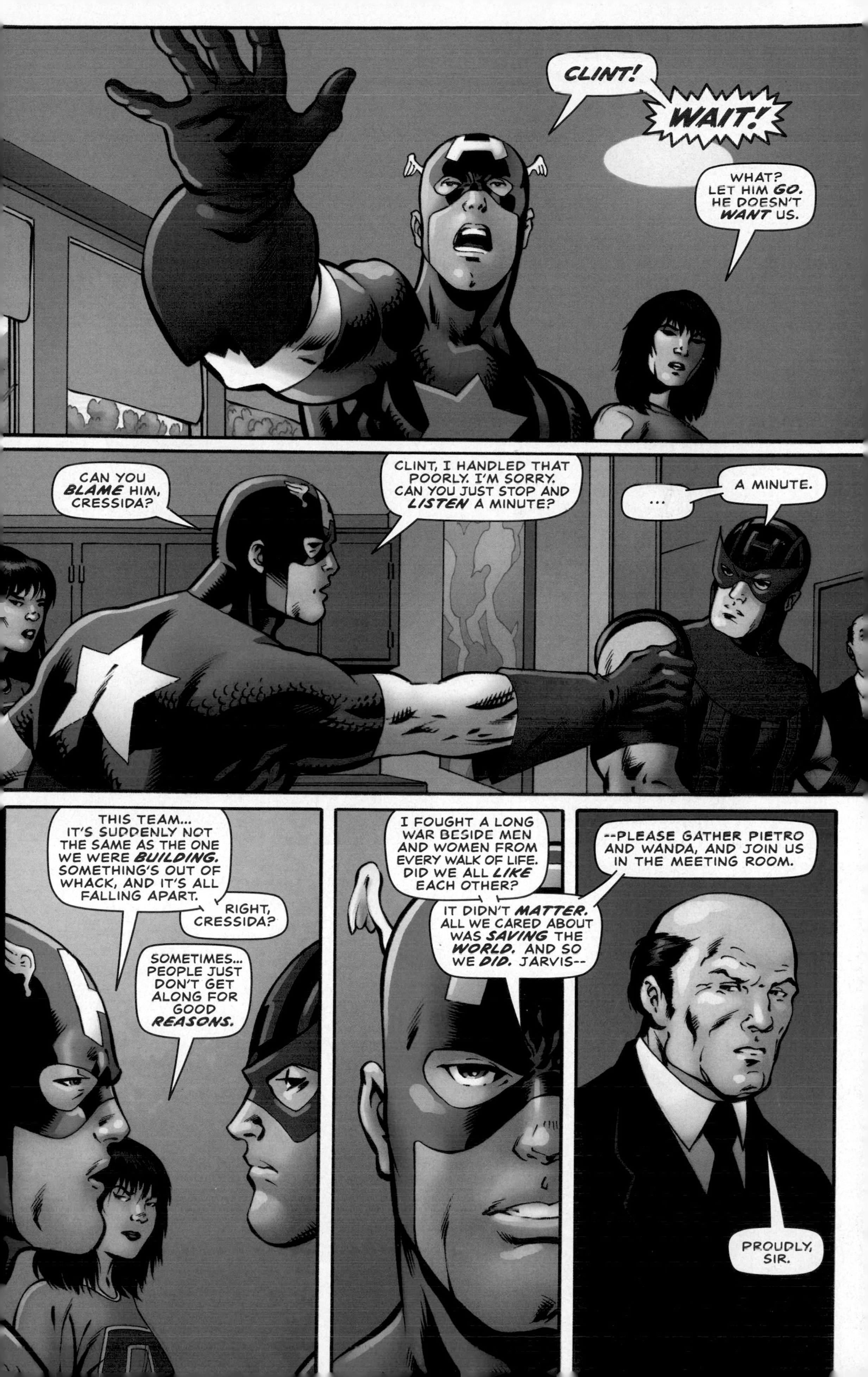
CLINT!
WAIT!
WHAT? LET HIM GO. HE DOESN'T WANT US.
CAN YOU BLAME HIM, CRESSIDA?
CLINT, I HANDLED THAT POORLY. I'M SORRY. CAN YOU JUST STOP AND LISTEN A MINUTE?
...
A MINUTE.
THIS TEAM... IT'S SUDDENLY NOT THE SAME AS THE ONE WE WERE BUILDING. SOMETHING'S OUT OF WHACK, AND IT'S ALL FALLING APART.
RIGHT, CRESSIDA?
SOMETIMES... PEOPLE JUST DON'T GET ALONG FOR GOOD REASONS.
I FOUGHT A LONG WAR BESIDE MEN AND WOMEN FROM EVERY WALK OF LIFE. DID WE ALL LIKE EACH OTHER?
IT DIDN'T MATTER. ALL WE CARED ABOUT WAS SAVING THE WORLD. AND SO WE DID. JARVIS--
--PLEASE GATHER PIETRO AND WANDA, AND JOIN US IN THE MEETING ROOM.
PROUDLY, SIR.

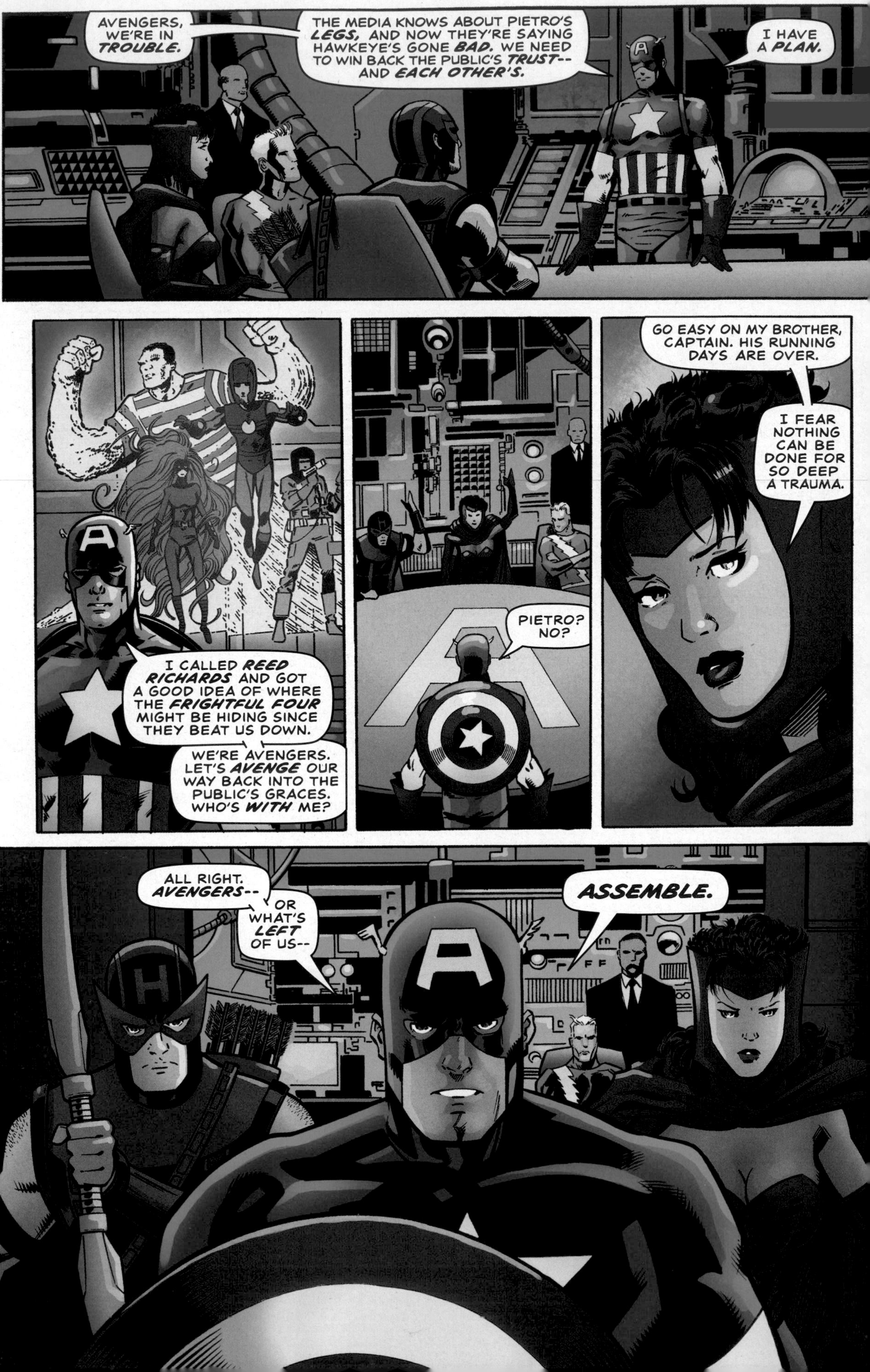

AVENGERS, WE'RE IN TROUBLE.
THE MEDIA KNOWS ABOUT PIETRO'S LEGS, AND NOW THEY'RE SAYING HAWKEYE'S GONE BAD. WE NEED TO WIN BACK THE PUBLIC'S TRUST-- AND EACH OTHER'S.
I HAVE A PLAN.
I CALLED REED RICHARDS AND GOT A GOOD IDEA OF WHERE THE FRIGHTFUL FOUR MIGHT BE HIDING SINCE THEY BEAT US DOWN.
WE'RE AVENGERS. LET'S AVENGE OUR WAY BACK INTO THE PUBLIC'S GRACES. WHO'S WITH ME?
PIETRO? NO?
GO EASY ON MY BROTHER, CAPTAIN. HIS RUNNING DAYS ARE OVER.
I FEAR NOTHING CAN BE DONE FOR SO DEEP A TRAUMA.
ALL RIGHT. AVENGERS--
OR WHAT'S LEFT OF US--
ASSEMBLE.

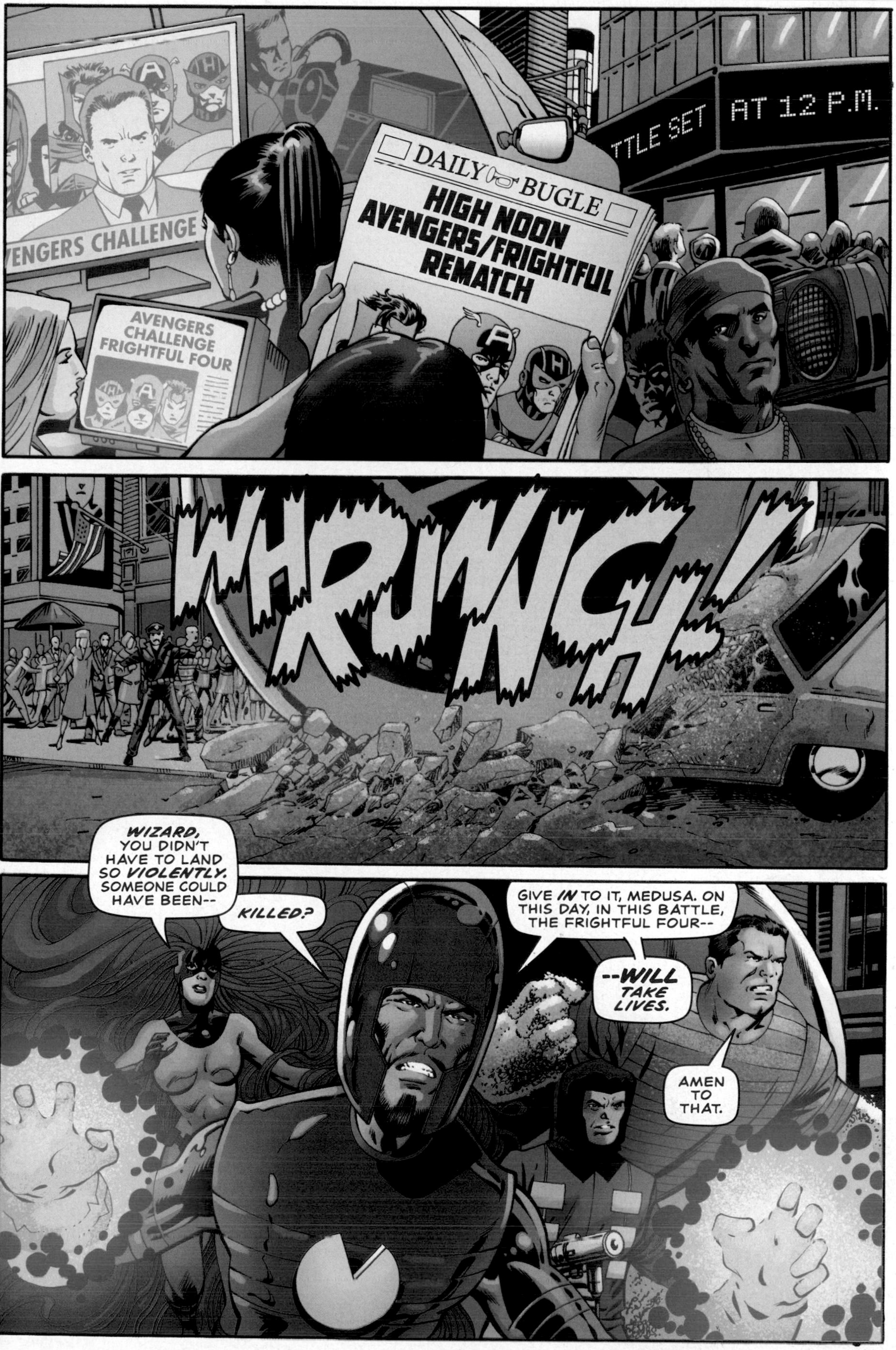
AVENGERS CHALLENGE
AVENGERS CHALLENGE FRIGHTFUL FOUR
DAILY BUGLE
HIGH NOON AVENGERS/FRIGHTFUL REMATCH
TTLE SET AT 12 P.M.
WHRUNCH!
WIZARD, YOU DIDN'T HAVE TO LAND SO VIOLENTLY. SOMEONE COULD HAVE BEEN--
KILLED?
GIVE IN TO IT, MEDUSA. ON THIS DAY, IN THIS BATTLE, THE FRIGHTFUL FOUR--
--WILL TAKE LIVES.
AMEN TO THAT.

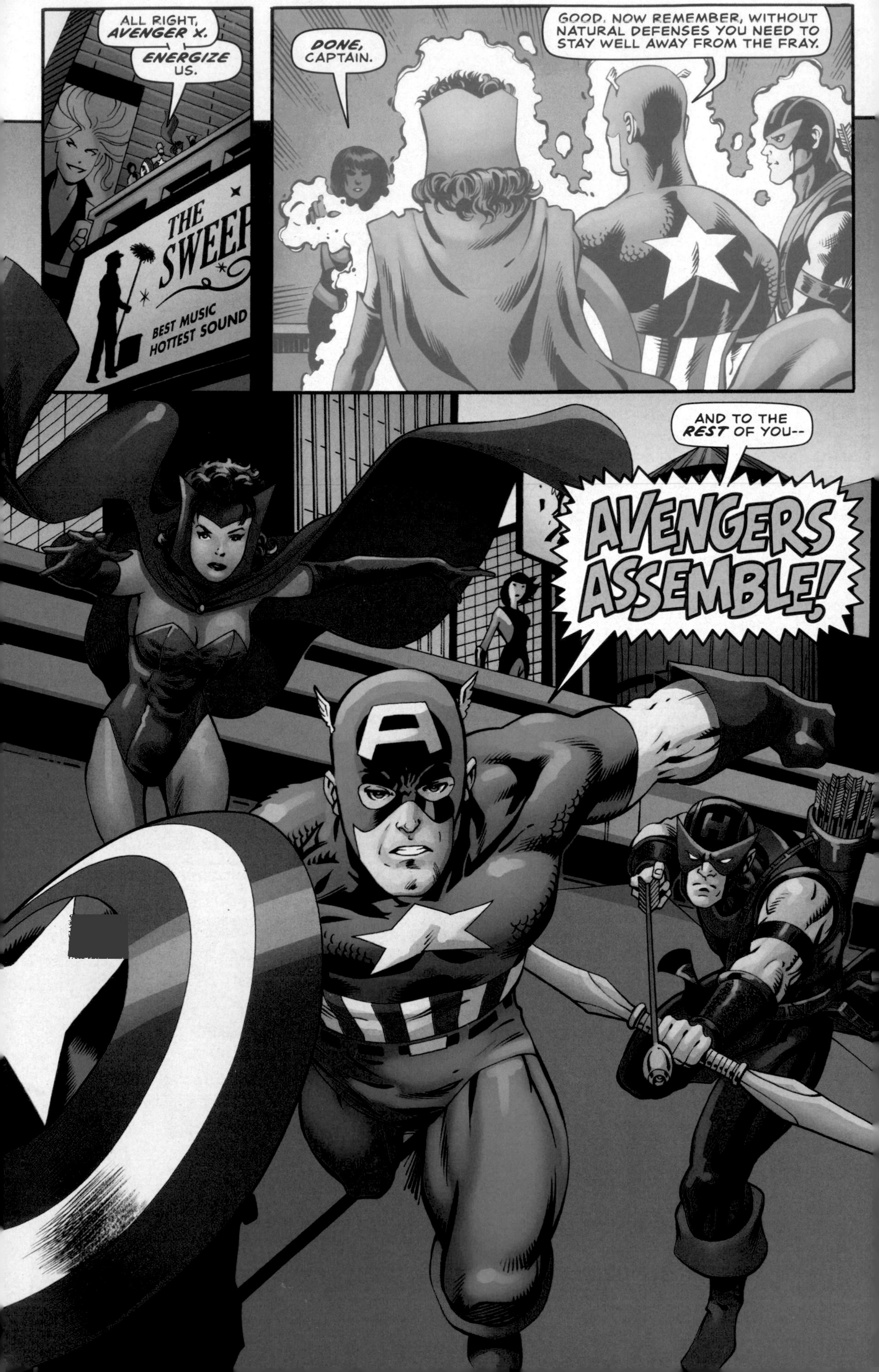
ALL RIGHT, *AVENGER X.*
ENERGIZE US.
THE SWEE
BEST MUSIC HOTTEST SOUND
DONE, CAPTAIN.
GOOD. NOW REMEMBER, WITHOUT NATURAL DEFENSES YOU NEED TO STAY WELL AWAY FROM THE FRAY.
AND TO THE *REST* OF YOU--
AVENGERS ASSEMBLE!

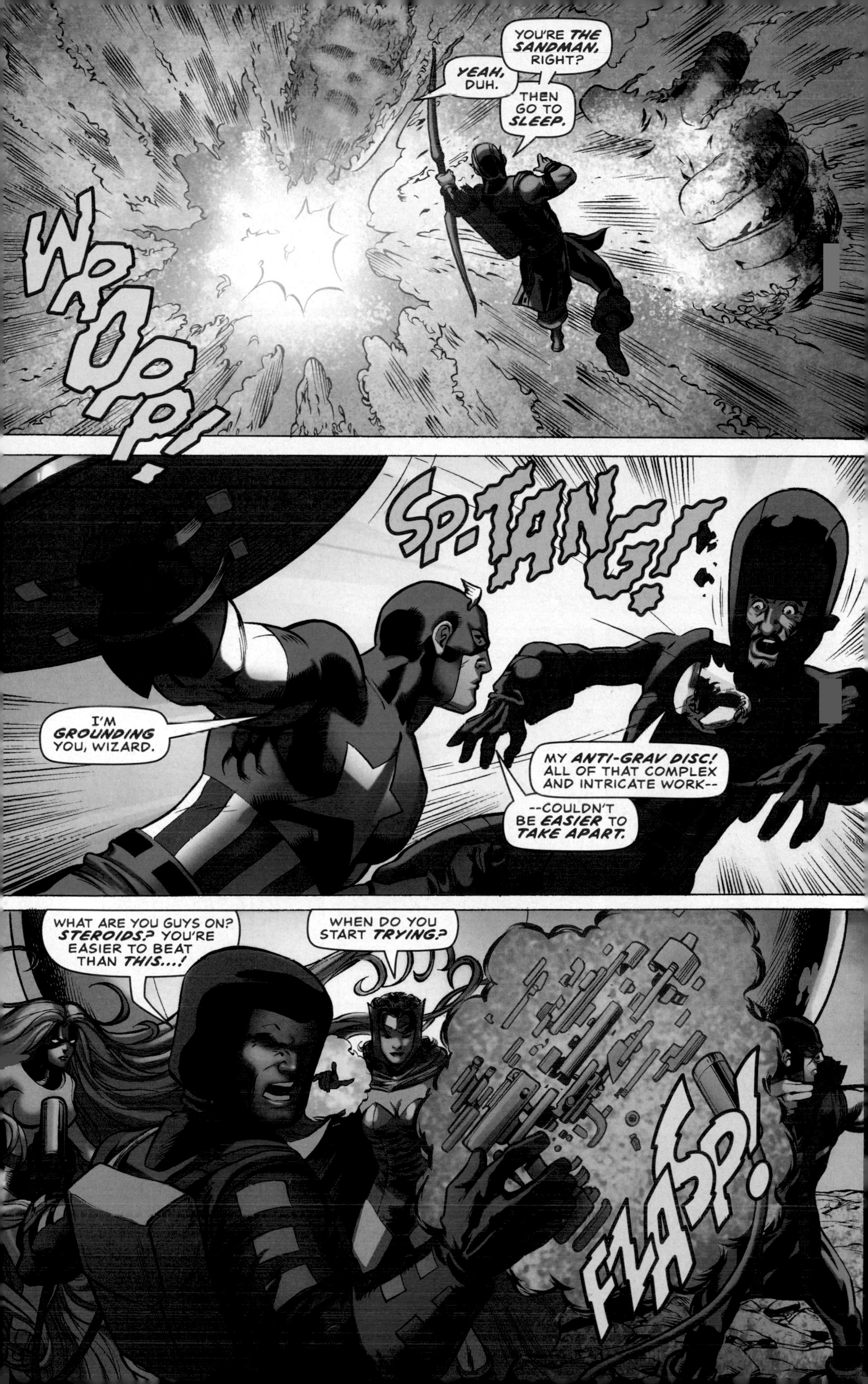
YOU'RE THE SANDMAN, RIGHT?
YEAH, DUH.
THEN GO TO SLEEP.
WROOPP!!
SP-TANG!!
I'M GROUNDING YOU, WIZARD.
MY ANTI-GRAV DISC! ALL OF THAT COMPLEX AND INTRICATE WORK--
--COULDN'T BE EASIER TO TAKE APART.
WHAT ARE YOU GUYS ON? STEROIDS? YOU'RE EASIER TO BEAT THAN THIS...!
WHEN DO YOU START TRYING?
FLASP!

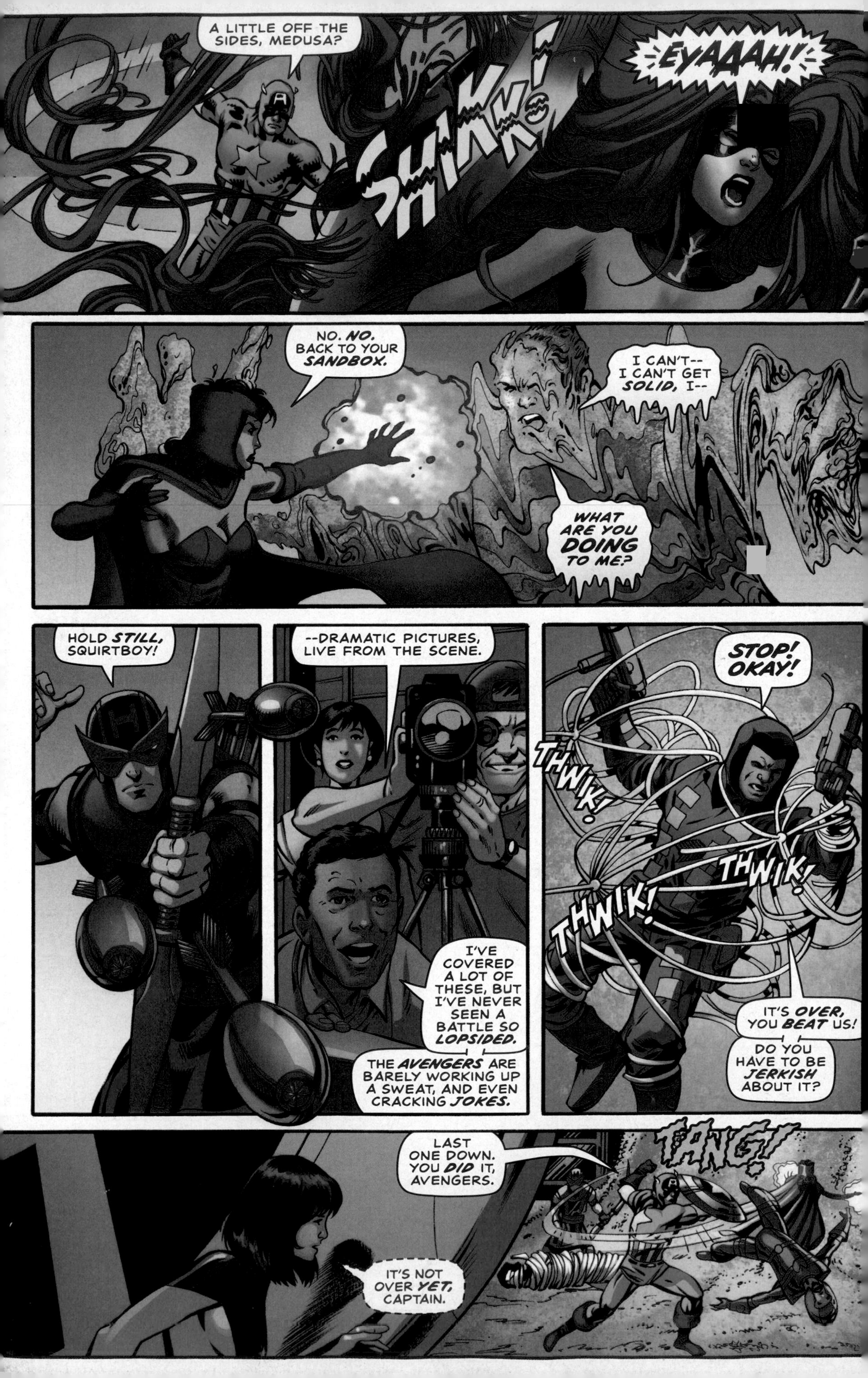
A LITTLE OFF THE SIDES, MEDUSA?
SHIKK!
EYAAAH!
NO. NO. BACK TO YOUR SANDBOX.
I CAN'T-- I CAN'T GET SOLID, I--
WHAT ARE YOU DOING TO ME?
HOLD STILL, SQUIRTBOY!
--DRAMATIC PICTURES, LIVE FROM THE SCENE.
I'VE COVERED A LOT OF THESE, BUT I'VE NEVER SEEN A BATTLE SO LOPSIDED.
THE AVENGERS ARE BARELY WORKING UP A SWEAT, AND EVEN CRACKING JOKES.
STOP! OKAY!
THWIK!
THWIK!
THWIK!
IT'S OVER, YOU BEAT US!
DO YOU HAVE TO BE JERKISH ABOUT IT?
LAST ONE DOWN. YOU DID IT, AVENGERS.
TANG!
IT'S NOT OVER YET, CAPTAIN.

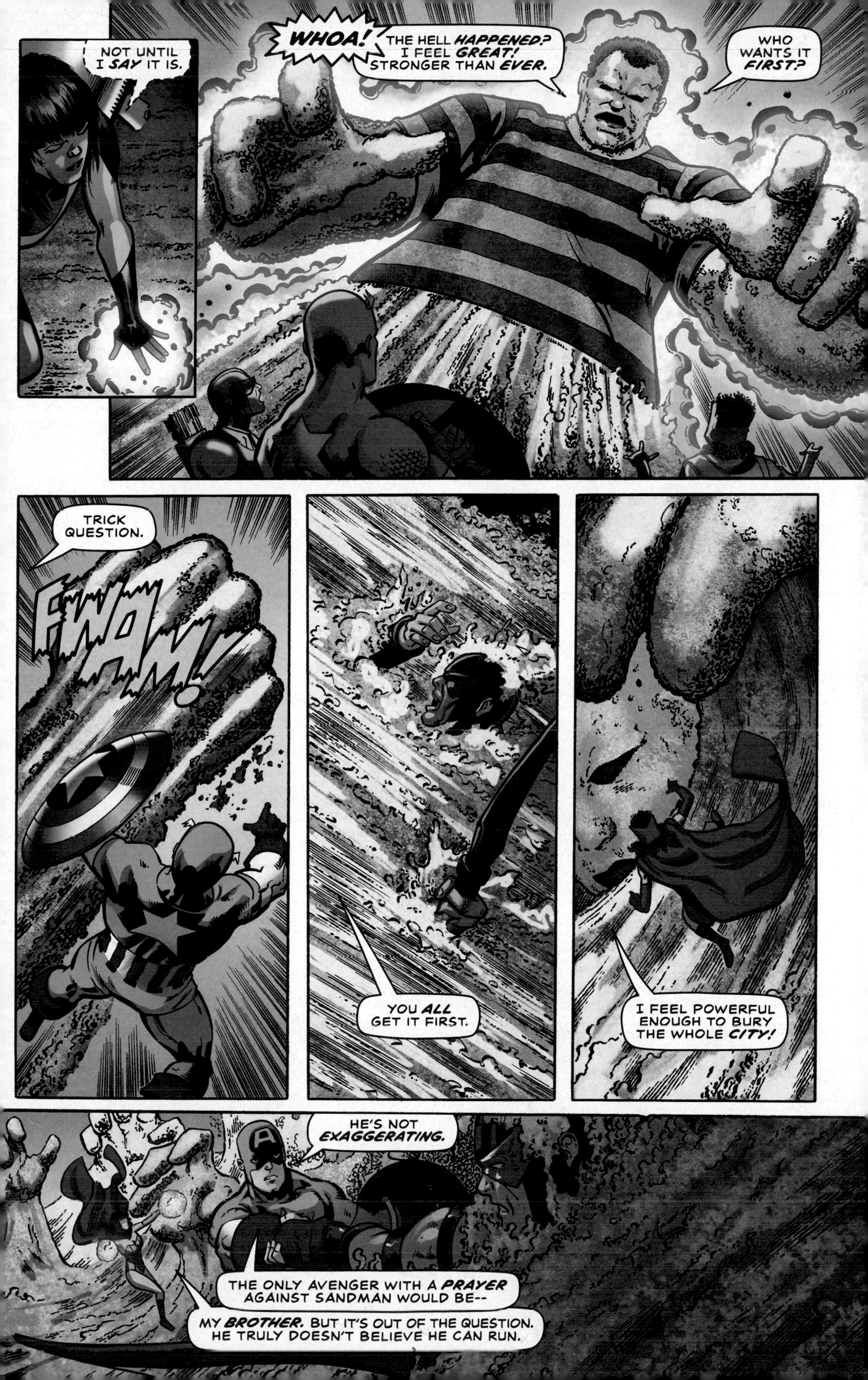
NOT UNTIL I SAY IT IS.
WHOA!
THE HELL HAPPENED? I FEEL GREAT! STRONGER THAN EVER.
WHO WANTS IT FIRST?
TRICK QUESTION.
FWAM!
YOU ALL GET IT FIRST.
I FEEL POWERFUL ENOUGH TO BURY THE WHOLE CITY!
HE'S NOT EXAGGERATING.
THE ONLY AVENGER WITH A PRAYER AGAINST SANDMAN WOULD BE--
MY BROTHER. BUT IT'S OUT OF THE QUESTION. HE TRULY DOESN'T BELIEVE HE CAN RUN.

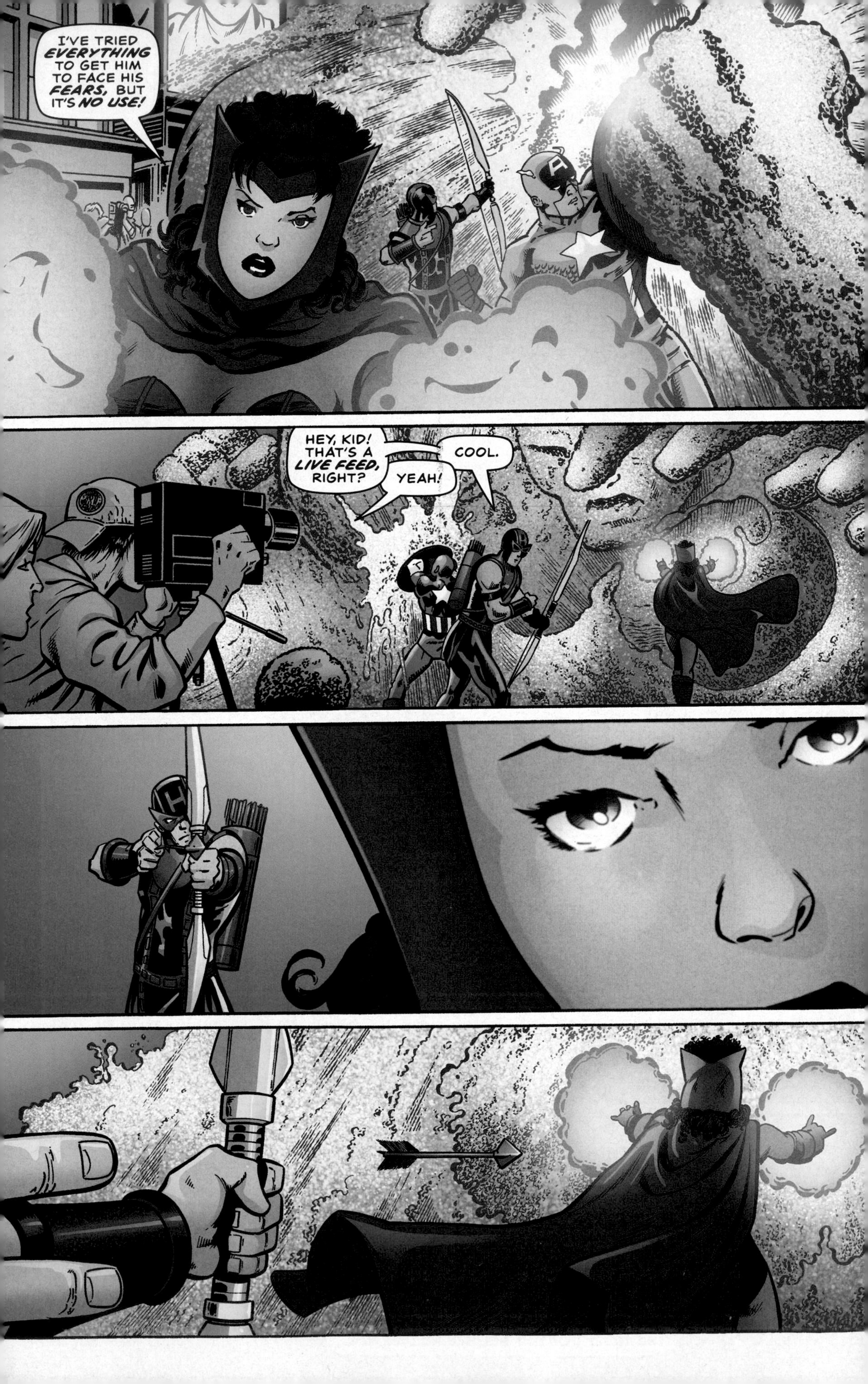
I'VE TRIED EVERYTHING TO GET HIM TO FACE HIS FEARS, BUT IT'S NO USE!
HEY, KID! THAT'S A LIVE FEED, RIGHT?
YEAH!
COOL.

THAK!

FORGET SANDMAN, I'LL TAKE YOU APART!

HOW DARE YOU ENDANGER MY SISTER?

WITH A PRACTICE ARROW?

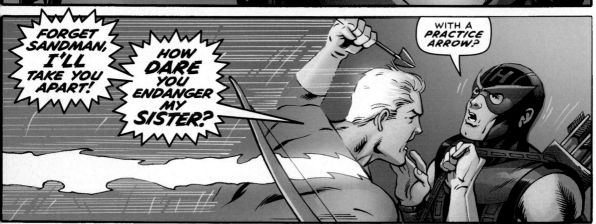

SNAP!

LOOK. BALSA WOOD. TONS MORE DELICATE THAN SAY, HMM, I DON'T KNOW, LEGS.

NOW QUIT BREATHING ON ME

--AND GO GET HIM!

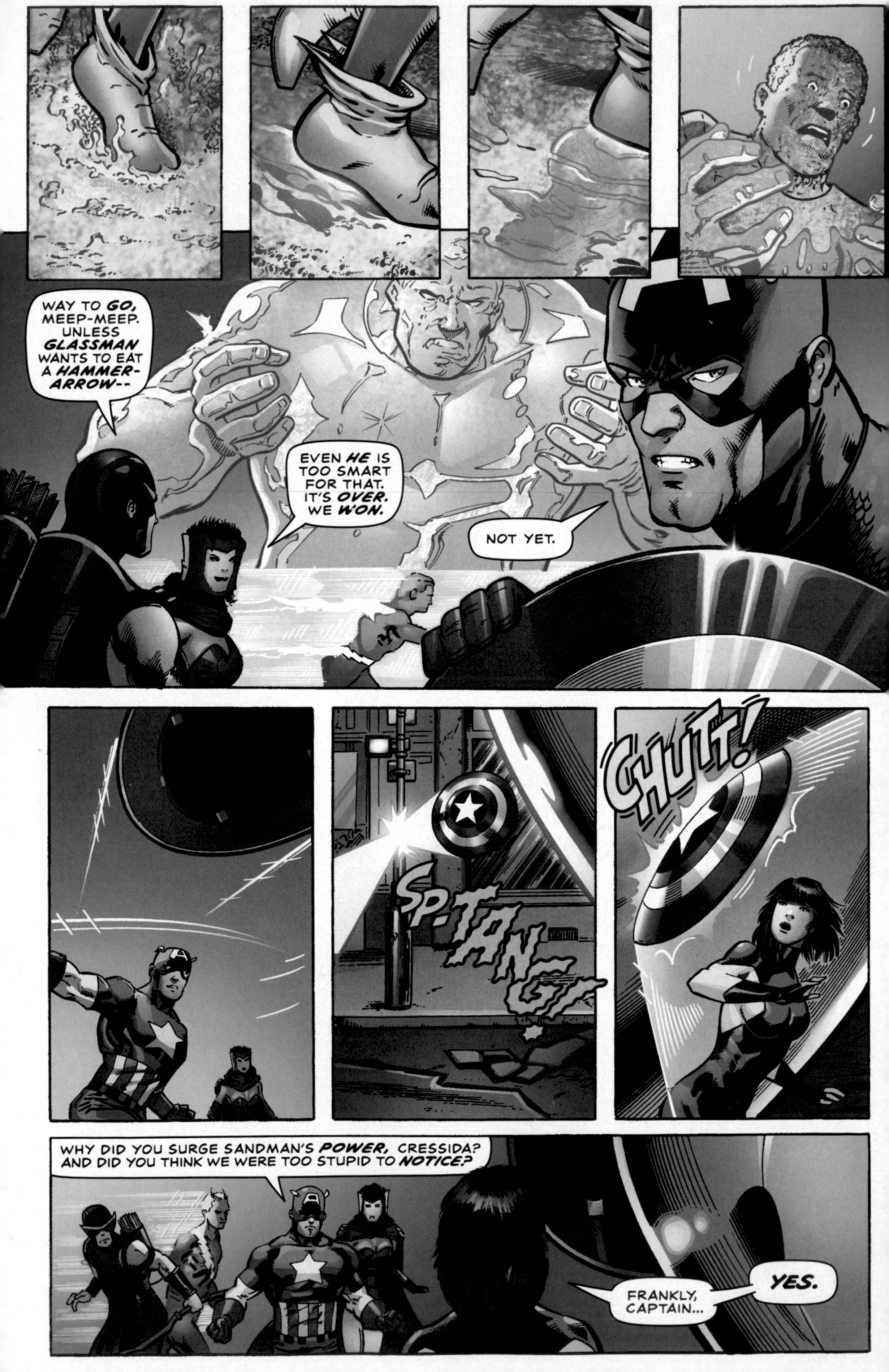
WAY TO GO, MEEP-MEEP. UNLESS GLASSMAN WANTS TO EAT A HAMMER-ARROW--
EVEN HE IS TOO SMART FOR THAT. IT'S OVER. WE WON.
NOT YET.
CHUTT!
SP-TANG!
WHY DID YOU SURGE SANDMAN'S POWER, CRESSIDA? AND DID YOU THINK WE WERE TOO STUPID TO NOTICE?
FRANKLY, CAPTAIN...
YES.

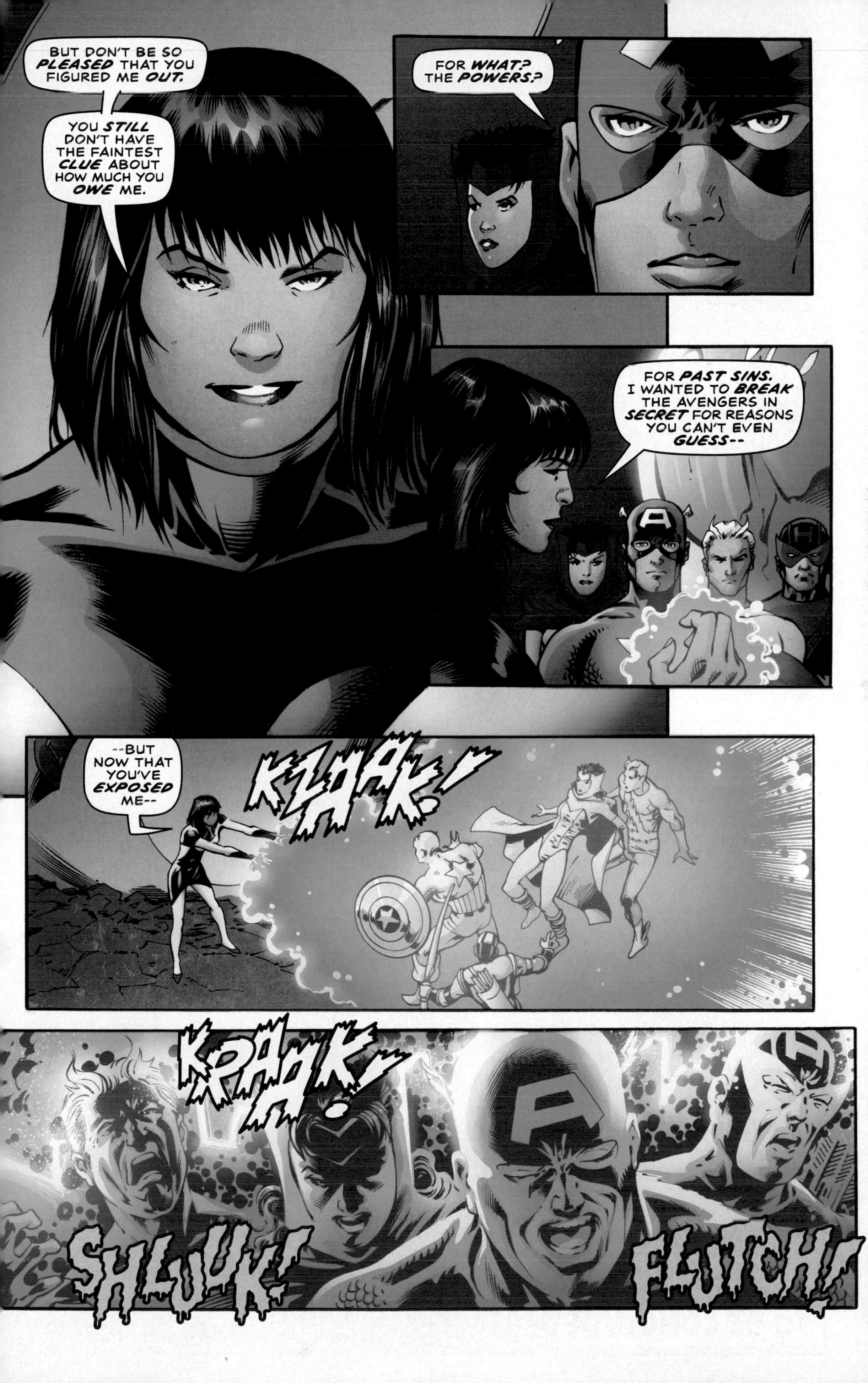
BUT DON'T BE SO PLEASED THAT YOU FIGURED ME OUT.
YOU STILL DON'T HAVE THE FAINTEST CLUE ABOUT HOW MUCH YOU OWE ME.
FOR WHAT? THE POWERS?
FOR PAST SINS. I WANTED TO BREAK THE AVENGERS IN SECRET FOR REASONS YOU CAN'T EVEN GUESS--
--BUT NOW THAT YOU'VE EXPOSED ME--
KLAAK!
KRAAK!
SHLUUK!
FLUTCH!

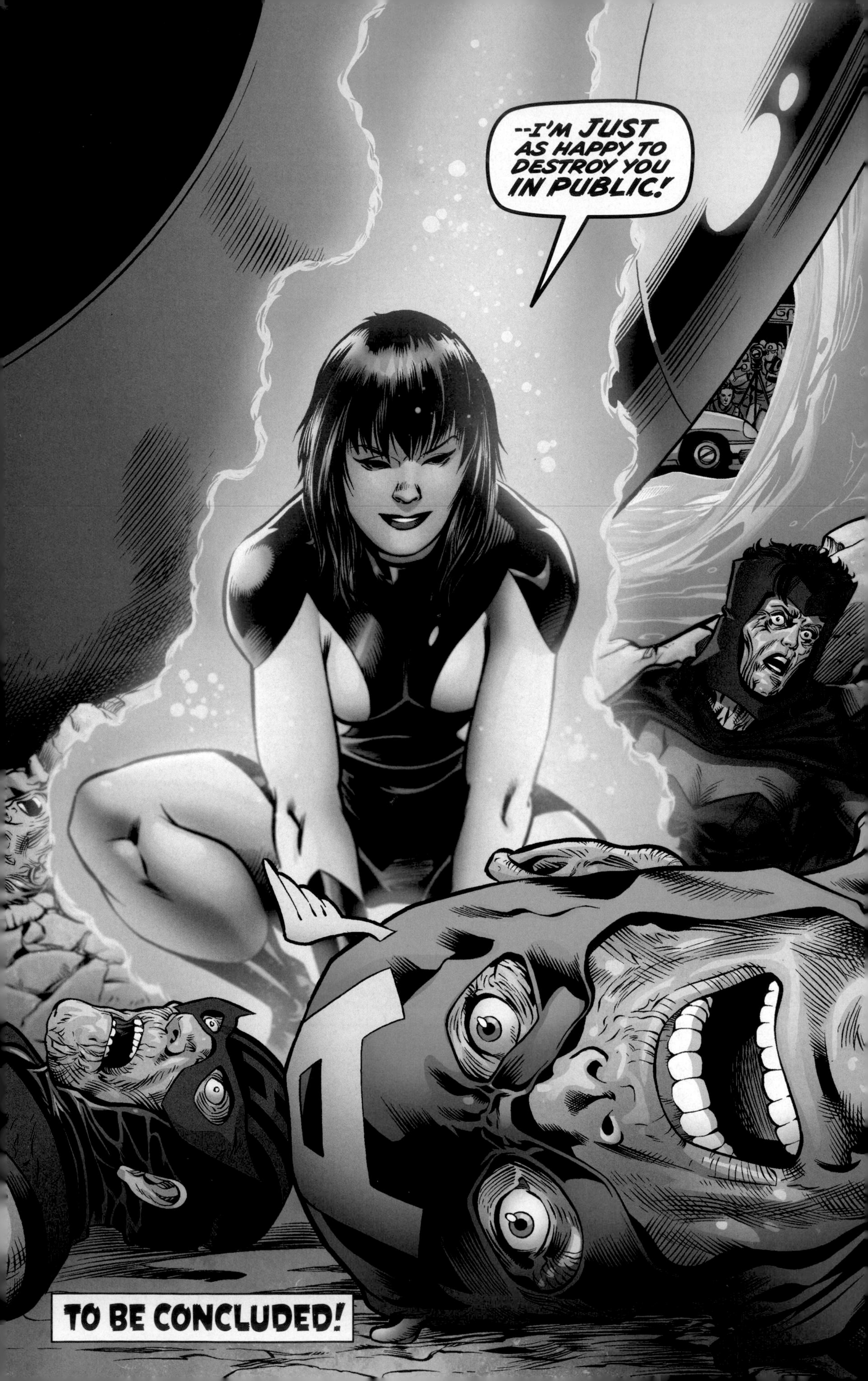
--I'M JUST AS HAPPY TO DESTROY YOU IN PUBLIC!
TO BE CONCLUDED!

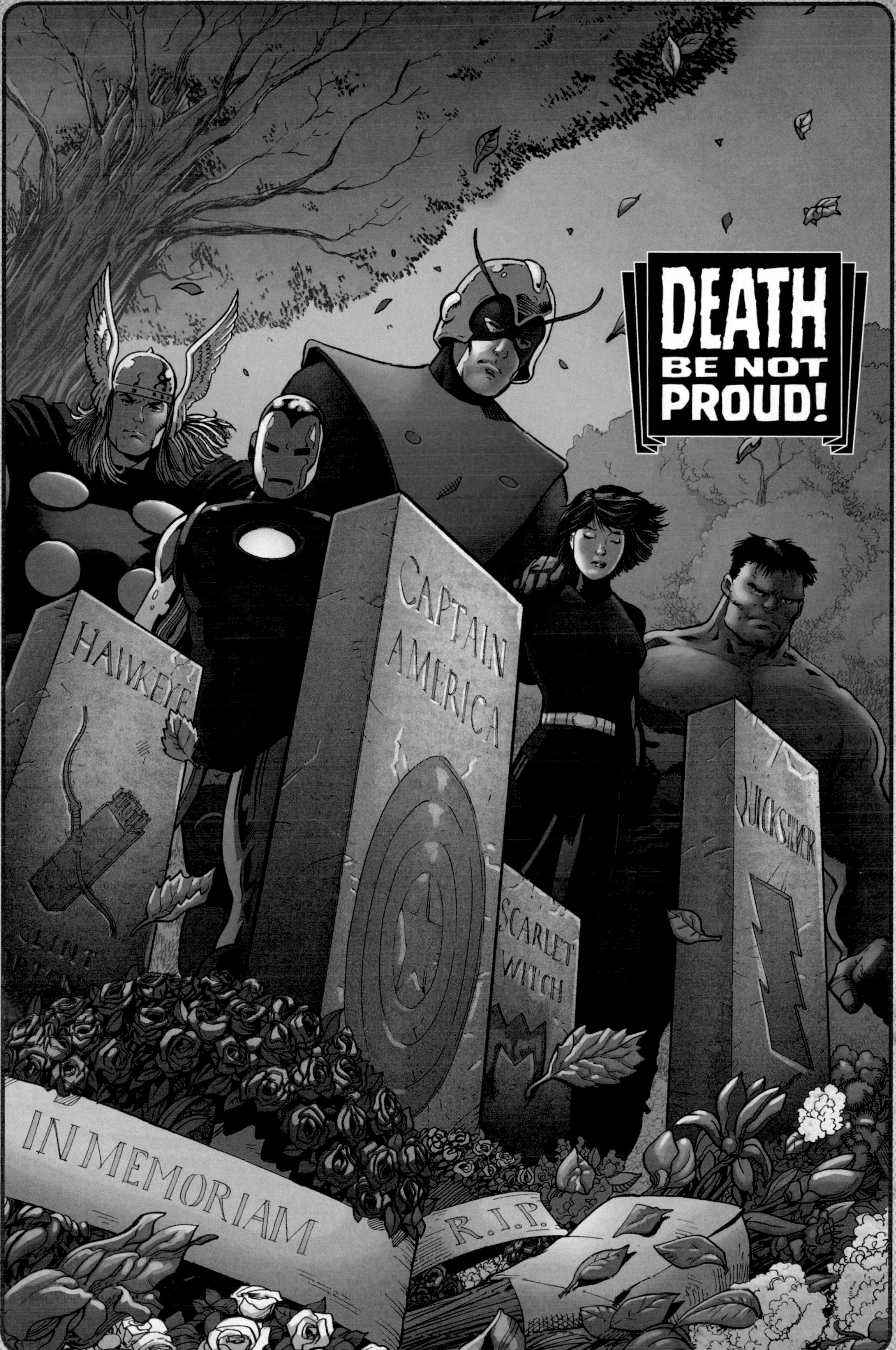
DEATH
BE NOT
PROUD!
HAWKEYE
CAPTAIN
AMERICA
SCARLET
WITCH
QUICKSILVER
IN MEMORIAM
R.I.P.

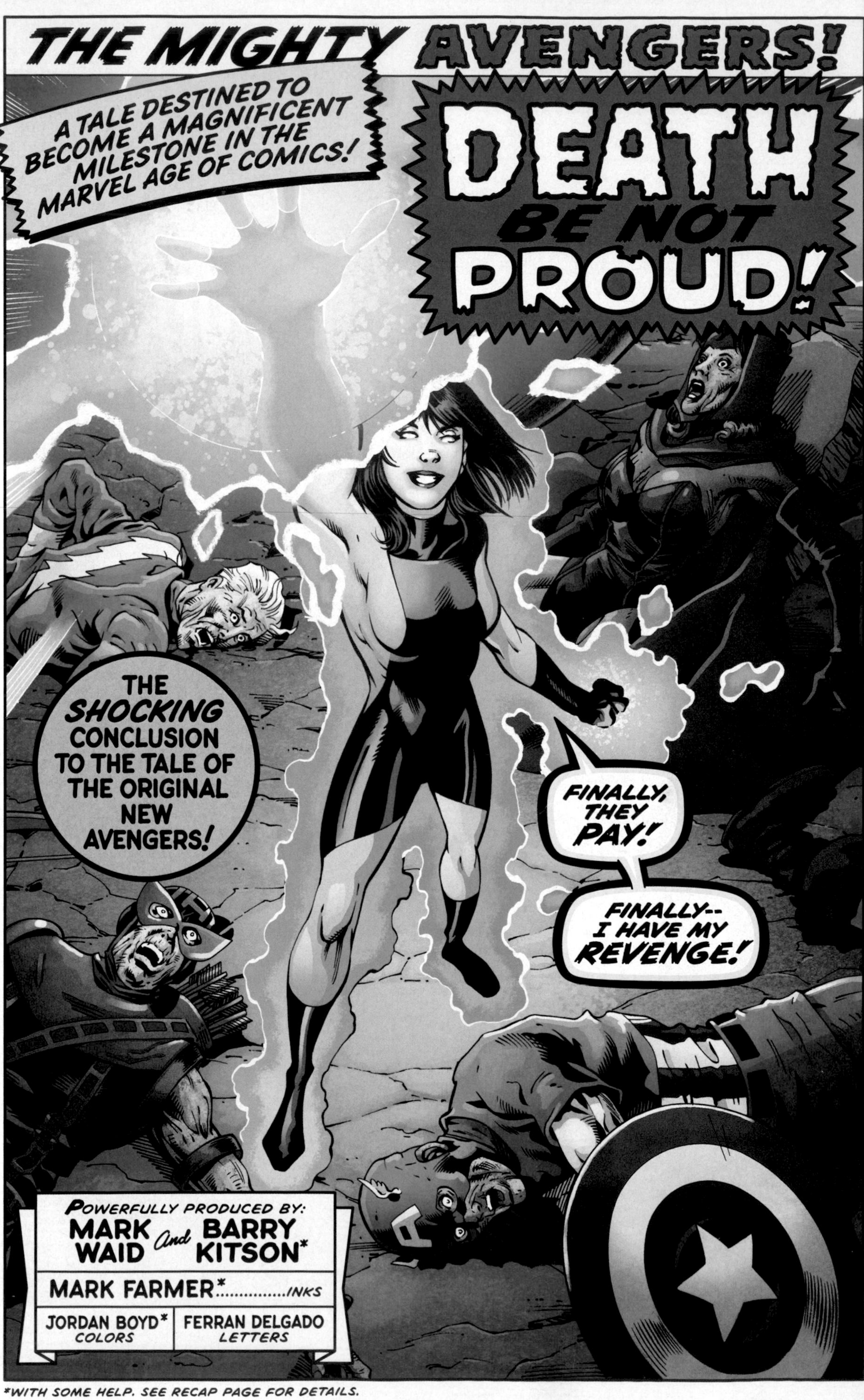
THE MIGHTY AVENGERS!
A TALE DESTINED TO BECOME A MAGNIFICENT MILESTONE IN THE MARVEL AGE OF COMICS!
DEATH BE NOT PROUD!
THE SHOCKING CONCLUSION TO THE TALE OF THE ORIGINAL NEW AVENGERS!
FINALLY, THEY PAY!
FINALLY-- I HAVE MY REVENGE!
POWERFULLY PRODUCED BY: MARK WAID And BARRY KITSON*
MARK FARMER*................INKS
JORDAN BOYD* COLORS
FERRAN DELGADO LETTERS

*WITH SOME HELP. SEE RECAP PAGE FOR DETAILS.

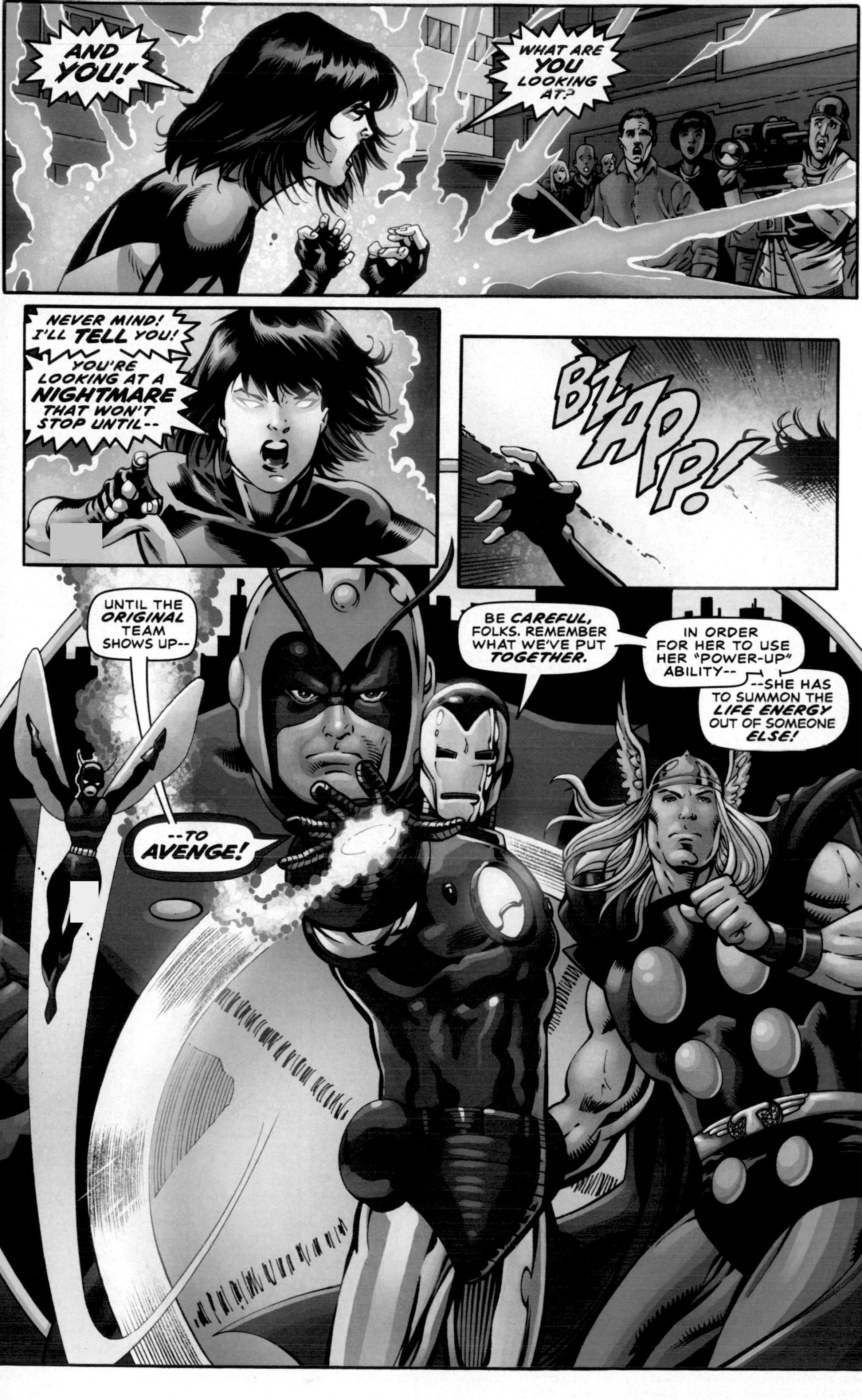
AND YOU!
WHAT ARE YOU LOOKING AT?
NEVER MIND! I'LL TELL YOU!
YOU'RE LOOKING AT A NIGHTMARE THAT WON'T STOP UNTIL--
BZAPP!
UNTIL THE ORIGINAL TEAM SHOWS UP--
--TO AVENGE!
BE CAREFUL, FOLKS. REMEMBER WHAT WE'VE PUT TOGETHER.
IN ORDER FOR HER TO USE HER "POWER-UP" ABILITY--
--SHE HAS TO SUMMON THE LIFE ENERGY OUT OF SOMEONE ELSE!

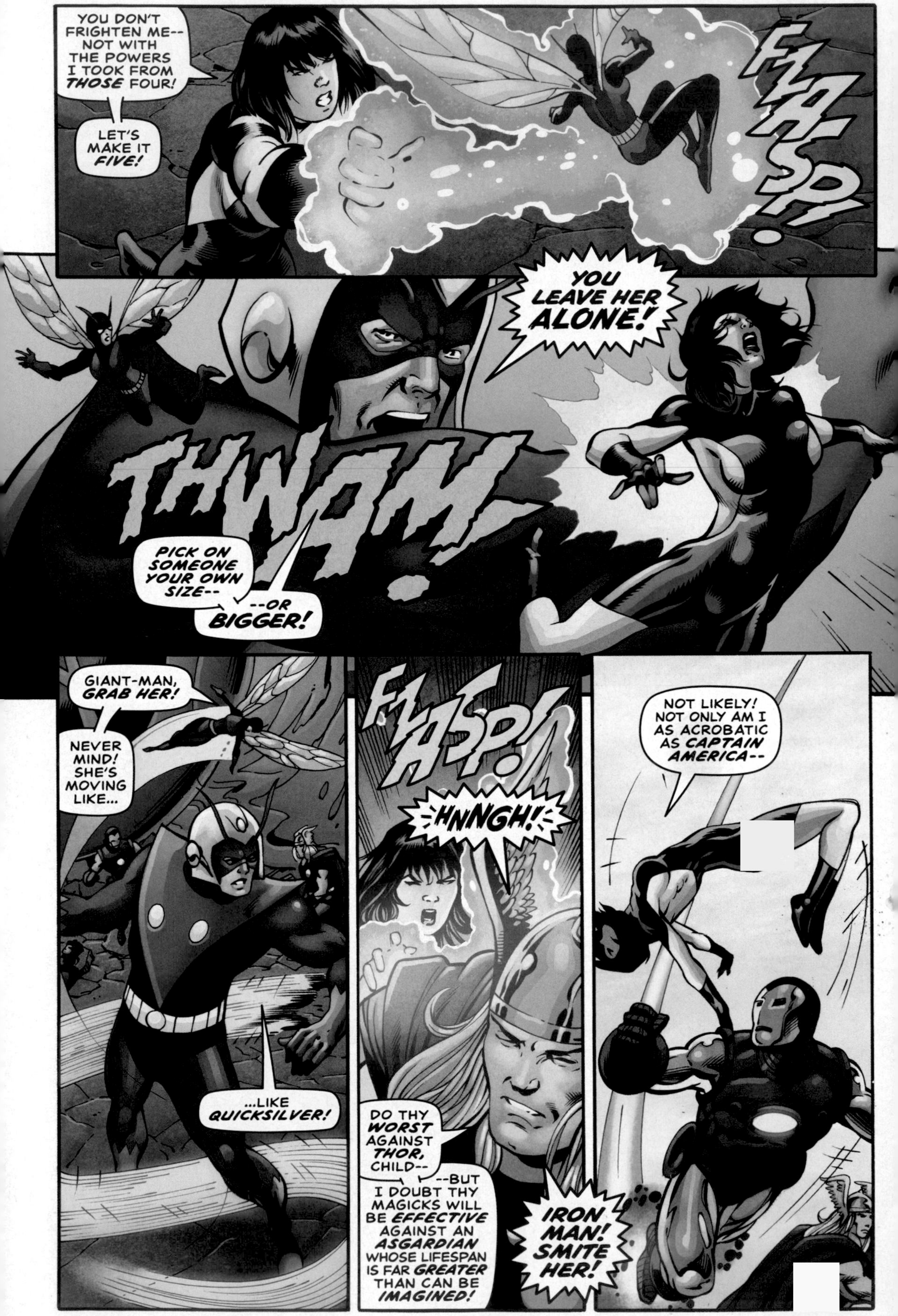
YOU DON'T FRIGHTEN ME--NOT WITH THE POWERS I TOOK FROM THOSE FOUR!
LET'S MAKE IT FIVE!
FLASP!!
YOU LEAVE HER ALONE!
THWAM!
PICK ON SOMEONE YOUR OWN SIZE--
--OR BIGGER!
GIANT-MAN, GRAB HER!
NEVER MIND! SHE'S MOVING LIKE...
...LIKE QUICKSILVER!
FLASP!
HNNGH!
DO THY WORST AGAINST THOR, CHILD--
--BUT I DOUBT THY MAGICKS WILL BE EFFECTIVE AGAINST AN ASGARDIAN WHOSE LIFESPAN IS FAR GREATER THAN CAN BE IMAGINED!
IRON MAN! SMITE HER!
NOT LIKELY! NOT ONLY AM I AS ACROBATIC AS CAPTAIN AMERICA--

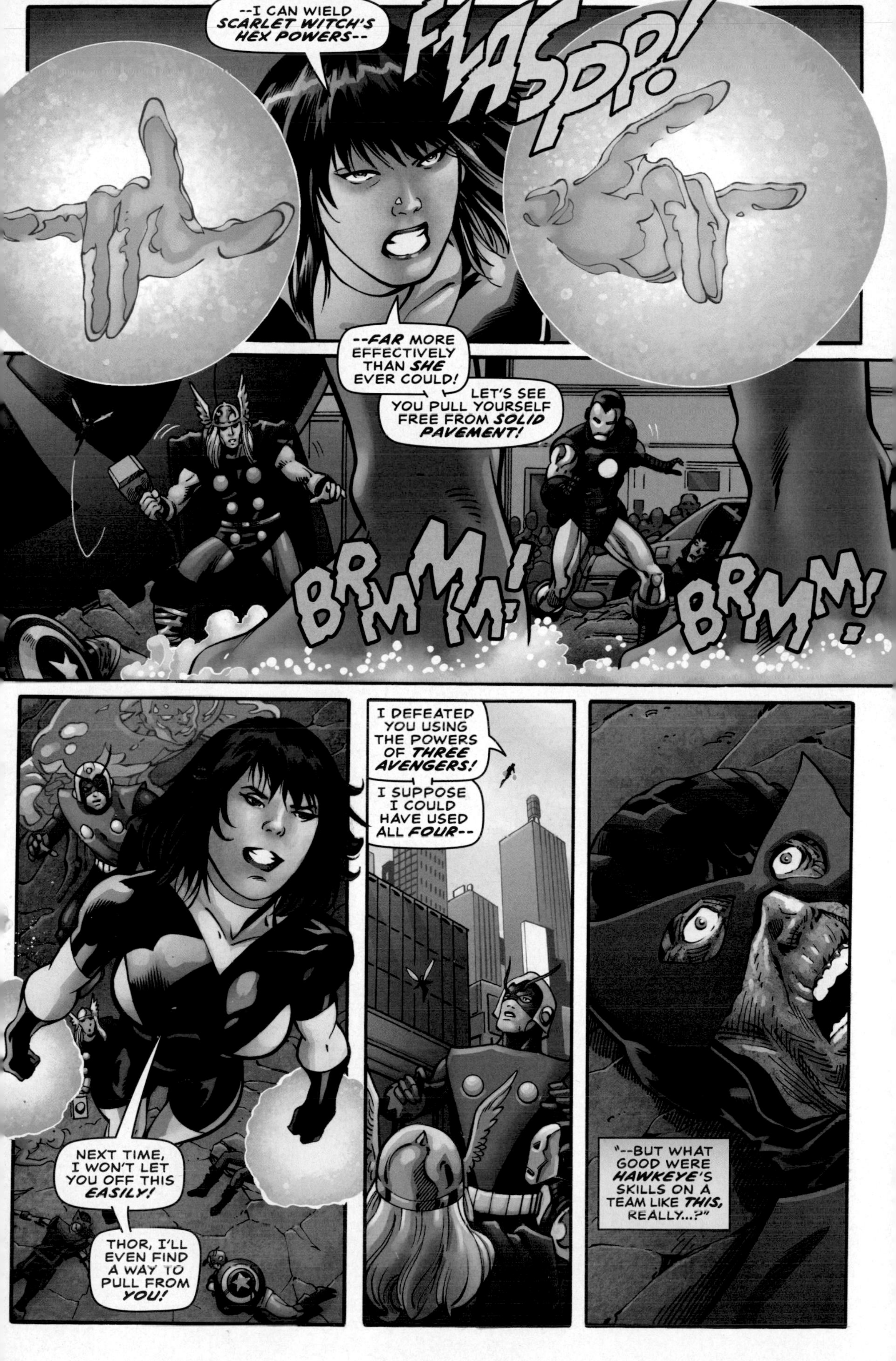
--I CAN WIELD SCARLET WITCH'S HEX POWERS--
FLASPP!
--FAR MORE EFFECTIVELY THAN SHE EVER COULD!
LET'S SEE YOU PULL YOURSELF FREE FROM SOLID PAVEMENT!
BRMMM!
BRMM!
NEXT TIME, I WON'T LET YOU OFF THIS EASILY!
THOR, I'LL EVEN FIND A WAY TO PULL FROM YOU!
I DEFEATED YOU USING THE POWERS OF THREE AVENGERS!
I SUPPOSE I COULD HAVE USED ALL FOUR--
"--BUT WHAT GOOD WERE HAWKEYE'S SKILLS ON A TEAM LIKE THIS, REALLY...?"

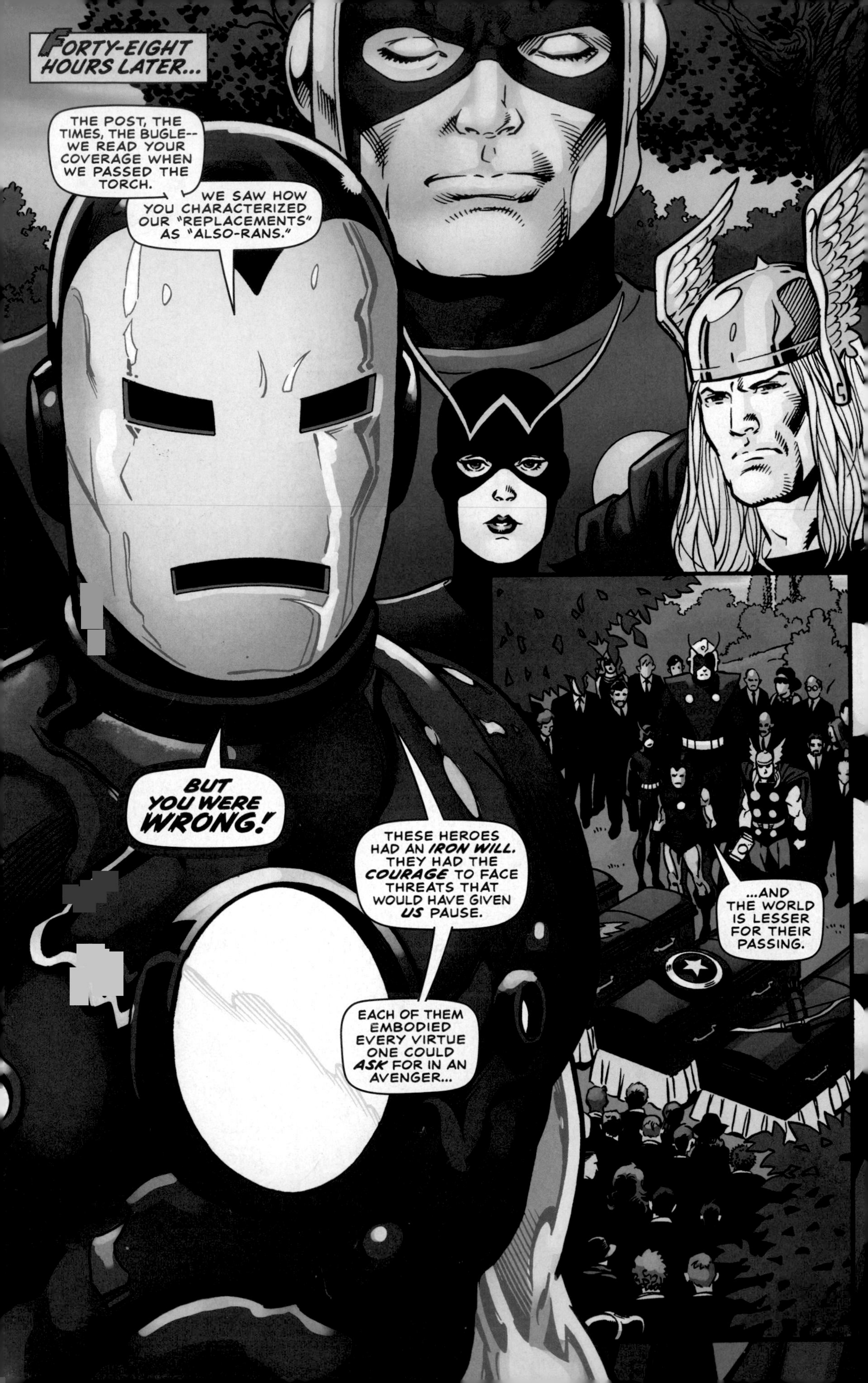
FORTY-EIGHT HOURS LATER...
THE POST, THE TIMES, THE BUGLE-- WE READ YOUR COVERAGE WHEN WE PASSED THE TORCH.
WE SAW HOW YOU CHARACTERIZED OUR "REPLACEMENTS" AS "ALSO-RANS."
BUT YOU WERE WRONG!
THESE HEROES HAD AN IRON WILL. THEY HAD THE COURAGE TO FACE THREATS THAT WOULD HAVE GIVEN US PAUSE.
EACH OF THEM EMBODIED EVERY VIRTUE ONE COULD ASK FOR IN AN AVENGER...
...AND THE WORLD IS LESSER FOR THEIR PASSING.

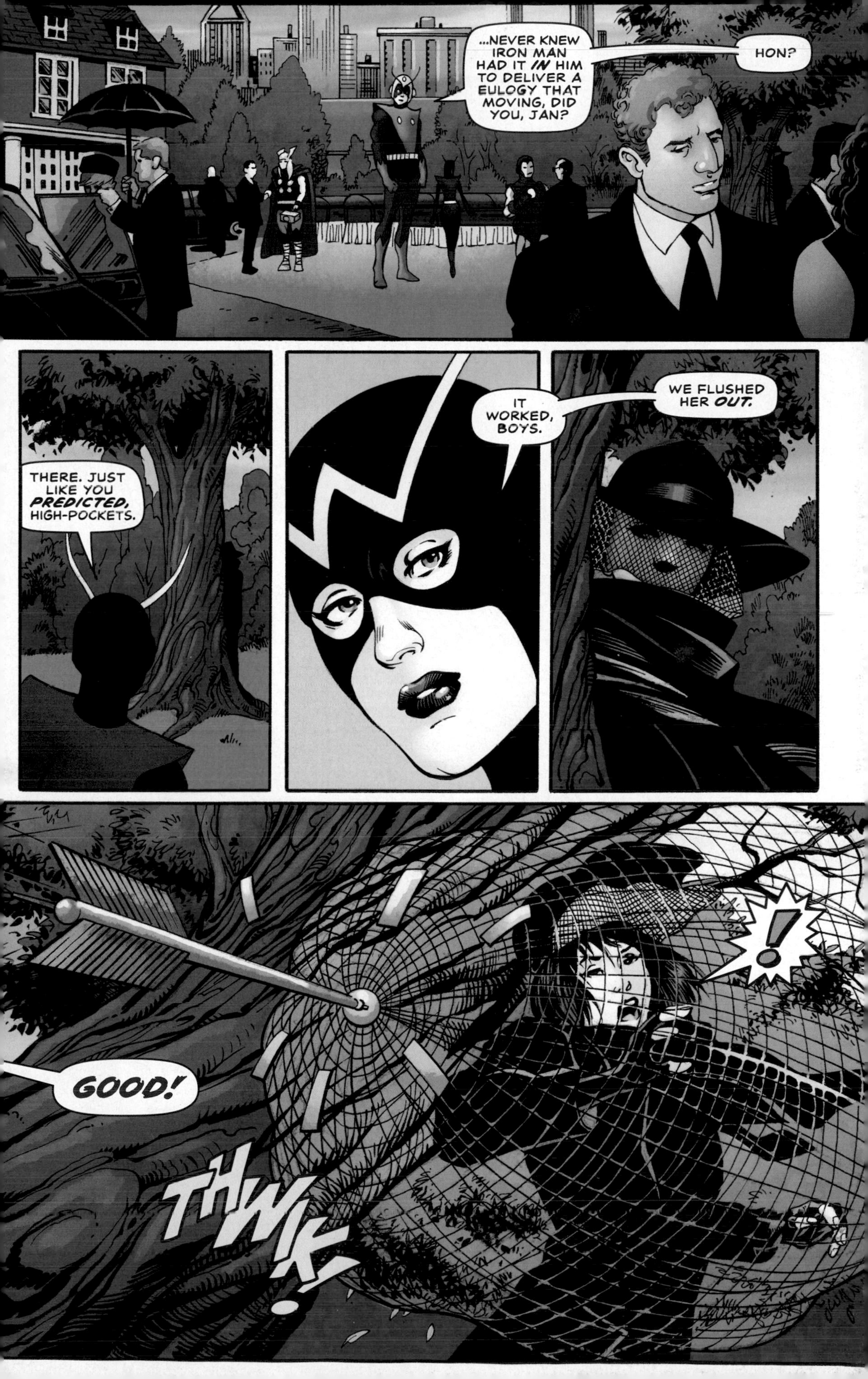
...NEVER KNEW IRON MAN HAD IT IN HIM TO DELIVER A EULOGY THAT MOVING, DID YOU, JAN?
HON?
THERE. JUST LIKE YOU PREDICTED, HIGH-POCKETS.
IT WORKED, BOYS.
WE FLUSHED HER OUT.
!
GOOD!
THWIK!

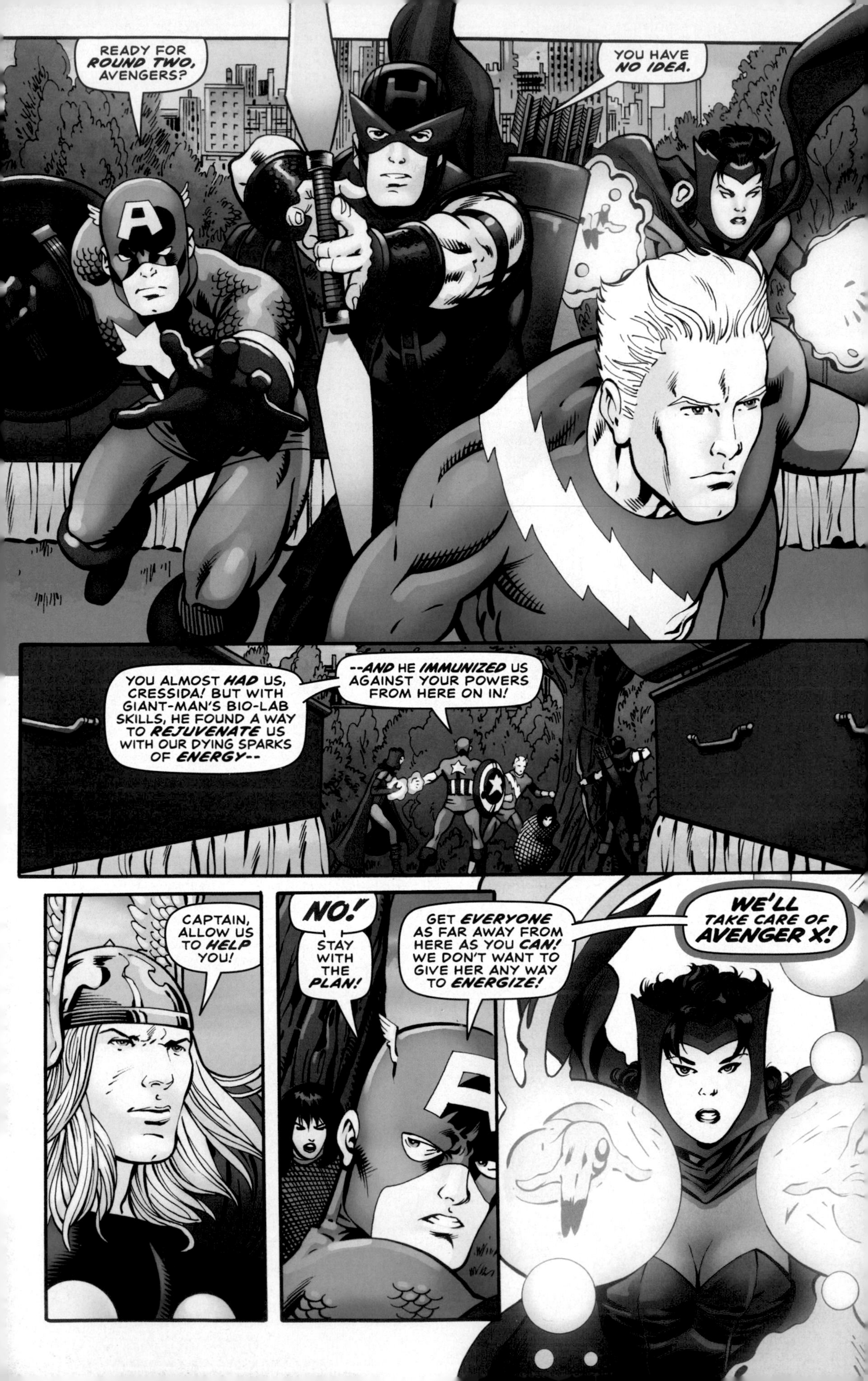
READY FOR ROUND TWO, AVENGERS?
YOU HAVE NO IDEA.
YOU ALMOST HAD US, CRESSIDA! BUT WITH GIANT-MAN'S BIO-LAB SKILLS, HE FOUND A WAY TO REJUVENATE US WITH OUR DYING SPARKS OF ENERGY--
--AND HE IMMUNIZED US AGAINST YOUR POWERS FROM HERE ON IN!
CAPTAIN, ALLOW US TO HELP YOU!
NO!
STAY WITH THE PLAN!
GET EVERYONE AS FAR AWAY FROM HERE AS YOU CAN! WE DON'T WANT TO GIVE HER ANY WAY TO ENERGIZE!
WE'LL TAKE CARE OF AVENGER X!

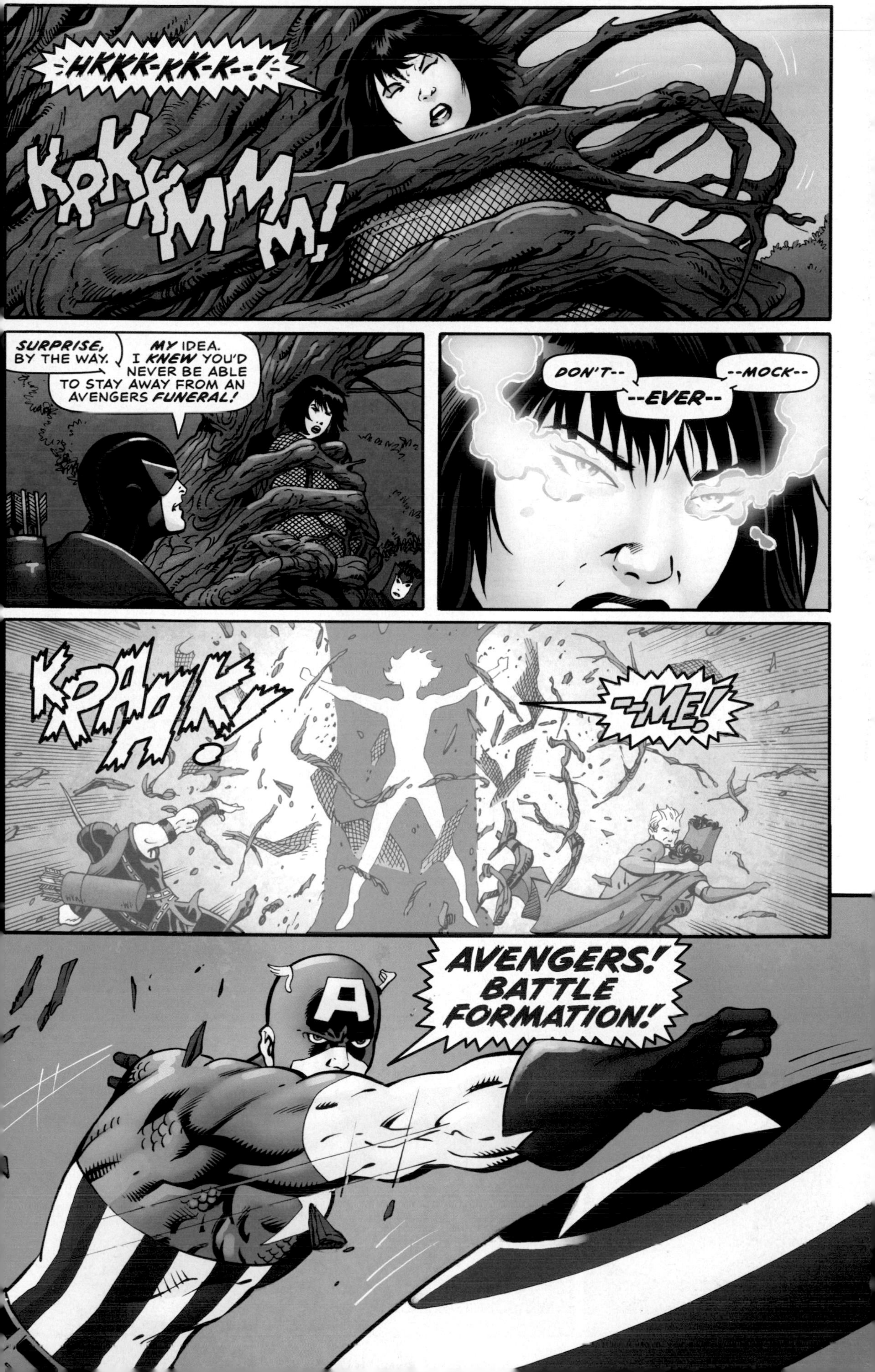
HKKK-KK-K--!
KRKKMMM!
SURPRISE, BY THE WAY.
MY IDEA. I KNEW YOU'D NEVER BE ABLE TO STAY AWAY FROM AN AVENGERS FUNERAL!
DON'T--
--EVER--
--MOCK--
KRAAK!
--ME!
AVENGERS! BATTLE FORMATION!

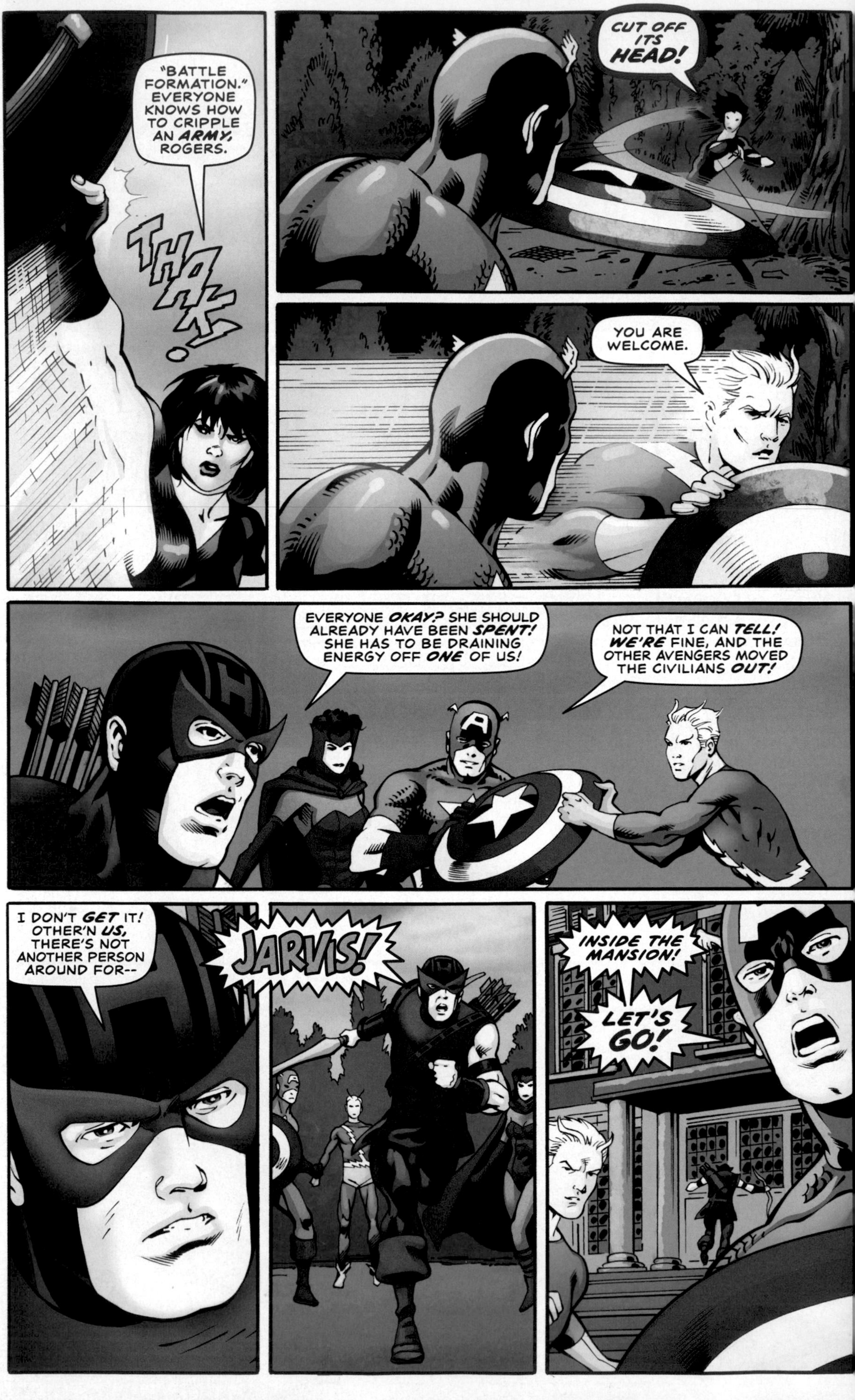

"BATTLE FORMATION." EVERYONE KNOWS HOW TO CRIPPLE AN ARMY, ROGERS.
THAK!
CUT OFF ITS HEAD!
YOU ARE WELCOME.
EVERYONE OKAY? SHE SHOULD ALREADY HAVE BEEN SPENT! SHE HAS TO BE DRAINING ENERGY OFF ONE OF US!
NOT THAT I CAN TELL! WE'RE FINE, AND THE OTHER AVENGERS MOVED THE CIVILIANS OUT!
I DON'T GET IT! OTHER'N US, THERE'S NOT ANOTHER PERSON AROUND FOR--
JARVIS!
INSIDE THE MANSION!
LET'S GO!

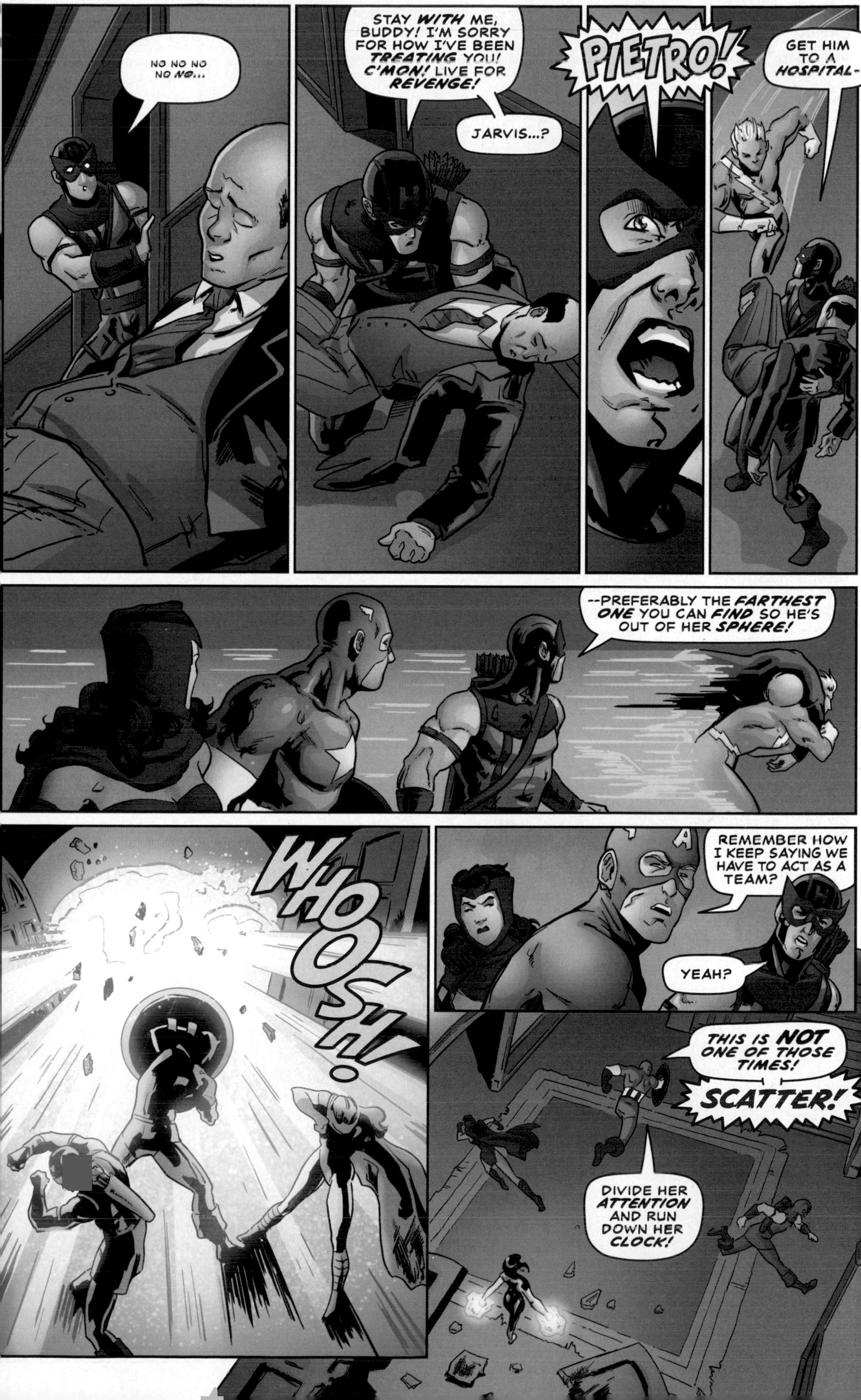
NO NO NO NO NO...
STAY WITH ME, BUDDY! I'M SORRY FOR HOW I'VE BEEN TREATING YOU! C'MON! LIVE FOR REVENGE!
JARVIS...?
PIETRO!
GET HIM TO A HOSPITAL--
--PREFERABLY THE FARTHEST ONE YOU CAN FIND SO HE'S OUT OF HER SPHERE!
WHOOSH!
REMEMBER HOW I KEEP SAYING WE HAVE TO ACT AS A TEAM?
YEAH?
THIS IS NOT ONE OF THOSE TIMES!
SCATTER!
DIVIDE HER ATTENTION AND RUN DOWN HER CLOCK!

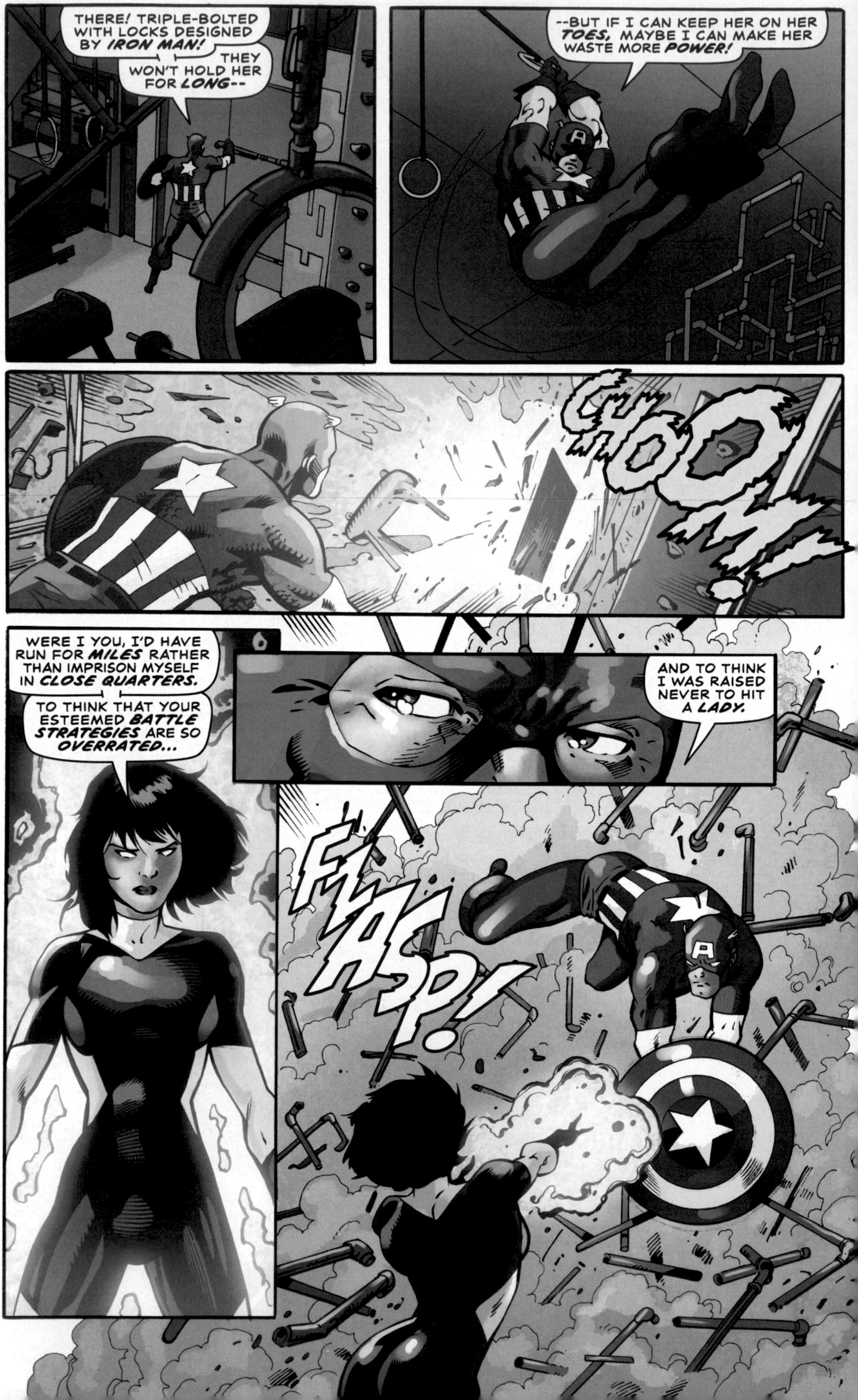
THERE! TRIPLE-BOLTED WITH LOCKS DESIGNED BY IRON MAN!
THEY WON'T HOLD HER FOR LONG--
--BUT IF I CAN KEEP HER ON HER TOES, MAYBE I CAN MAKE HER WASTE MORE POWER!
CHOOM!
WERE I YOU, I'D HAVE RUN FOR MILES RATHER THAN IMPRISON MYSELF IN CLOSE QUARTERS.
TO THINK THAT YOUR ESTEEMED BATTLE STRATEGIES ARE SO OVERRATED...
AND TO THINK I WAS RAISED NEVER TO HIT A LADY.
FLASP!

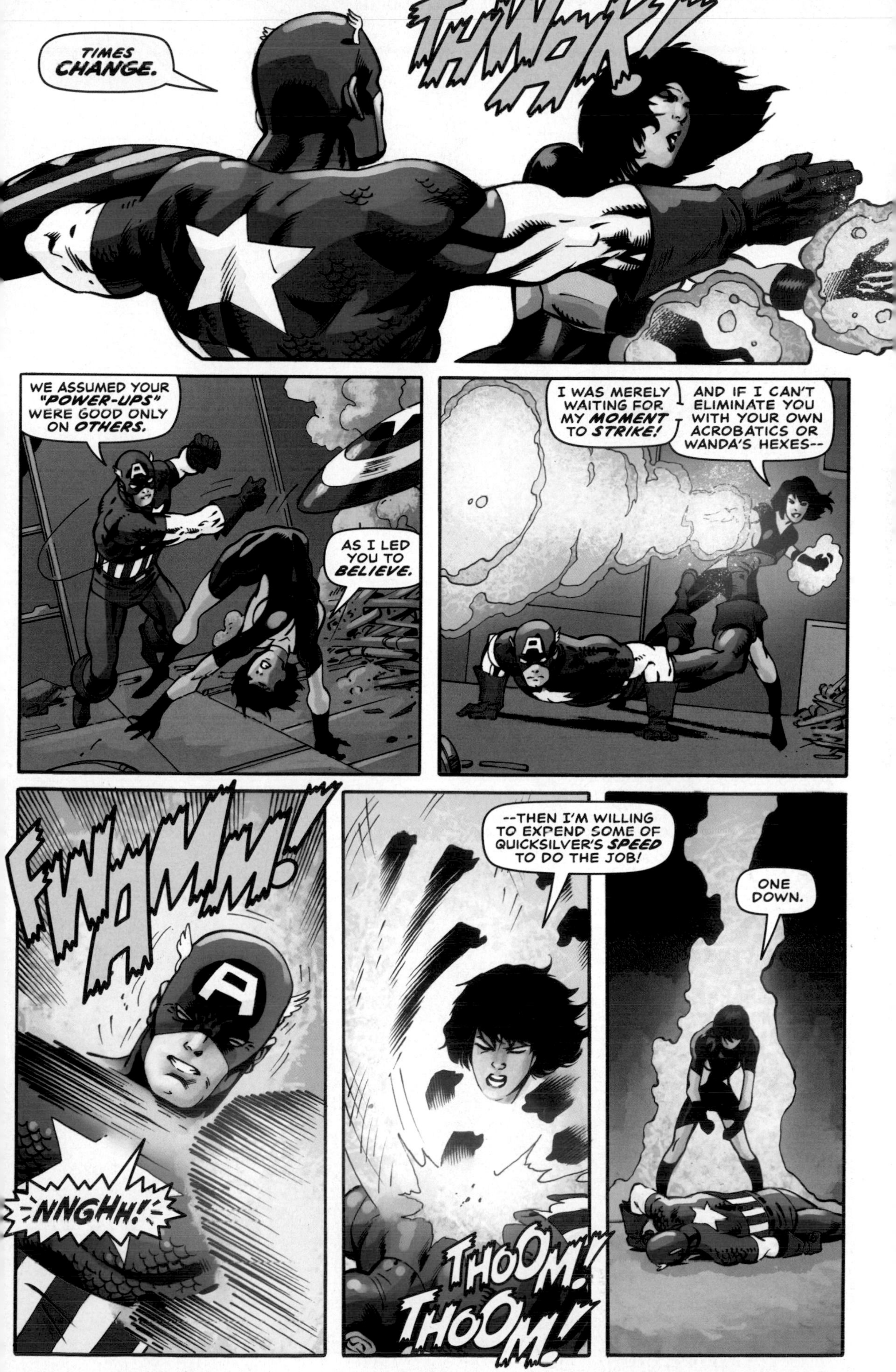
TIMES CHANGE.
THWOK!
WE ASSUMED YOUR "POWER-UPS" WERE GOOD ONLY ON OTHERS.
AS I LED YOU TO BELIEVE.
I WAS MERELY WAITING FOR MY MOMENT TO STRIKE!
AND IF I CAN'T ELIMINATE YOU WITH YOUR OWN ACROBATICS OR WANDA'S HEXES--
FWAMMM!
NNGHH!
--THEN I'M WILLING TO EXPEND SOME OF QUICKSILVER'S SPEED TO DO THE JOB!
THOOM! THOOM!
ONE DOWN.

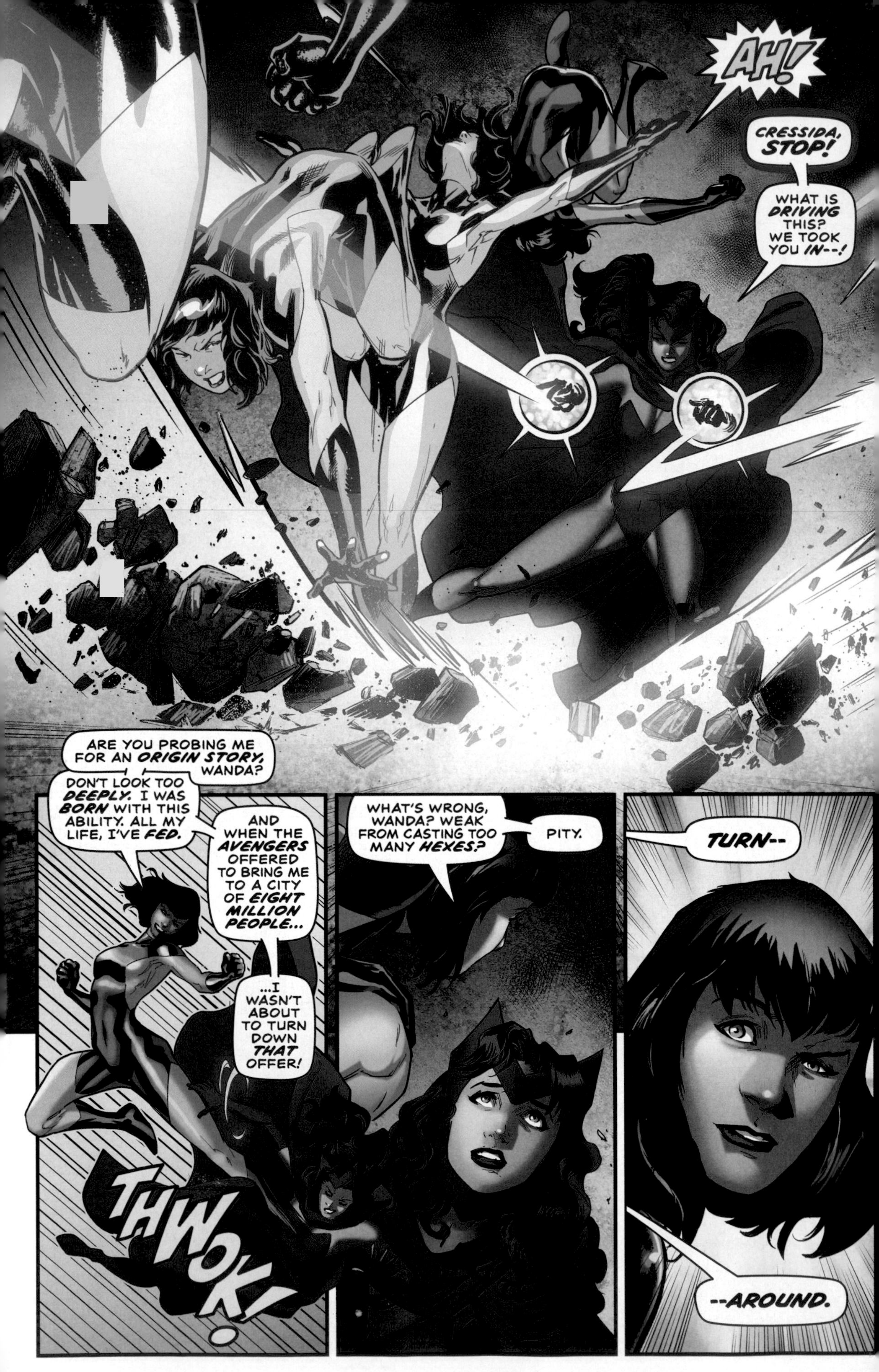
AH!
CRESSIDA, STOP!
WHAT IS DRIVING THIS? WE TOOK YOU IN--!
ARE YOU PROBING ME FOR AN ORIGIN STORY, WANDA?
DON'T LOOK TOO DEEPLY. I WAS BORN WITH THIS ABILITY. ALL MY LIFE, I'VE FED.
AND WHEN THE AVENGERS OFFERED TO BRING ME TO A CITY OF EIGHT MILLION PEOPLE...
...I WASN'T ABOUT TO TURN DOWN THAT OFFER!
THWOK!
WHAT'S WRONG, WANDA? WEAK FROM CASTING TOO MANY HEXES?
PITY.
TURN--
--AROUND.

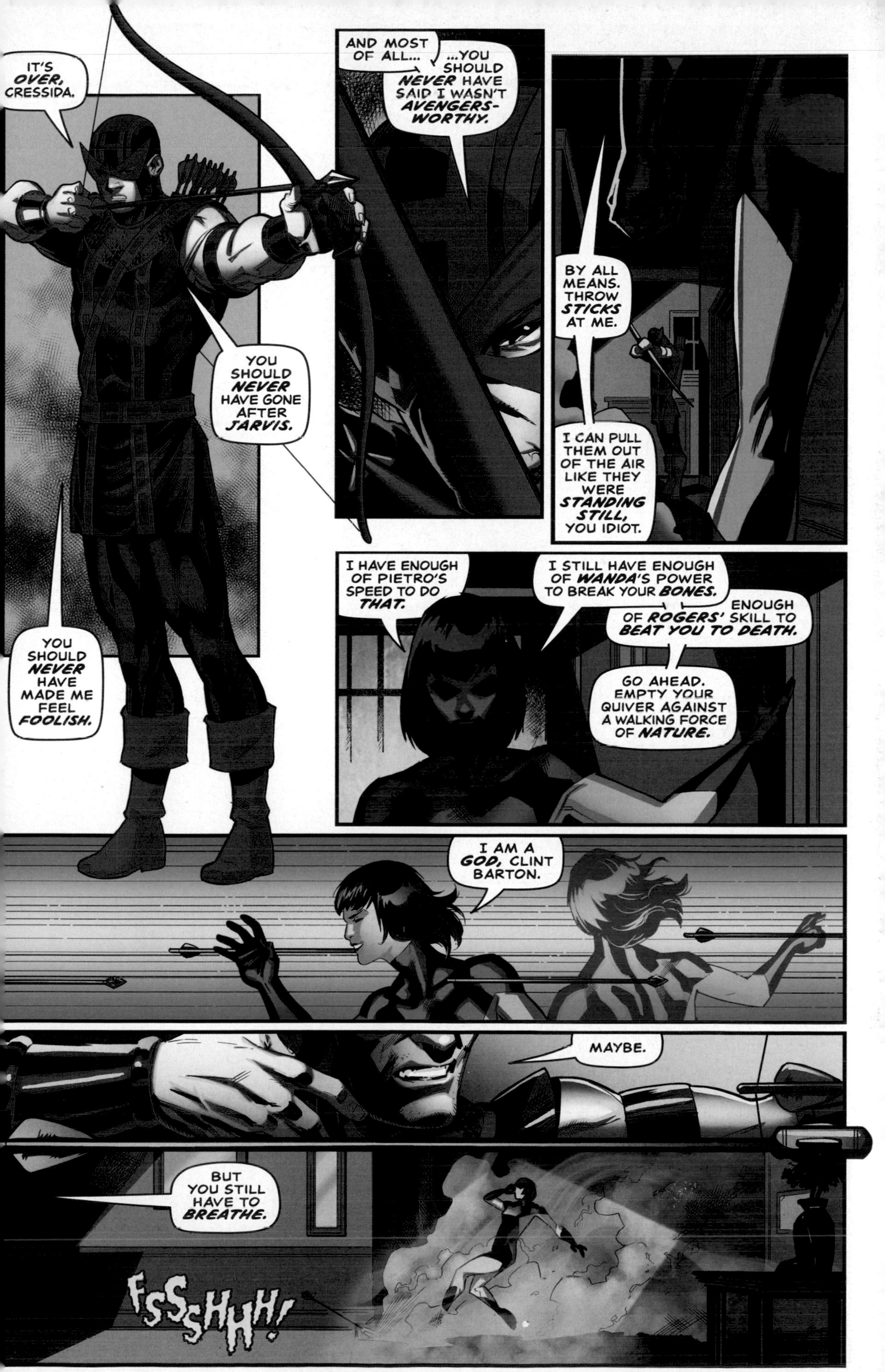
IT'S OVER, CRESSIDA.
YOU SHOULD NEVER HAVE GONE AFTER JARVIS.
YOU SHOULD NEVER HAVE MADE ME FEEL FOOLISH.
AND MOST OF ALL...
...YOU SHOULD NEVER HAVE SAID I WASN'T AVENGERS-WORTHY.
BY ALL MEANS. THROW STICKS AT ME.
I CAN PULL THEM OUT OF THE AIR LIKE THEY WERE STANDING STILL, YOU IDIOT.
I HAVE ENOUGH OF PIETRO'S SPEED TO DO THAT.
I STILL HAVE ENOUGH OF WANDA'S POWER TO BREAK YOUR BONES.
ENOUGH OF ROGERS' SKILL TO BEAT YOU TO DEATH.
GO AHEAD. EMPTY YOUR QUIVER AGAINST A WALKING FORCE OF NATURE.
I AM A GOD, CLINT BARTON.
MAYBE.
BUT YOU STILL HAVE TO BREATHE.
FSSSHHH!

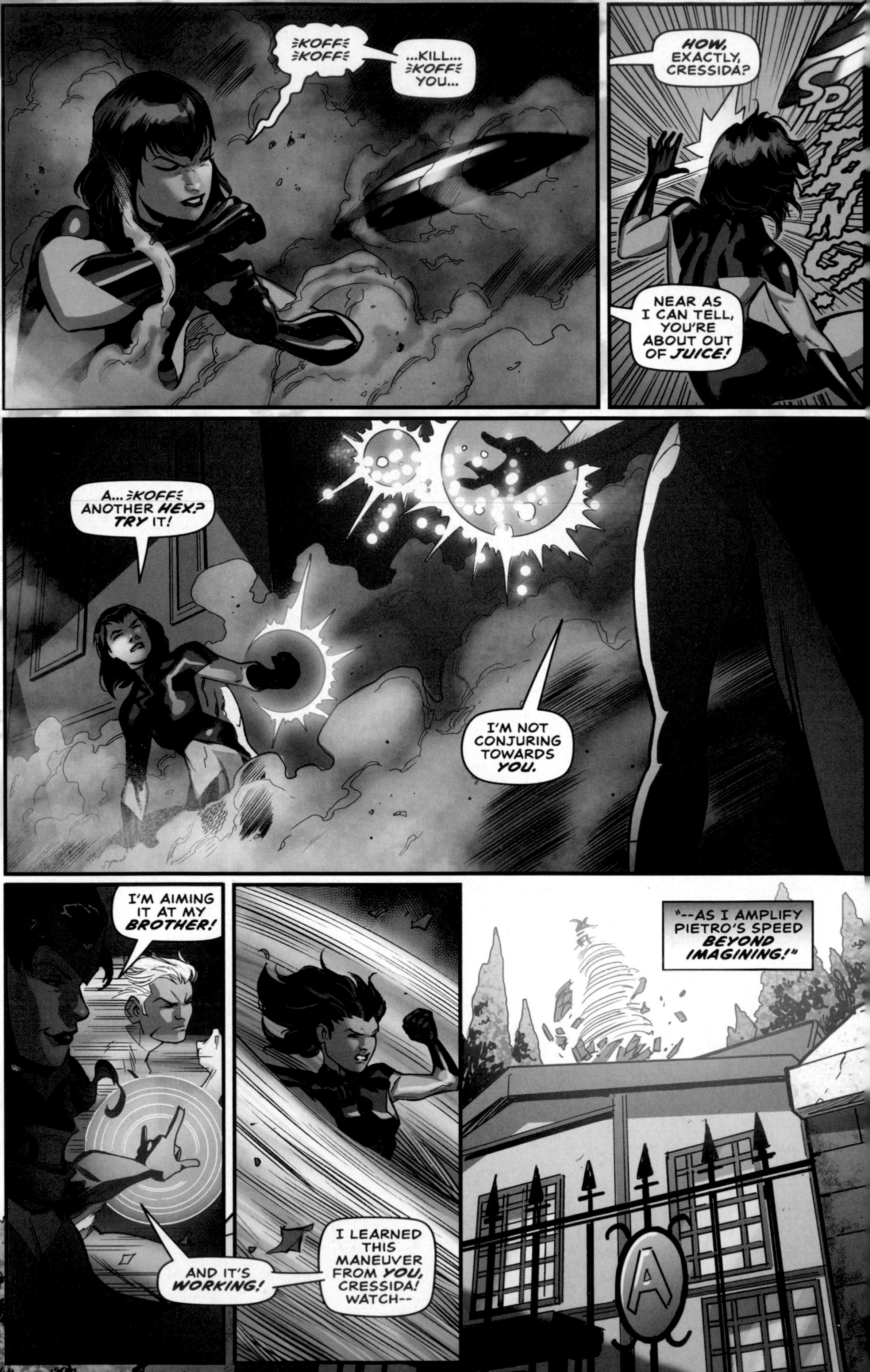

≶KOFF≷ ≶KOFF≷
...KILL... ≶KOFF≷ YOU...
HOW, EXACTLY, CRESSIDA?
SP-TANG
NEAR AS I CAN TELL, YOU'RE ABOUT OUT OF JUICE!
A... ≶KOFF≷ ANOTHER HEX? TRY IT!
I'M NOT CONJURING TOWARDS YOU.
I'M AIMING IT AT MY BROTHER!
AND IT'S WORKING!
I LEARNED THIS MANEUVER FROM YOU, CRESSIDA! WATCH--
"--AS I AMPLIFY PIETRO'S SPEED BEYOND IMAGINING!"
A

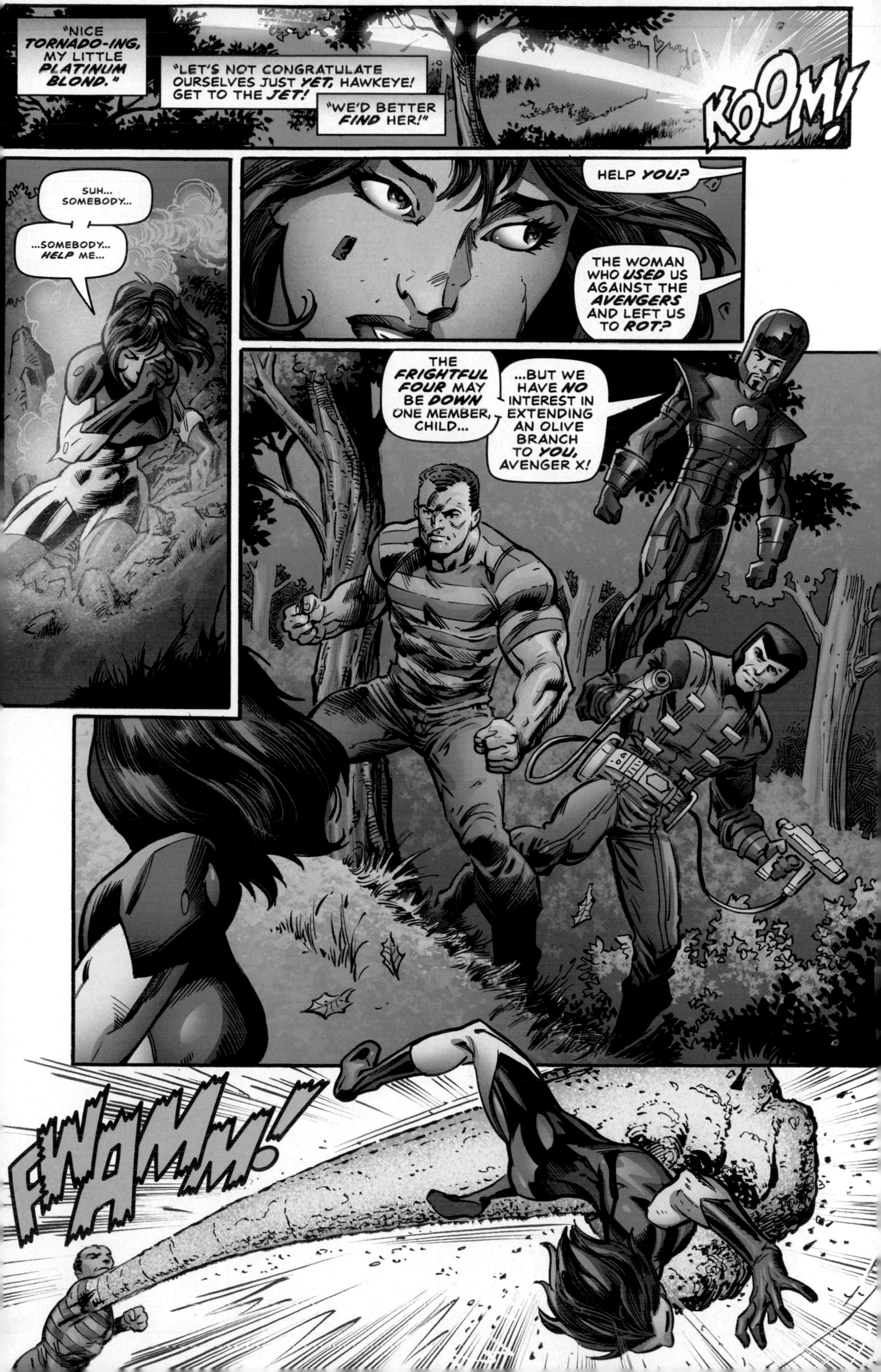
"NICE TORNADO-ING, MY LITTLE PLATINUM BLOND."
"LET'S NOT CONGRATULATE OURSELVES JUST YET, HAWKEYE! GET TO THE JET!
"WE'D BETTER FIND HER!"
KOOM!
SUH... SOMEBODY...
...SOMEBODY... HELP ME...
HELP YOU?
THE WOMAN WHO USED US AGAINST THE AVENGERS AND LEFT US TO ROT?
THE FRIGHTFUL FOUR MAY BE DOWN ONE MEMBER, CHILD...
...BUT WE HAVE NO INTEREST IN EXTENDING AN OLIVE BRANCH TO YOU, AVENGER X!
FWAMM!

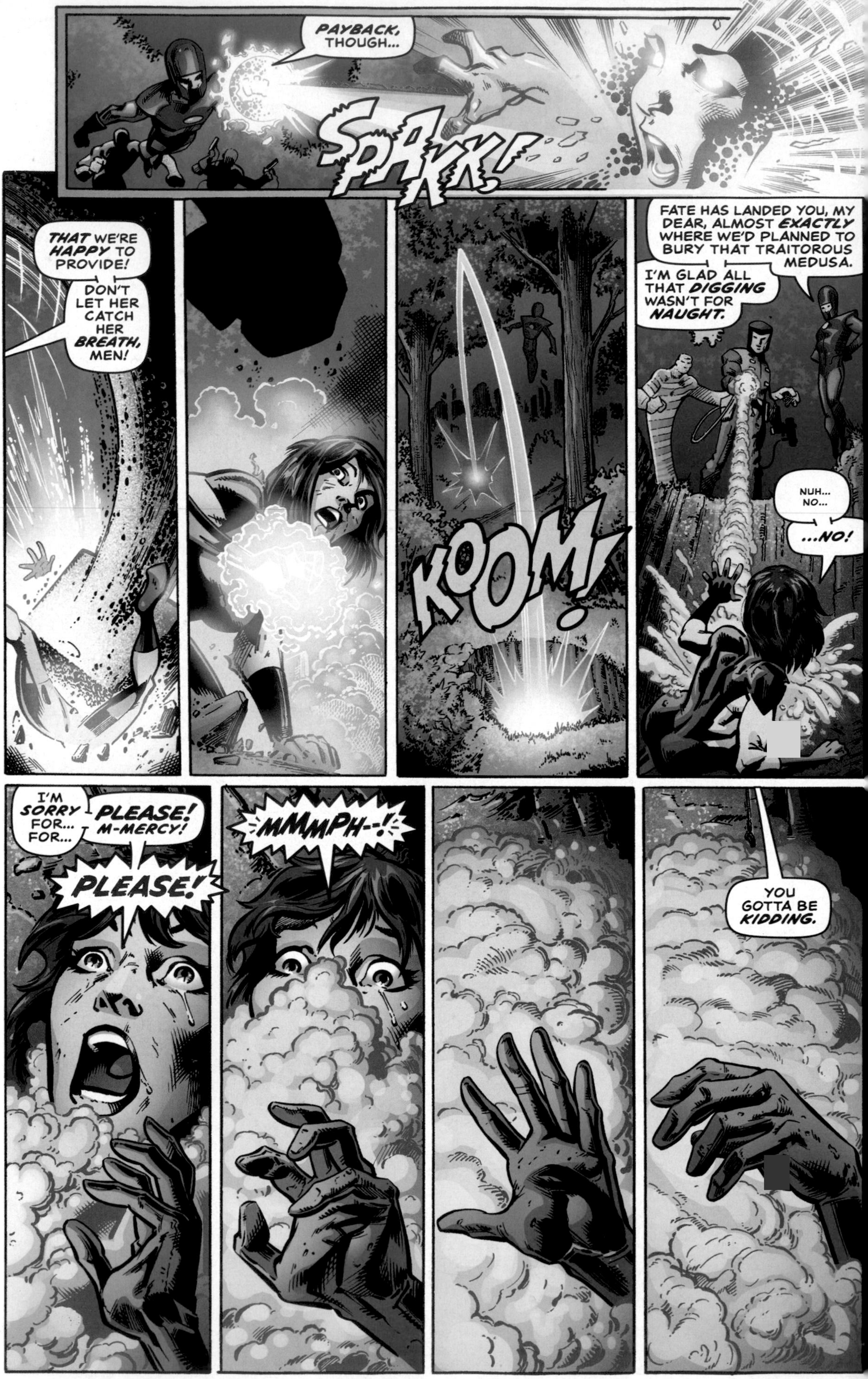
PAYBACK, THOUGH...
SPAKK!
THAT WE'RE HAPPY TO PROVIDE!
DON'T LET HER CATCH HER BREATH, MEN!
KOOM!
FATE HAS LANDED YOU, MY DEAR, ALMOST EXACTLY WHERE WE'D PLANNED TO BURY THAT TRAITOROUS MEDUSA.
I'M GLAD ALL THAT DIGGING WASN'T FOR NAUGHT.
NUH... NO...
...NO!
I'M SORRY FOR... FOR...
PLEASE! M-MERCY!
PLEASE!
MMMPH--!
YOU GOTTA BE KIDDING.

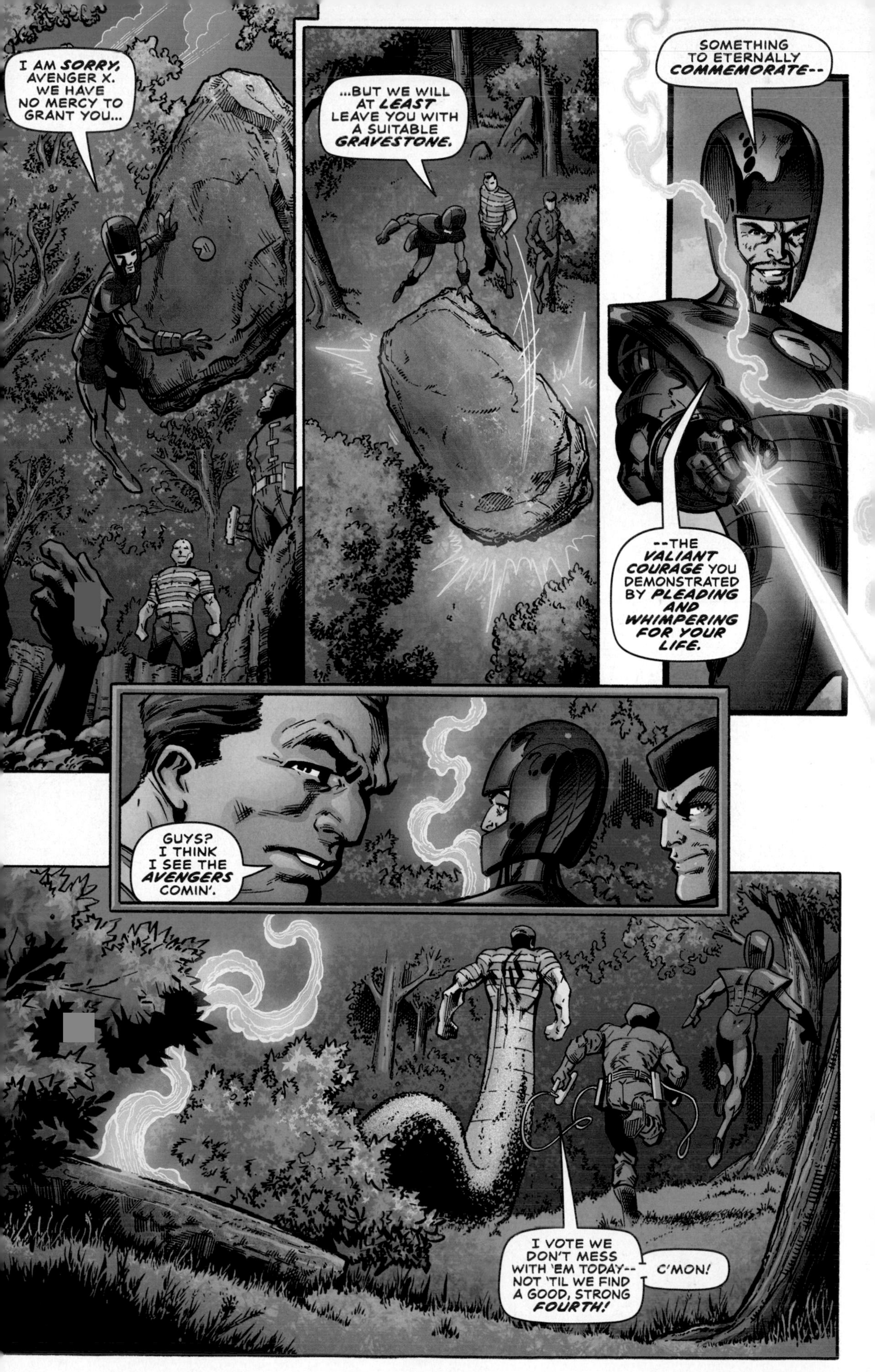
I AM SORRY, AVENGER X. WE HAVE NO MERCY TO GRANT YOU...
...BUT WE WILL AT LEAST LEAVE YOU WITH A SUITABLE GRAVESTONE.
SOMETHING TO ETERNALLY COMMEMORATE--
--THE VALIANT COURAGE YOU DEMONSTRATED BY PLEADING AND WHIMPERING FOR YOUR LIFE.
GUYS? I THINK I SEE THE AVENGERS COMIN'.
I VOTE WE DON'T MESS WITH 'EM TODAY-- NOT 'TIL WE FIND A GOOD, STRONG FOURTH!
C'MON!

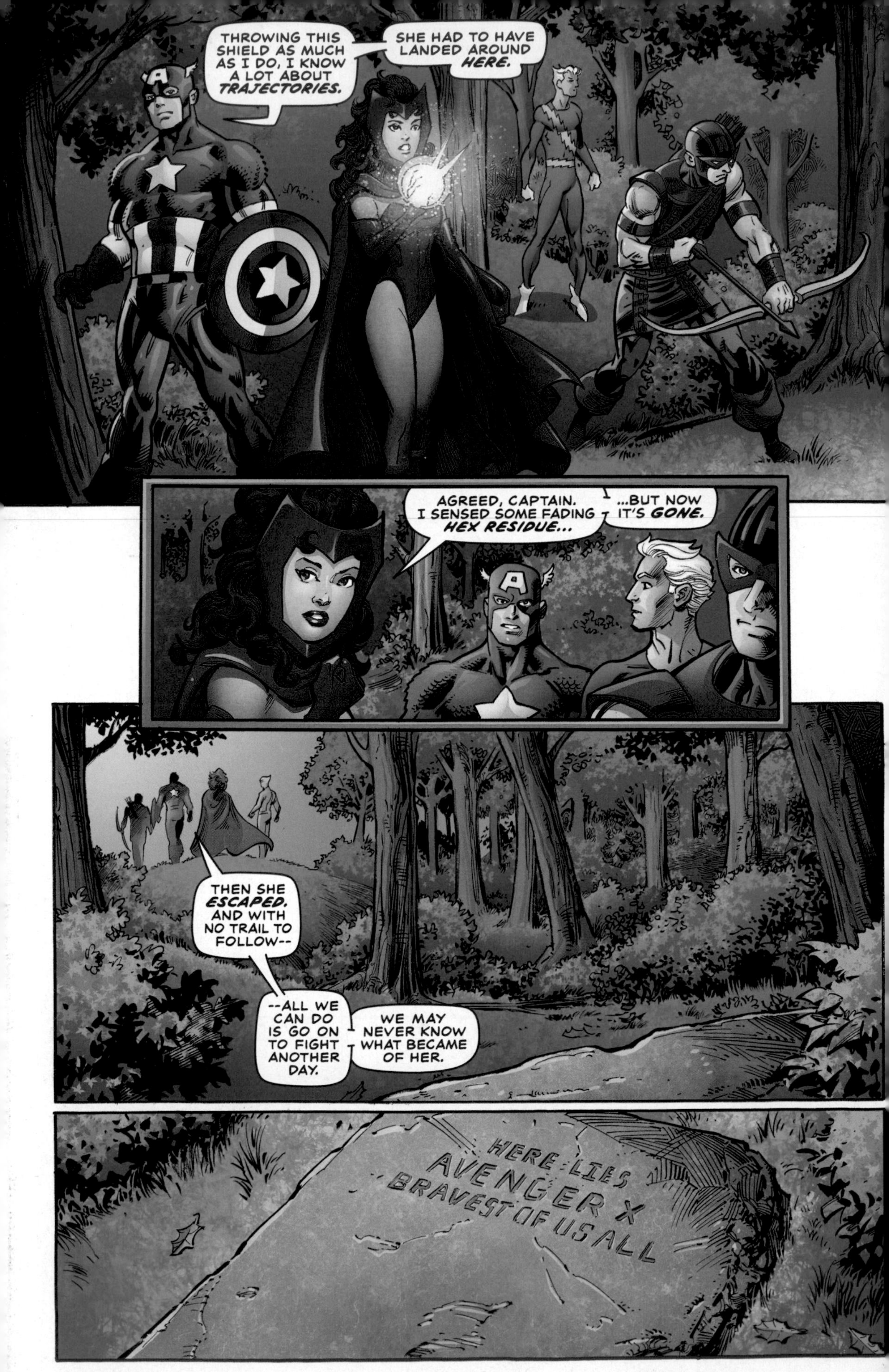
THROWING THIS SHIELD AS MUCH AS I DO, I KNOW A LOT ABOUT TRAJECTORIES.
SHE HAD TO HAVE LANDED AROUND HERE.
AGREED, CAPTAIN. I SENSED SOME FADING HEX RESIDUE...
...BUT NOW IT'S GONE.
THEN SHE ESCAPED. AND WITH NO TRAIL TO FOLLOW--
--ALL WE CAN DO IS GO ON TO FIGHT ANOTHER DAY.
WE MAY NEVER KNOW WHAT BECAME OF HER.
HERE LIES AVENGER X BRAVEST OF US ALL

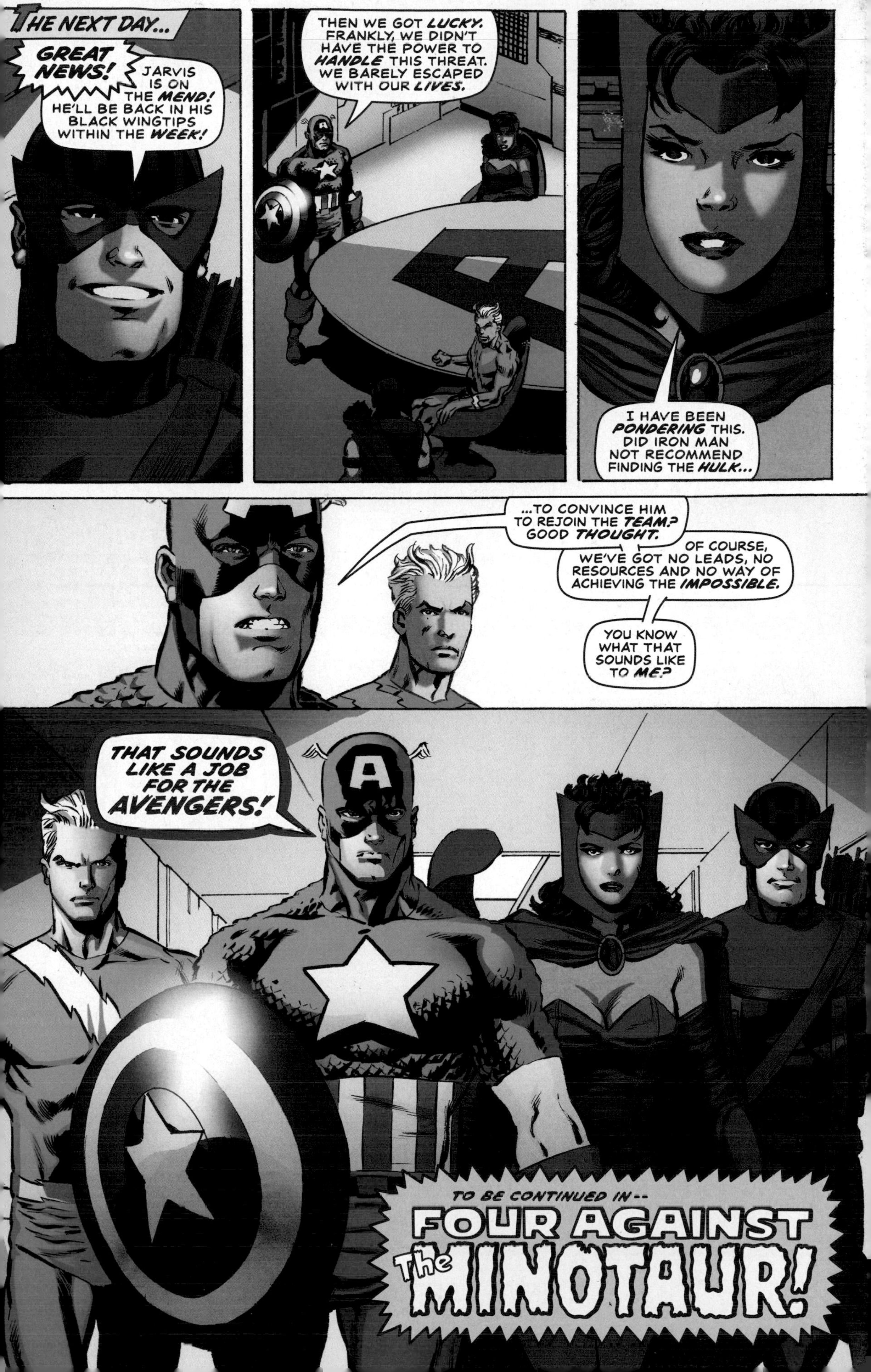
THE NEXT DAY...
GREAT NEWS!
JARVIS IS ON THE MEND! HE'LL BE BACK IN HIS BLACK WINGTIPS WITHIN THE WEEK!
THEN WE GOT LUCKY. FRANKLY, WE DIDN'T HAVE THE POWER TO HANDLE THIS THREAT. WE BARELY ESCAPED WITH OUR LIVES.
I HAVE BEEN PONDERING THIS. DID IRON MAN NOT RECOMMEND FINDING THE HULK...
...TO CONVINCE HIM TO REJOIN THE TEAM? GOOD THOUGHT.
OF COURSE, WE'VE GOT NO LEADS, NO RESOURCES AND NO WAY OF ACHIEVING THE IMPOSSIBLE.
YOU KNOW WHAT THAT SOUNDS LIKE TO ME?
THAT SOUNDS LIKE A JOB FOR THE AVENGERS!
TO BE CONTINUED IN--
FOUR AGAINST The MINOTAUR!

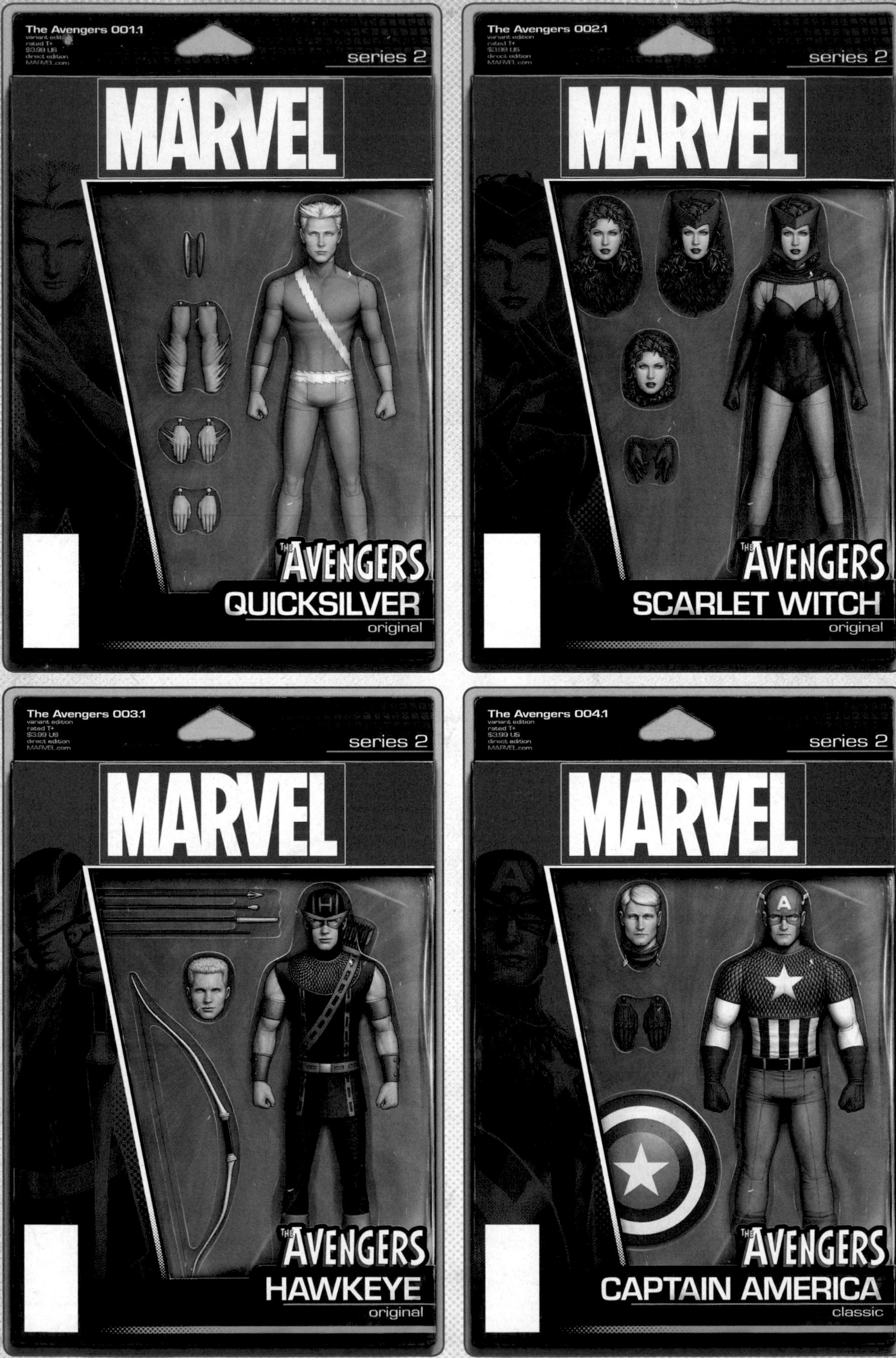
The Avengers 001.1
series 2
MARVEL
THE AVENGERS
QUICKSILVER
original
The Avengers 002.1
series 2
MARVEL
THE AVENGERS
SCARLET WITCH
original
The Avengers 003.1
variant edition
rated T+
$3.99 US
direct edition
MARVEL.com
series 2
MARVEL
THE AVENGERS
HAWKEYE
original
The Avengers 004.1
variant edition
rated T+
$3.99 US
direct edition
MARVEL.com
series 2
MARVEL
THE AVENGERS
CAPTAIN AMERICA
classic

JOHN TYLER CHRISTOPHER

#1-4 action figure variants

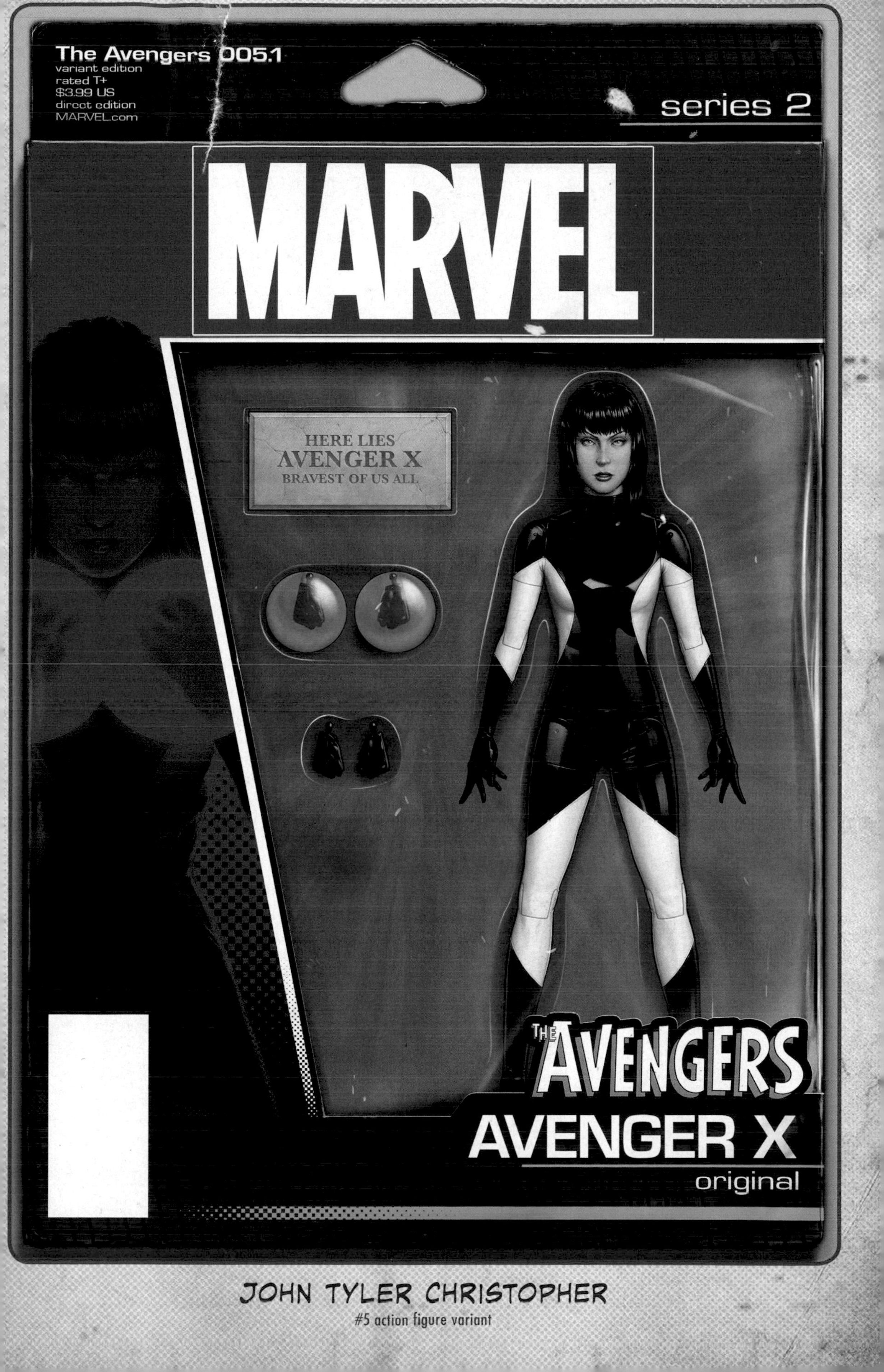
The Avengers 005.1
variant edition
rated T+
$3.99 US
direct edition
MARVEL.com
series 2
MARVEL
HERE LIES
AVENGER X
BRAVEST OF US ALL
THE AVENGERS
AVENGER X
original

JOHN TYLER CHRISTOPHER

#5 action figure variant

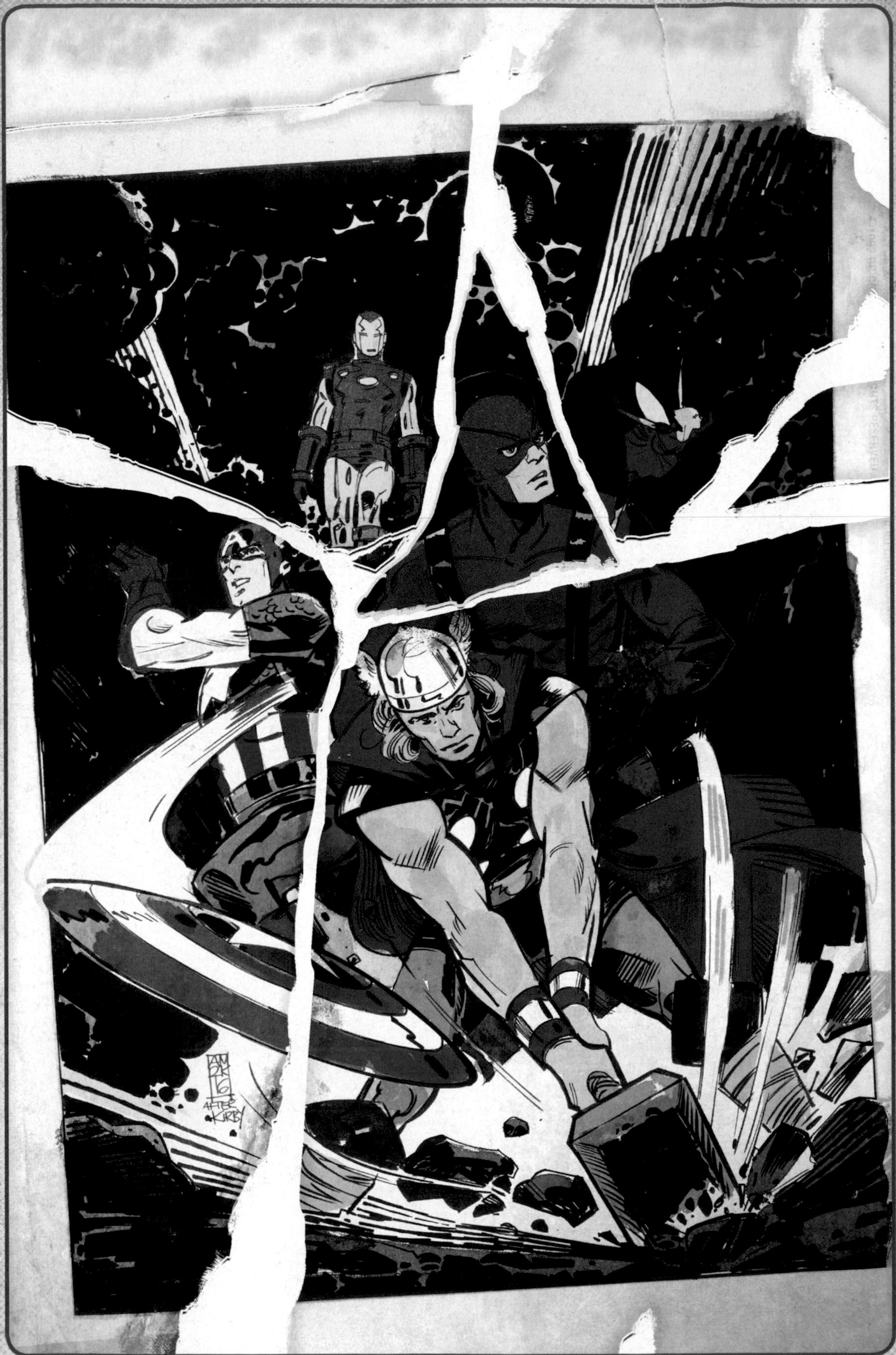
AM 2K 16 AFTER KIRBY

ALEX MALEEV

#1 variant

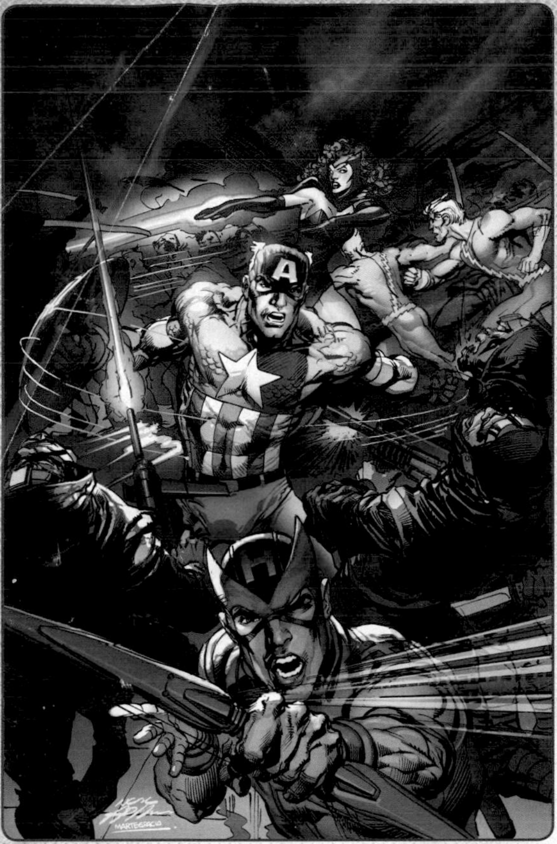

NEAL ADAMS & MARTE GRACIA
#2 variant

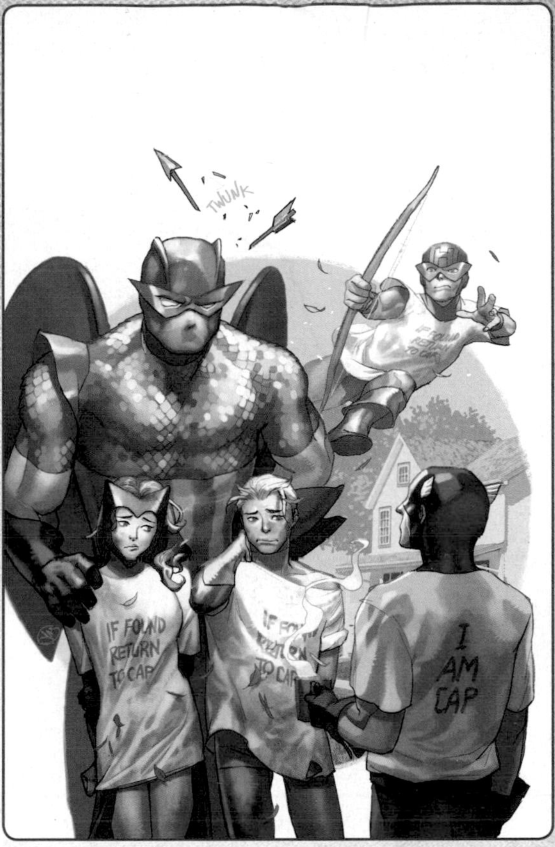
TWUNK
IF FOUND RETURN TO CAP
I AM CAP

YASMINE PUTRI
#2 variant

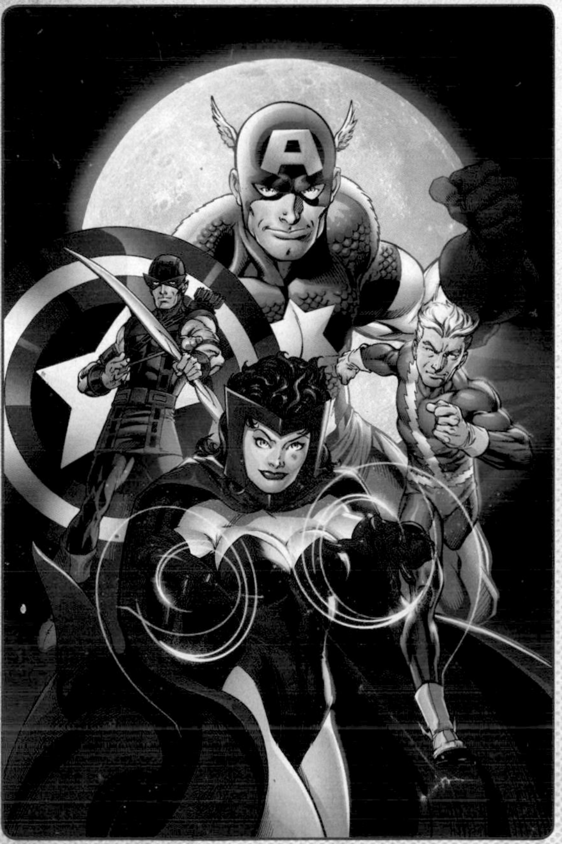

MARK BAGLEY, JOHN DELL & MATT YACKEY
#3 variant

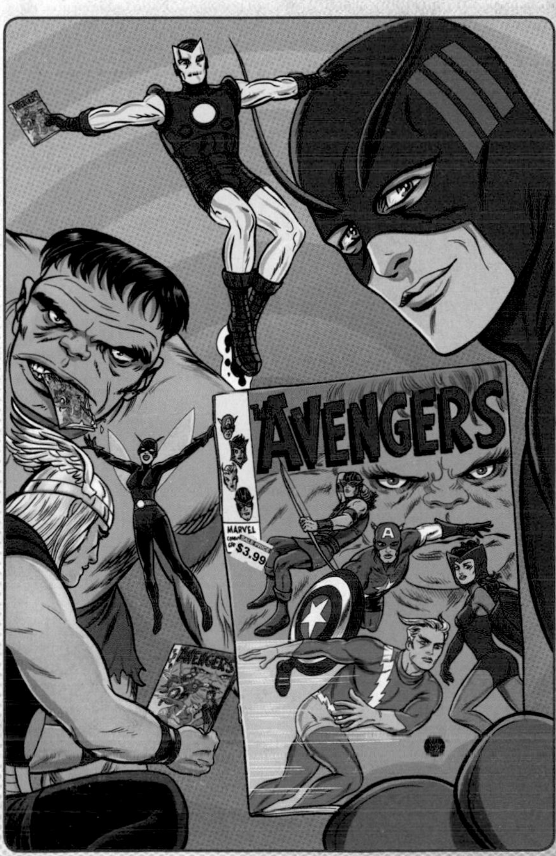
AVENGERS
MARVEL
$3.99

MIKE ALLRED & LAURA ALLRED
#4 variant

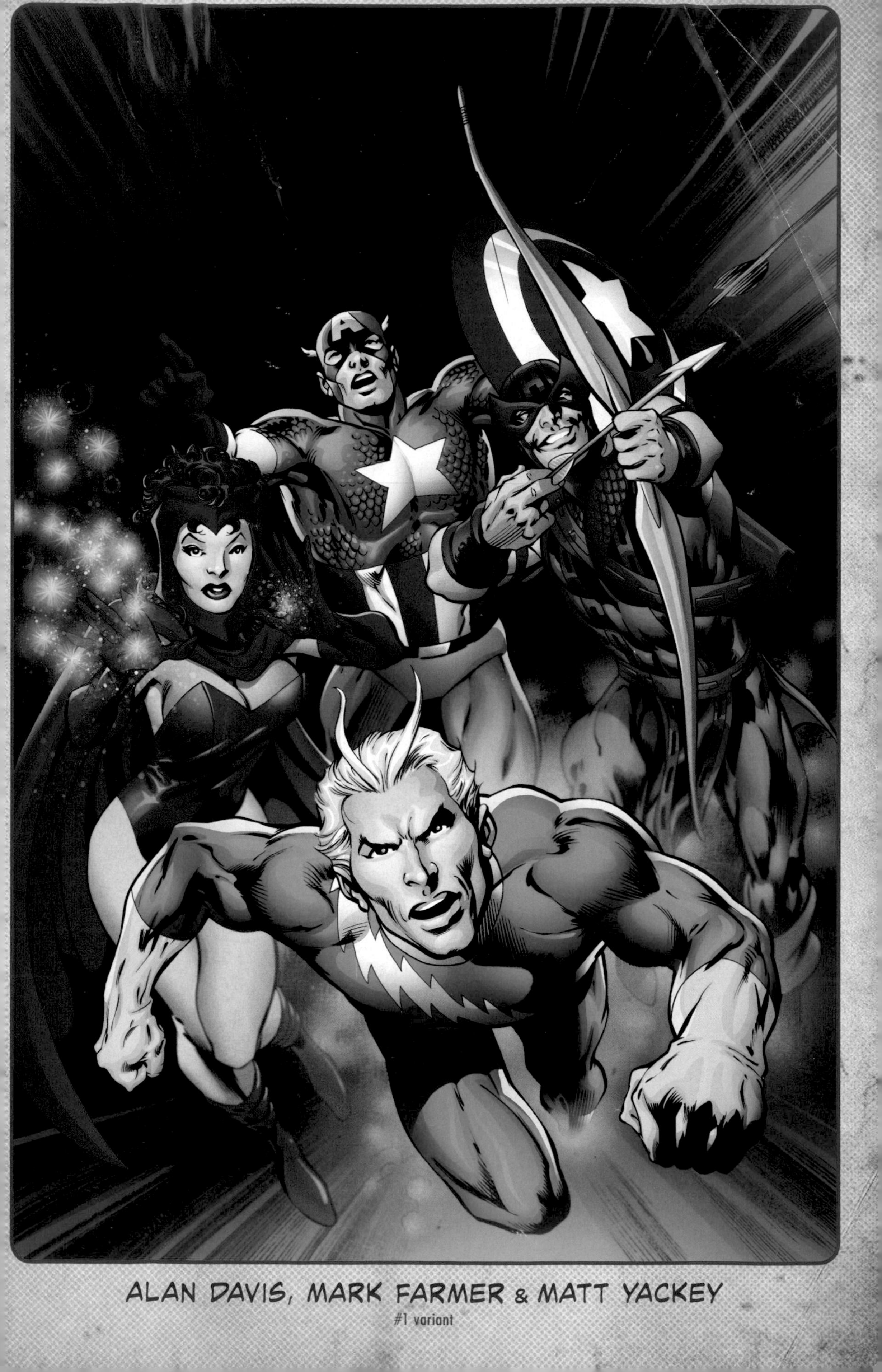

ALAN DAVIS, MARK FARMER & MATT YACKEY

#1 variant